Profiting from Diversity

GEORGIAN COLLEGE LIBRARY

Profiting from Diversity

The Business Advantages and the Obstacles to Achieving Diversity

Edited by

Gloria Moss
Senior Lecturer, Bucks New University

Editorial matter, selection and introduction © Gloria Moss 2010
Chapters © their authors 2010

All rights reserved. No reproduction, copy or transmission of this publication may be made without written permission.

No portion of this publication may be reproduced, copied or transmitted save with written permission or in accordance with the provisions of the Copyright, Designs and Patents Act 1988, or under the terms of any licence permitting limited copying issued by the Copyright Licensing Agency, Saffron House, 6-10 Kirby Street, London EC1N 8TS.

Any person who does any unauthorized act in relation to this publication may be liable to criminal prosecution and civil claims for damages.

The authors have asserted their rights to be identified as the authors of this work in accordance with the Copyright, Designs and Patents Act 1988.

First published 2010 by
PALGRAVE MACMILLAN

Palgrave Macmillan in the UK is an imprint of Macmillan Publishers Limited, registered in England, company number 785998, of Houndmills, Basingstoke, Hampshire RG21 6XS.

Palgrave Macmillan in the US is a division of St Martin's Press LLC, 175 Fifth Avenue, New York, NY 10010.

Palgrave Macmillan is the global academic imprint of the above companies and has companies and representatives throughout the world.

Palgrave® and Macmillan® are registered trademarks in the United States, the United Kingdom, Europe and other countries.

ISBN-13: 978-0-230-51616-8 hardback

This book is printed on paper suitable for recycling and made from fully managed and sustained forest sources. Logging, pulping and manufacturing processes are expected to conform to the environmental regulations of the country of origin.

A catalogue record for this book is available from the British Library.

A catalog record for this book is available from the Library of Congress.

10 9 8 7 6 5 4 3 2 1
19 18 17 16 15 14 13 12 11 10

Printed and bound in Great Britain by
CPI Antony Rowe, Chippenham and Eastbourne

Contents

List of Figures	vii
List of Tables	viii
Notes on Contributors	ix

Part I The Background

1 Introduction — *Gloria Moss* ... 3

Part II Profiting from Diversity

2 Diversity, Innovation, and Corporate Strategy — *Alan H. David* ... 19

3 Eastward Enlargement, Cultural and National Identity, and Diversity in the European Union — *Heather Skinner and Krzysztof Kubacki* ... 45

4 Knowledge Management and the Positive Impact of a Collectivist Culture — *Gloria Moss, Krzysztof Kubacki, Marion Hersh, and Rod Gunn* ... 59

5 Gender-Based Motives for Purchasing Fair Trade Products in France — *Florence de Ferran* ... 75

6 Women Managers in Latvia: A Universal Footprint for the Future? — *Gloria Moss, David Farnham, and Caryn Cook* ... 91

7 Variety is the Spice of Life: How Design Diversity Can Enhance Profitability — *Gloria Moss* ... 119

Part III Obstacles to Diversity Initiatives

8 Embedding Diversity: The Obstacles Faced by Equality and Diversity Specialists — *Alison Preece* ... 137

9	Design Diversity: The Organisational Obstacles *Gloria Moss*	149
10	Obstacles to Greater Design Diversity: Gender and Webdesign Software *Gabor Horvath, Gloria Moss, Rod Gunn and Eszter Vass*	171
11	Tackling Ageism in Employment: Age the Final Frontier of Discrimination? *David Farnham*	194
12	Disabled People and Employment: Barriers to Potential Solutions *Marion Hersh*	215
13	Barriers to Diversity: The Case of Advertising Creatives *Jim Blythe*	241

Name Index 256

Subject Index 263

List of Figures

2.1	Diversity, structure, and the value chain	21
2.2	Diversity and the 'learning organisation' a complimentary approach. Adapted from Kandola and Fullerton (1998)	28
2.3	Absorptive Capacity within the Context of Diversity. Adapted from Hopkins *et al.* (2008)	35
2.4	Diversity strategic process measurement model	36
5.1	(a) Hierachical value map of fair trade coffee purchase by men ($n = 180$/ threshold$= 5$) and (b) hierarchical value map of fair trade coffee purchase by women ($n = 400$/ threshold$= 8$)	83
7.1	Model showing the links needed between performance and preference in order to create congruence (Moss, 2007)	131
9.1	The gains to be derived from achieving a match between production and preference aesthetics	150
9.2	The gains to be derived from achieving a match between production and preference aesthetics	151
10.1	Gender characteristics of grocery websites	177
10.2	The Gender Index of grocery homepages	178
10.3	Shapes on the templates	185
10.4	Layout of the templates	186
10.5	Number of different text colours used	187
10.6	Types of different text colours used	187
10.7	Typography of the templates	188
10.8	Visual gender index	189
10.9	Index of gender – summary	189
12.1	The context component of the comprehensive assistive technology model	217
12.2	The main barriers to employment of disabled people related to the context component of the comprehensive assistive technology model	218
12.3	The relationships between the main barriers to the employment of disabled people	235

List of Tables

1.1	Correlations between perceived diversity in the senior management and outputs (taken from Allen *et al.*, 2008)	13
2.1	Claimed benefits of diversity	23
2.2	Proposed framework by author adapted from Wheeler (1998) and Hubbard (2004)	31
2.3	Scorecard perspectives proposed by the author adapted from Hubbard (2004) and Kaplan and Norton (1996)	40
4.1	Percentage of Australians and Slovenians citing certain constructs as important in team research	69
6.1	Percentage of the Latvian working population employed in different sectors, 1997 and 2000	93
6.2	Comparison of the attributes of men's and women's leadership styles noted in the literature, with the corresponding features of Latvian men's and women's management noted by the respondents	113
6.3	Comparison of the benefits the literature ascribes to transformational leadership and the benefits respondents attribute to women managers	115
7.1	Summary of the views of researchers as to ways in which personality is manifested in graphic expression, and the gender with which a particular form of graphic expression is associated	126
7.2	The sex with which various graphic features are associated	128
7.3	Differences in male and female graphic expression over a number of studies (Moss 2009)	129
7.4	The strength of male and female preferences for websites and elements of websites produced by people of the same gender as themselves (Moss and Gunn 2009)	130
9.1	The proportion of men and women members (and by grade of membership) according to membership statistics held by the Chartered Society of Designers	154
10.1	The scoring system	184
13.1	The processes of a grounded theory study	243
13.2	Categories of data	244

Notes on Contributors

Dr. Jim Blythe is Visiting Reader in Marketing at Plymouth Business School, and a Visiting Professor at Fachhochschule Nordhausen, Germany. He is the author of over 50 academic papers and 14 textbooks. His work has been published in the *Journal of Marketing Management*, *Industrial Marketing Management*, the *Journal of Business and Industrial Management*, *Marketing Intelligence and Planning*, and many more. He is the editor of the *Marketing Review*, and is on the editorial panels of four other academic journals, as well as being Chair of the Academy of Marketing Special Interest Group for Qualitative Inquiry in Marketing.

Caryn E. Cook, MSc, Chartered FCIPD, PGCE, is a senior lecturer with the Business School at the University of Wales, Newport, teaching Employee Relations on the CIPD Professional Development Programme, Human Resource Management and general management. She is a chartered fellow of the Chartered Institute of Personnel Development. A joint paper with Gloria Moss and David Farnham on 'Lessons on Gender and Management from Latvia' was presented at the International Conference, New socio-economic challenges of development in Europe at the University of Latvia in October 2008. Prior to entering the Higher Education Sector Caryn was a training manager within the Railway. Her research interests are within Employee Relations and conceptual frameworks of HRM.

Alan David is Senior Lecturer in Strategic Management at the University of Westminster. He worked at Courtaulds in the head office Strategic Planning team and, following an MBA, attended the Advanced Management Programme International run by faculty at Harvard Business School. His main teaching interests relate to Corporate Strategy, the Management of Innovation and Change and Systems Dynamics and Strategic Modelling. His research interests focus on how systems thinking interventions impact on organisational learning and how a range of intervention techniques, from 'Soft Systems' approaches and Scenario Thinking, enrich management thinking about strategy.

David Farnham is Professor at the University of Portsmouth. He has held visiting academic appointments at the Universities of Glamorgan,

Greenwich, East London, the Ecole Supérieure de Commerce Paris and the Katholieke Universiteit Leuven. His current research interests include new forms of employment relationship, the changing faces of HRM, public management reform, diversity and theories of work, management and employment. He is currently a chief examiner for a professional body, a board member of a housing association, a harbour commissioner for a trust port and a trustee of a social enterprise, with special interests in HR policy and corporate governance.

Florence de Ferran joined the University of La Rochelle in 2008 as an assistant professor. Prior to joining La Rochelle, she served in ESG Paris Graduate School of Management, in Avignon and Aix-Marseille Universities. She earned a Master and a PhD in Marketing from IAE Aix-en-Provence Graduate School of Management. Her primary research interests include consumer behaviour, socially responsible buying behaviour, and advanced data analysis. Prior to entering academe, she worked in an advertising agency.

Rod Gunn was a principal lecturer in Quantitative Methods at Glamorgan University Business School, where he carried out research into the use of the web in Business, Commerce and Education.

Marion Hersh is a senior lecturer in the University of Glasgow. Her research interests relate to the use of technology to achieve social change and include assistive technology for people for sensory impairments and technology and ethical issues. She organises a conference series on assistive technology for people with hearing and vision impairments. Dr Hersh's recent publications include a book on Mathematical Modelling for Sustainable Development, two co-authored books on Assistive Technology for the Hearing Impaired, Deafblind and Deaf and Visually Impaired and Blind People and a presentation of and applications of the Comprehensive Assistive Technology (CAT) model which she co-developed.

Gabor Horvath is Senior Lecturer in Marketing at the Glamorgan Business School. His research focuses on the extent to which present web-designs reflect the different aesthetic expectations of the two genders, that is whether they were tailored to suit the preferences of the target markets.

Krzysztof Kubacki is a lecturer in Marketing at the School of Economic and Management Studies, Keele University. He is a graduate of the School of Music in Legnica, Poland, and before joining academia was working as a musician for the Helena Modrzejewska Theatre in Legnica and the Opera Theatre in Wrocław, Poland. Although his main research interests lie in the relationship between marketing and music, he carries out research projects on a variety of marketing issues in Poland and Central Europe. He has published extensively across a number of marketing areas, including music, culture, hospitality industry and knowledge management.

Gloria Moss is a Senior Lecturer in Human Resources at Buckinghamshire New University and a Visiting Professor at the Ecole Superieure de Gestion (ESG), Paris. She combines a background in Human Resource, as Training Manager for Courtaulds and Eurotunnel where she was responsible for management training, with research on leadership, teamwork and design. She has published more than 30 peer-reviewed articles investigating the impact of gender, nationality and personality on behaviour with a book, *Gender, Design and Marketing* (2009), focusing on design and marketing. Clients have included M&S, BT, Bounty and Ford. She is a Chartered FCIPD.

Alison Preece is an equality and diversity manager at the University of Wales, Newport. Prior to this Alison worked with disadvantaged groups, specifically disabled people and lone parents, to enable them to overcome barriers to entering education, training or employment. Alison is a member of the Equality Challenge Unit's Welsh Liaison Group and is currently Vice Chair of the South East Wales Equality Network.

Heather Skinner is Principal Lecturer in Marketing at the Glamorgan Business School, specialising in the marketing of services where her main research interests focus on internal marketing and employee empowerment in service settings. Heather is particularly interested in non-profit and public sector services marketing, and the marketing of leisure, sport, heritage and tourism where her main research interests are in the marketing of place, and the representation of national identity into the national brand.

Eszter Vass is a former MSc Female Entrepreneurship student of the Glamorgan Business School, University of Glamorgan, Wales. At the moment she is a full-time mum, taking care of her three children.

Part I
The Background

1
Introduction

Gloria Moss

The case for diversity would appear to be compelling. The customer base of organisations is increasingly diverse, driven to great extent by population changes (Kandola and Fullerton, 2003) and globalisation (Stockdale and Crosby, 2004: 15) and this, coupled with the fact that organisations 'need employees that can read their customers and interact with them in a near-flawless manner' (Jackson and Alvarez, 1992: 14), presents organisations with a vital source of competitive advantage. As Kandola and Fullerton assert (2003: 46), 'the ability of an organisation to provide products and services to all potential markets is a bottom-line concern' creating a need for organisations to be 'more responsive to the diverse needs of its customer base'.

Whilst Kandola and Fullerton assert the important role diversity can play in achieving a better customer focus, they say that as yet 'the evidence is slight'. This book fills the gap by exploring some of the specific business benefits to be achieved by diversity. At the same time, it explores some of the specific obstacles which stand in the way of achieving diversity. It is important to do this since without a grasp of the problems involved in achieving a diverse workforce, managing the change involved in introducing diversity will be extremely difficult.

The starting point to a consideration of diversity involves a historical understanding of the way that a diversity approach emerged out of the earlier Equal Opportunities (EO) approach.

The limitations of an Equal Opportunities approach

In the 1960s and 1970s, EO policies were introduced to complement anti-discrimination and equal pay legislation and to equalise opportunities and outcomes in the workplace (Kirton and Greene, 2000).

EO policies were predicated on the assumption of ontological equality, a belief in the fundamental sameness of individuals (Miller, 1996; Gagnon and Cornelius, 2000; Kirton and Greene, 2000), and this EO mindset produced an acceptance that white, non-disabled, heterosexual men's experiences and interpretations of organisational life were universally applicable (Alvesson and Billing, 1997). This way of thinking led to organisational analyses that 'occurred through a lens which is primarily white and male' (Cianni and Romberger, 1997), producing organisational cultures constructed around a 'white, male norm' (Kirton and Greene, 2000). A practical consequence was that minorities were required to adopt the norms and practices of the majority (Nkomo, 1992).

Success was, for instance, all about having women at senior levels of the company – even if none of them had children and they all behaved exactly like men. The message seemed to be: if they want to join us, they can, but they need to fit in and play by our rules (Schneider, 2001).

In a similar way, Thomas (1990: 308) writes that

> the governing assumption appeared to be that they [the minorities, women] would assimilate... the adjustment burden has been on individuals.

Discussion of 'merit' and of the 'brightest' people rising to the top are often problematic in fact given that these terms assume a common norm and there is no questioning as to whether the norm is that of a particular group. If, however, we are to scrutinise the concept of 'merit' of the term, it is easy to see how suspect the term is. In Imperial China, for example, for a period from the first century to 1905, an examination was established which offered access to the highest levels of government office in the country. The appearance of neutrality and impartiality was reinforced by a system in which candidates' scripts were recopied by a third person to prevent the candidate's handwriting being recognised and the topics in which the lucky 5 per cent of successful candidates had to excel included the scholastic arts (music, arithmetic, writing, and knowledge of the rituals and ceremonies in both public and private life) as well as the militaristic arts (archery and horsemanship). To modern eyes, the set of skills demanded of successful applicants makes the concept of merit used here somewhat problematic and throws into relief the biases inherent in certain concepts of merit.

Turning to the present day, at the time that this book went to press, an issue appeared in France concerning the type of knowledge that it was reasonable to expect aspiring civil servants to have. The French President, Nicolas Sarkozy, took the view that an entrance exam for civil servants included questions on a seventeenth-century novel the *Princesse de Cleves*. He joked that only a 'sadist or an idiot' could have inserted such questions (Bremner, 24 March 2009: 30) and whilst the public furore that surrounded these comments may have been inflamed by anti-government feeling, the issue raised serious questions about how best to assess merit. The different views expressed show the widespread divergence of opinions and the fact that one culture's idea of merit, and indeed one person's idea of merit, may be very different from the next.

Despite the contingent nature of the concept of merit, there is a constant flow of references in academic literature and elsewhere to 'the best' people for the job. Dickson, for example, writing in the *Harvard Business Review*, speaks of the need in business for the 'best and the brightest, regardless of race' (1992: 46). The authors of a CIPD book on diversity, Kandola and Fullerton (2003: 129) write that 'those who are selected in situations where preferential selection appears to be operating experience more stress than people selected by merit' (129) and this confidence in the objective nature of the standards shines through in many other pieces of writing. Dickson writing in the prestigious *Harvard Business Review* (1992) notes that

> business needs the best and the brightest, regardless of race and ethnic Background.

And writing in the same journal in the same year, Drake (1992: 142) states that

> If a corporation is committed to working objectively to hire the best and brightest in a diverse culture, many inequalities will take care of themselves.

They are by no means alone in making appeals to the concept of 'merit' and we find this again in the work of Heilman (1994: 129) who invokes this concept as a reason for rejecting positive discrimination:

> Preferential selection may be interpreted as an indication that the recipient is not competent enough to be selected on his/her/own merits.

In summer 2009, there was a sprat in the British Press which turned on these very issues. The deputy leader of the Labour Party, Harriet Harman, announced that 'it's a thoroughly bad thing to have a men-only leadership' and that 'a balanced team of men and women makes better decisions' (Oakeshott, 2009). A former member of parliament, Edwina Currie took issue with her, saying that 'I'd need the best people to run the country, irrespective of gender. I'd have thought that was a statement of the obvious, but it has passed Ms Harman by (Currie, 2009).

What Edwina Currie and a myriad other commentators who rest their faith on appointment by 'merit' tend to overlook is the problematic nature of the concepts of 'merit', 'potential', 'best' and 'brightest'. For what frequently goes unmentioned is the extent to which notions of 'the best' are frequently fashioned around the preferences of those determining the standards, thereby undermining their value as dispassionate benchmarks of merit and ability. This is something that the rare commentator appears to grasp:

> The meritocracy myth... has created a societal climate that discourages diversity and privileges homogeneity and the defined norm of the dominant group. (Stockdale and Crosby, 2004: 51, quoting Wildman and Davis, 1996)

Several of the chapters in this book, in fact, illustrate the extent to which concepts of excellence are rooted in the judgements of a single sector of society. For example, the chapter by Gabor Horvath, Gloria Moss, Rod Gunn and Eszter Vass, on webdesign software (Chapter 10), demonstrates the extent to which the free webdesign software available is anchored in the male aesthetic rather than the female. Any concepts of 'merit' operated by the software firms producing this software is likely to be anchored, equally, at the male end of the design continuum. Similar points can be inferred from many of the other chapters.

Where management is concerned, for example, the chapter on knowledge management by Gloria Moss, Krzysztof Kubacki, Marion Hersh and Rod Gunn (Chapter 4) shows the extent to which the practice of teamwork is valued and facilitated in a collectivist country and the way it can assist in the development of Knowledge. This is demonstrated through a study of the views of academics in an individualistic (Australia) and collectivist country (Slovenia), with subjects in Slovenia showing a greater willingness to engage in teamwork than those in an individualistic country (Australia). Significantly, it is shown that respondents in Slovenia have a significantly higher *per capita* research output than those in Australia. It is not difficult to infer from this data that concepts of excellence regarding teamworking may be culture-specific and cultural diversity in the workforce may enhance the potential for teamwork, and through that, Knowledge Creation. A similar point arises from the chapter on leadership by Gloria Moss, David Farnham and Caryn Cook (Chapter 6) which focuses on the way in which women leaders in Latvia use a different set of leadership skills from men, relying to a greater extent on transformational skills. Evidence gathered from the respondents (male and female managers) links such use of transformational skills with improved performance and this provides evidence of the merit in employing a more diverse management grouping than is usually found outside Latvia.

Where marketing is concerned, Jim Blythe shows (Chapter 13) how the personality of the creative influences the character of the work produced and, moreover, how the acceptance of this work will be influenced by the personality of the client. In a similar way, a grasp of the diversity of people's reactions inspired Florence De Ferran's research on men and women's motivations to purchase Fair Trade products. Her chapter (Chapter 5) highlights subtle differences in the motivations of men and women and leads her to suggest that the marketing of Fair Trade Products should take account of these differences. The need to take account of the differing needs of the market are the subject of Heather Skinner and Krzysztof Kubacki's chapter on the differences between the cultures of central European states (Chapter 3). Rather than assume a homogeneous culture across central European states, this chapter argues for the heterogeneous nature of these states and the importance of factoring these differences into any marketing campaign.

The chapters on design by Gloria Moss (Chapters 7 and 9) likewise show the importance of understanding the diversity that can exist in the designs that men and women produce (their so-called production aesthetic) and prefer (the so-called preference aesthetic). They also discuss the importance of factoring an understanding of these differences into a design and marketing strategy as well as a firm's recruitment and promotion strategy. For, of course, divergences in men and women's productions, and preferences are at odds with a single concept of 'merit' difficult to concretise.

The complex process involved in weaving diversity into business strategy is explored by Alan H. David in a chapter (Chapter 2) that takes a resource-based view, examining the role that diversity can bring to building strategic resources for competitive advantage. The author also makes the point that single-threaded diversity initiatives will not be successful without a supporting infrastructure within the organisation. A scorecard approach which makes explicit the relationship between organisational diversity and performance is explained.

Equal Opportunities give way to diversity

The evidence for diversity in people's preferences militates against a single concept of merit and, by the same token, the notion of sameness implied within Equal Opportunities policies has given way to discussions of diversity, with the emphasis alternatively on individual and group differences. In the case of group differences, some discussions, for example those relating to gender, have been held back by a fear that emphasising differences between the genders will be used, as it arguably has in the past, to reassert inferiority and exclusion (Webb, 1997), thus maintaining the power of the dominant groups (Liff, 1996). A further inhibitor to such discussions has been the extent to which people may be simultaneously members of several diverse groupings (for example, a disabled person of a racial minority).

This reticence to discuss the features that may unite members of a diverse group is one of the prompts to this book. Where others may fear to discuss group-based characteristics, the authors here examine the case for identifying group-based features either in a workforce or in a customer base. The case for doing this is succinctly summarised by Alison Preece in her chapter (Chapter 8) on the obstacles faced by Equality and Diversity specialists:

> It may be worth asking whether, by concentrating on the needs of the individual, we weaken the case for making changes by losing the critical mass of support of people who identify closely as a group. Stereotype has become a word associated with the negative aspects of large group characteristics whereas in reality there may still be some value in considering the needs of the majority of people who belong to a certain group. We may not be willing to change society for one person but pressure from large numbers can make a more powerful argument which may achieve results.

We can see that describing the diverse characteristics of different groupings provides powerful evidence for an organisation seeking to harness the strengths available in the workforce. If organisations are not aware of the features that characterise certain diverse groups, how can they for example harness the strengths available in a given workforce? We know that managers may be involved in the psychological, rather than simple objective construction of the world, leading them to, singly or collectively, produce different cognitive maps (Eden, 1989) and the information on psychological types available through psychometric tests such as the MBTI or Kirton's Adaptor/Innovator instrument (Kirton, 1999) offers data on cognitive type segmented by occupation and this isolation of group characteristics can assist in management and training decisions.

In a similar way, research on leadership has shown that men and women often favour and practice different leadership styles (Rosener, 1990; Nkomo, 1992; Kirton and Greene, 2000; Alimo-Metcalfe and Alban-Metcalfe, 2003) and this finding has important implications for leadership in organisations (Moss and Daunton, 2006). Some of the implications of these differences are explored in the chapter by Gloria Moss, David Farnham and Caryn Cook on men and women as leaders in Latvia (Chapter 6). At the time the research was conducted, Latvia had a higher proportion of female managers than any other country in the European Union and the near parity of male and female managers made it less likely that women might seek to do what they are credited with doing when in a minority situation, namely model their style on men, and more likely that people would have some experience of seeing women in a management role. This chapter therefore describes in-depth interviews with managers in which they were asked to comment on men and women's style of leadership and if they were different, how these differences impacted on the organisation.

The results reveal that the overwhelming majority of respondents refer to differences in the management style of male and female managers. In fact, only one of the 27 respondents considered there to be no difference between the management style of men and women with the remaining 26 respondents speaking of differences. These coalesced around seven themes which were: decision-making style, focus on results, long- or short-term focus, consensual approach to management, focus on teamwork, attitude to risk, and emotionality. Overall, the male and female styles of management were perceived as different and as bringing distinct and separate advantages to organisations.

The significance of gaining an understanding of differences between people extends to marketing as well as to management and the former is particularly important given the advantages of shaping products around the 'unique and particular needs' of the customer (Hammer, 1995: 21). Without an understanding of differences between people, any attempt to create appropriate products must, to a large extent, be guesswork. However, a study of difference can help remove some of the uncertainty as shown in Chapter 10. This chapter, under its lead author Gabor Horvath, reveals the fact that free webdesign software is masculine in its orientation regardless of the audience to whom it is being addressed. Were the creators of this software to be aware of women's preference for websites anchored in a female aesthetic, they might create software capable of delivering this alternative style but as it is, unbeknown probably to the creators of the software, the software is optimised for producing websites targeted at male rather than female consumers. This is an important finding and the chapter illustrates the benefits of mapping the features of a product against the preferences of a group of end-users. In the case of webdesign software, the chapter points out that the widespread presence of webdesign software more geared to delivering the male than the female aesthetic constitutes a major obstacle to achieving greater diversity.

Further obstacles to achieving diversity are examined by Gloria Moss in her chapter on the obstacles to greater gender diversity in the design and advertising professions (Chapter 9). One of the obstacles discussed concerns the impediments to parachuting staff with a new perspective into organisations. As she writes: '...for as long as organisations are unbalanced demographically (for example employing a higher proportion of men than women), it will be difficult for new people with a different way of seeing not to feel tempted to model their performance on that of the majority'. The pressure towards conformity places impediments in the way of employing people who stand outside the prevailing culture, a disturbing fact given 'people's limited ability to think beyond their ways of seeing into that of other's'.

These limitations could well lie at the root of the attempt to open up workforces to a diversity of generations and David Farnham, in his chapter on age (Chapter 11), examines some of the issues reinforcing ageism in employment and the workplace. These are complex since, as he writes:

> Discrimination on the grounds of age can take place between individuals, within and between groups, in organisations, in communities, and in society-at-large. An elderly person, for example, may typically stereotype younger persons as being 'immature', 'irresponsible' or 'reckless.' Similarly, a young person may typically stereotype older persons as being 'inflexible', 'old fashioned' or 'forgetful.'

It is not surprising, given this complexity, that a 'series of obstacles' are encountered in attempting to root out ageism. As Professor Farnham writes:

> Re-writing all policies to remove age discrimination is necessary to comply with age legislation but this is not sufficient to safeguard

employers from challenges of ageism. There needs to be a fundamental shift in everyone's perception of age and where the boundaries of acceptable behaviour are.

Marion Hersh, similarly, highlights the obstacles encountered in attempting to open up employment opportunities for disabled people (Chapter 12). She writes of the largely socially constructed negative identity of disability, writing that 'There seems to be a de facto assumption in a number of countries that people who become disabled or have long term sickness absence will not return to work.' She goes onto say that

> Due to the continuing prevalence of myths that disabled people are not able to work (Stanley and Regan, 2003) or are not highly competent and productive workers, very little consideration has been given to overcoming the barriers to promotion of disabled people or obtaining a career which is interesting and suited to the particular disabled person's interests and skills.

Business benefits of diversity

The contributors to this book show how greater diversity in the workforce can reap substantial benefits for organisations and this new information adds greatly to our understanding of the benefits that can flow from a more diverse workforce. The value of these new insights can perhaps best be gauged from an understanding of the benefits previously ascribed to a diverse workforce. In this remaining section, we outline some of the information currently available on the benefits.

According to a recent article on diversity (Allen *et al.*, 2008) the benefits of diversity include:

> the ability to attract and retain the best talent available; reduced costs due to lower turnover and fewer lawsuits; enhanced market understanding and marketing ability; greater creativity and innovations; better problem solving; greater organisational flexibility, better decision making and better overall performance.... These benefits have the potential to affect organizational performance and the bottom line.

In the course of listing these resource-based benefits, a number of studies are referred to (Cox and Blake, 1991; Cox, 1993; Watson *et al.*,

1993; McAllister, 1997; Robinson and Dechant, 1997; Carlozzi, 1999; Griscombe and Mattis, 2002) and elsewhere we find reference to other resource-based benefits, including diversity in knowledge, skills and competences leading to enhanced innovation and creativity (Milliken and Martins, 1996), gender and age diversity leading to superior commitment, satisfaction, creativity and innovation (Jehn *et al.*, 1999), non-homogeneous workgroups leading to improved creativity and decision making (Jackson, 1992) and the employment of women and minorities leading to a better understanding of a demographically diverse customer base (Jackson and Alvarez, 1992; Cox, 1993).

Despite this research detailing the resource-based benefits of diversity, Weigand writes in 2007 that 'surprisingly, there is little evidence of a relation between workplace diversity and firm performance'. This echoes the earlier view of Kandola and Fullerton (2003: 46) as to the lack of 'conclusive data' on the relationship between diversity and the bottom line. Likewise, it echoes the findings of a 2004 study which showed that having employees in retail with demographic characteristics similar to customers does not necessarily produce a significant increase in sales (Leonard *et al.*, 2004: 733). In fact, the authors of this last study claim that:

> Despite the lack of consistent evidence, proponents of diversity routinely advocate that employers must hire a diverse workforce to attract diverse customers.

Moreover, if we revisit the article by Allen *et al.* (2008) on the advantages of diversity we find that all but two of the seven studies cited were conducted 12 or more years ago.

Fortunately, other more recent studies do find a link between diversity and profitability. For example, Ng and Tung found in a 1998 study that culturally heterogeneous branches of a bank experienced lower levels of absenteeism and higher levels of productivity and financial profitability than more homogeneous branches. Another study from the same year found that organisations with the highest proportion of female and minority directors had appreciably higher investor returns than those with no women or minority directors (Hillman *et al.*, 1998).

In a similar way, a study by Robert Weigand in 2007, comparing the profitability of 50 companies singled out for exemplary diversity practices in 2004 with 50 matching firms from the Fortune 1000 list, found that the diversity-award winners had higher profit margins, return on assets, return on equity and economic value-added compared to matching organisations. Then, a study by Richard Allen and

Table 1.1 Correlations between perceived diversity in the senior management and outputs (taken from Allen *et al.*, 2008)

Factor with which a perceived diversity in senior management is correlated	Extent of the correlation
Overall firm performance	$p < 0.001$
Quality	$p < 0.001$
Productivity	$p < 0.001$
Profitability	$p < 0.001$

co-authors at the University of Tennessee at Chattanooga (2008) interviewed employees in 130 companies in the southeast United States and found highly significant correlations between perceived diversity at the senior management level and firm performance (see Table 1.1). These studies provide an explicit link between diversity and profitability and the contributions in this book extend our understanding of the resource-based benefits of diversity. It is to be hoped that future work will continue to research these links.

Meanwhile, this book extends the information available on specific resource-based benefits of diversity. In this way, the reader will find chapters focusing on the positive benefits that a collectivist culture can bring to knowledge creation (Chapter 4); on the distinct features that men and, separately, women can bring to management and business (Chapter 6); on the specific way in which gender can impact on designs and design preferences (Chapter 7); on the different ways in which men and women conceive of fair trade coffee (Chapter 5); and finally on the distinct social and economic features that distinguish Central European economies (Chapter 3).

It is hoped that this identification of the benefits diversity can bring to management and marketing will increase as organisations and markets become increasingly diverse.

References

Alimo-Metcalfe, B. and Alban-Metcalfe, J. (2003), 'Leadership: A Masculine Past, but a Feminine Future?', Paper presented at the BPS Occupational Psychology Conference, Bournemouth, 8–10 January.

Allen, R., Dawson, G., Wheatley, K. and White, C. (2008), Perceived diversity and organisational performance, *Employee Relations*, 30 (1), 20–33.

Alvesson, M. and Billing, Y. (1997), *Understanding Gender and Organizations*, Sage, London.

Bremner, C. (2009), Sarkozy sentenced to ridicule for failing to mind his language, *The Times*, 24 March, 30.

Carlozzi, C. (1999), Diversity is good for business, *Journal of Accountancy*, 188 (3), 81–86.

Cianni, M. and Romberger, B. (1997), Life in the corporation: A multi-method study of the experiences of male and female Asian, Black Hispanic and white employees, *Gender, Work and Organization*, 4 (2), 116–127.

Cox, T. (1993), *Cultural Diversity in Organizations: Theory, Research and Practice*, Berrett-Koehler Publishers, San Francisco, CA.

Cox, T. and Blake, S. (1991), Managing cultural diversity: Implications for organizational effectiveness, *Academy of Management Executive*, 5 (3), 45–55.

Currie, E. (2009), Harriet Harman's rabid nonsense that has no regard for real needs, *The Times*, 3 August.

Dickson, R. (1992), The business of equal opportunity, *Harvard Business Review*, 46–53, January/February.

Drake, L. (1992), Can equal opportunities by made more equal? *Harvard Business Review*, March–April, 142.

Eden, C. (1989), Using cognitive mapping for strategic options development and analysis. In Rosenhead, J. (Ed.), *Rational Analysis for a Problematic World*, John Wiley, Chichester.

Gagnon, S. and Cornelius, N. (2000), Re-examining workplace equality: The capabilities approach, *Human Resource Management Journal*, 10 (4), 68–87.

Griscombe, K. and Mattis, M. (2002), Levelling the playing field for women of color in corporate management: Is the business case enough?, *Journal of Business Ethics*, 37, 103–109.

Hammer, M. (1995), *Reengineering the Corporation*. Nicholas Brealey Corporation, London.

Heilman, M. (1994), Affirmative action: Some unintended consequences for working women, *Research in Organizational Behaviour*, 16, 125–169.

Hillman, A., Harris, I., Cannella, A. and Bellinger, L. (1998), 'Diversity on the Board: An Examination of the Relationship Between Director Diversity and Firm Performance', Paper presented at the annual meeting of the Academy of Management, San Diego, CA.

Jackson, S.E. (1992), Consequences of group composition for the interpersonal dynamics of strategic issue processing. In P. Shrivastava, A. Huff and J. Dutton (Eds), *Advances in Strategic Management*, 8, 345–382. JAI Press, Greenwich, CT.

Jackson, S.E. and Alvarez, E.B. (1992), Working through diversity as a strategic imperative. In Jackson, S.E., Associates (Eds), *Diversity in the Workplace: Human Resource Initiatives*, Society for Industrial and Organisational Psychology: The Professional Practice Series, The Guildford Press, New York.

Jehn, K., Northcraft, G. and Neale, M. (1999), Why differences make a difference: A field study of diversity, conflict, and performance in work groups, *Administrative Science Quarterly*, 44, 741–763.

Kandola, R. and Fullerton, J. (2003), *Diversity in Action: Managing the Mosaic*, Chartered Institute of Personnel and Development, London.

Kirton, G. and Greene, A. (2000), *The Dynamics of Managing Diversity*, Butterworth-Heinemann, Oxford.

Kirton, M.J. (1999), *Manual: Kirton Adaptation-Innovation Inventory*, 3rd ed. Occupational Research Centre, Hatfield, UK.

Leonard, J., Levine, D. and Joshi, A. (2004), Do birds of a feather shop together? The effects on performance of employees' similarity with one another and with customers. *Journal of Organizational Behavior*, 25, 731–754.

Liff, S. (1996), Two routes to managing diversity: Individual differences or social group characteristics, *Employee Relations*, 19 (1), 11–26.

McAllister, M. (1997), Profiting from diversity, *Equal Opportunities International*, 16 (5), 23–33.

Miller, D. (1996), Equality management: Towards a materialist approach, *Gender, Work and Organisation*, 3 (4), 202–214.

Milliken, F. and Martins, L. (1996), Searching for common threads: Understanding the multiple effects of diversity in organizational groups, *Academy of Management Review*, 21, 402–433.

Moss, G. and Daunton, L. (2006), The discriminatory impact of deviations from selection criteria in Higher Education selection, *Career Development International*, 11 (6), 504–521.

Ng, E.S.W. and Tung, R.L. (1998), Ethno-cultural diversity and organizational effectiveness: A field study, *International Journal of Human Resource Management*, 9 (6), 980–995.

Nkomo, S. (1992), The emperor has no clothes: Rewriting 'race in organizations', *Academy of Management Review*, 17 (3), 487–513.

Oakeshott, I. (2009), Harriet Harman: You can't trust men in power, The *Times*, 2 August.

Robinson, G. and Dechant, K. (1997), Building a business case for diversity, *Academy of Management Executive*, 11 (3), 21–31.

Rosener, J. (1990), Ways women lead, *Harvard Business Review*, November/December, 119–125.

Schneider, R. (2001), Variety performance, *People Management*, 7 (9), 27–31.

Stanley, K. and Regan, S. (2003), The Missing Millions: Supporting Disabled People into Work, London, IPPR.

Stockdale, M.S. and Crosby, F.J. (2004), *The Psychology and Management of Workplace Diversity*, Blackwell Publishing, Oxford.

Thomas, R. (1990), From affirmative action to affirming diversity, *Harvard Business Review*, March–April, 107–117.

Watson, W., Kumar, K. and Michaelsen, L. (1993), Cultural diversity's impact on interaction process and performance: Comparing homogeneous and diverse task groups, *Academy of Management Journal*, 36, 590–602.

Webb, J. (1997), The politics of equal opportunity, *Gender, Work and Organisation*, 4 (3), 159–167.

Weigand, R. (2007), Organizational diversity, profits and returns in US firms, *Problems and Perspectives in Management*, 5 (3), 69–83.

Wildman, S. and Davis, A. (1996), Making systems of privilege visible. In S.M. Wildman (Ed.), *Privilege Reveal: How Invisible Preference Undermines America*, 25–42. New York University Press, New York.

Part II
Profiting from Diversity

2
Diversity, Innovation, and Corporate Strategy

Alan H. David

Introduction

Demographic changes in the workforce and customer populations, combined with global markets and international competition, result in increasingly diverse markets and workplaces. Many diversity specialists argue that competitive advantage can be obtained from acknowledging diversity, internally and externally (Cox, 2001), and if this is true, it would be important for executives to broaden their understanding of both these aspects of diversity and include diversity as an integrated strand within corporate strategy.

This chapter provides an overview of the way that organisations can broaden their understanding of diversity so that it moves beyond legal compliance to become a major component of strategy with a distinct contribution to competitive advantage. Where forces in the external market are concerned, global competition, instant communication or customised market niches and products, make it imperative that resources and opportunities are tapped on a multi-national scale in differing cultural/ethnic environments (Senge and Sterman, 1991; Golembiewski, 1995). Organisations need to respond in a proactive way to these environmental trends by developing internal sensitivity to market diversities and recognising signals from their customer base. This ability to 'read' diversities in the environment and respond in an agile way is embodied in the concept of absorptive capacity (Cohen and Levinthal, 1990) and corporate agility (Sambamurthy et al., 2003; Mathiyalakan et al., 2005).

These observations indicate that while a philosophy of managing diversity should pervade the entire organisation, it should also be more than simply another Human Resources policy as it needs to be an integrated part of the organisation's strategy. In order to integrate diversity elements within the strategy process, an organisation needs to consider those diversity attributes that are crucial to competitive strategy. These would include teams with a capacity for diverse thinking and paradigm-shifting ideas and the presence of a 'diversity mindset' in the senior management group (Hopkins *et al.*, 2008; Moss, 2009) and an appropriate level of diversity density within the organisation (Hopkins *et al.*, 2008). The case is made that diversity is one of the factors underpinning the development of deeper-seated competences over time and that these in turn facilitate the accumulation of competitive strategic resources (Barney, 2001; Haberberg and Rieple, 2008). Things an organisation has, such as retail branches or a customer database, may be considered assets, but it is the existence of competencies that enables the organisation to effectively do things with these assets so that they become over time strategic resources that contribute within the value chain of the organisation to give competitive advantage.

The link between diversity, absorptive capacity, and competencies in the value chain will be explored later in the chapter.

The strategic diversity roadmap

This chapter will produce four main learning outcomes for the reader.

- Broadening the scope and definition of diversity
- Explaining the role of diversity within the learning organisation
- Propose a model that explains how diversity is one of the factors underpinning the development of competencies over time that facilitates the accumulation of strategic resources in the value chain
- Explain the diversity scorecard approach as a tool for evaluating diversity's contribution

We will now present an expanded explanation of these four learning outcomes.

The first encourages a broadening of the scope of diversity beyond the traditional Human Resource Management (HRM) race and gender definition of diversity and the 'visible differences' that distinguish people (DeEtta Jones, 1999) to include four types of diversity. These four types of interdependent and sometimes overlapping aspects of diversity identified by Hubbard (2004) relate to the workforce, behavioral and cognitive diversity, structural diversity, and strategy. A model is

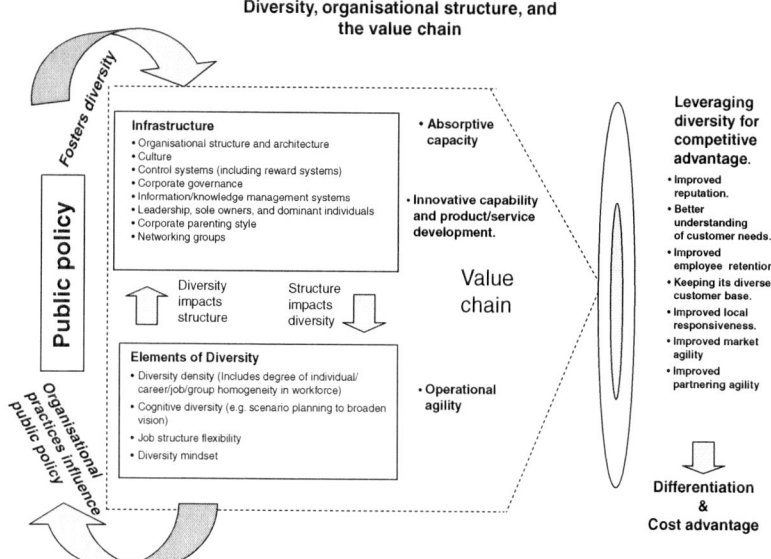

Figure 2.1 Diversity, structure, and the value chain

presented summarising these points in Figure 2.1 and a table showing the four types is shown at Table 2.2. It is useful to introduce and explain these four types of diversity here before moving on to the other remaining three learning outcomes:

Workforce Diversity encompasses group and situational identities of the organisation's employees (i.e. gender, race, physical ability, economic background, and status, etc.) and also includes changes in labour market demographics.

Cognitive and Behavioral Diversity encompasses work styles, learning styles, communication styles, aspirations, beliefs/value system, as well as employees' attitudes and expectations. It also includes the degree of diversity in thinking at both the individual and group level and the subsequent richness of 'mental models' that are developed through diverse thinking over time that enable the reading of signals from diverse environments.

Structural Diversity encompasses interactions across functions, across organisational levels in the hierarchy, and across divisions. It also includes the 'strategic styles' (Goold and Campbell, 1987) that characterise the relationship between the corporate parent and organisation's divisions as well as strategic alliances and cooperative ventures. The extent to which corporate governance systems reflect diverse stakeholders is also included in this type of diversity. As organisations become increasingly flexible and agile, adopting cross-functional teams, networked structures, and a more global strategic posture, measuring this type of diversity will become increasingly important.

Business and Global Diversity encompasses the expansion and segmentation of customer markets, the diversification of products and services offered, and the variety of operating environments in which organisations work and compete. These environments are defined by community and societal expectations as well as by business cultures, and norms. Day and Van den Bulte (2002) claimed that the heterogeneity of internal resources enriches the 'diversity orientation' of an organisation and enhanced its ability to conduct a dialogue across diverse customer contact points, thus improving marketing effectiveness in diverse market environments and conferring competitive advantage.

The second learning outcome establishes a link between the concepts of 'diversity' and the 'learning organisation'. This is useful because it helps build a richer picture of the way that diversity can contribute to competitive advantage and innovation in organisations. In this context, the concept of 'absorptive capacity' (Cohen and Levinthal, 1990; Zahra and George, 2002) will be used to indicate how 'diversity density' and a 'diversity mindset' can make knowledge derived from 'diverse' markets intelligible.

Hopkins *et al.* (2008) provide a well articulated definition of the terms 'diversity density' and 'diversity mindset'; The concept of diversity density refers not only to the percentage of diverse employees in an organisation's workforce, but also to the extent to which individuals from these diverse groups (including diverse professional groupings) are represented at all levels of the organisation. The concept of diversity mindset refers to the extent to which an organisation's senior executives view diversity as a business strategy rather than a management (or HRM department) issue.

The third learning outcome is supported by proposing a model (Figure 2.1) that explains how the structural aspects such as information system architecture, networking groups, control and reward systems, and corporate governance both influence and are influenced by the 'diversity orientation' (diversity density) in the organisation. The link between diversity, absorptive capacity, and competencies in the value chain will be explained in a later section.

The fourth learning outcome is the importance of having systems of measurement with which the benefits of diversity (sometimes intangible) can be measured. This measurement is based on standard measures (Sambamurthy et al., 2003; Mathiyalakan et al., 2005) as well as on a 'diversity scorecard' approach (Kaplan and Norton, 1996; Wheeler, 1998; Hubbard, 2004).

Before moving onto examining these points in detail, we will consider some of the claimed benefits of diversity.

The claimed benefits of diversity

The literature claims a number of benefits for diversity and these are summarised in Table 2.1. In doing this, the benefits have been mapped against the 'diversity scorecard' perspectives suggested by Edward Hubbard (2004). A brief definition of a 'scorecard' would be helpful to the reader here and more detailed explanation will follow later in the chapter. The scorecard approach is designed to provide a systematic approach to developing strategic management performance measurements. The scorecard provides a series of 'perspectives' that provide a rational basis for grouping the various metrics that help identify the contribution that diversity makes to competitive advantage. It should be emphasised that the headings provided by writers in the 'scorecard' literature provide generic examples and typically, each organisation would design and demonstrate a set of measures that reflect its unique circumstances.

As seen from Table 2.1, numerous benefits have been ascribed to diversity ranging from internal cost savings, to greater learning and flexibility, a more diverse mindset and better understanding of the customer. These are significant claims and an understanding of the

Table 2.1 Claimed benefits of diversity

Workplace climate/culture

Reduced inter-group conflict (Kandola and Fullerton, 1998)
Positive consequences for recruitment and retention (Baldiga, 2005; Lockwood, 2005)
Improved employee relations (McEnrue, 1993)

Financial impact

Reduced labour costs, recruitment, turnover and training (McEnrue, 1993)

Diversity Leadership Commitment

Better 'diversity mindset' within in the senior management team (Hopkins et al., 2008)

Table 2.1 (Continued)

Learning and growth

New product development (McEnrue, 1993)
Greater creativity (McEnrue, 1993)
Improved innovation capability (Nieto and Quevedo, 2005)
Increased capacity for establishing and establish and maintaining inter-organisational relationships. (McEnrue, 1993).
Improved 'absorptive capacity' (Cohen and Levinthal, 1990; also Zahra and George, 2002) i.e. its ability to apply new, external knowledge
Improved strategic 'diversity mindset' and strategic planning (David et al., 1999)
Improved 'corporate agility' (Sambamurthy et al., 2003; Mathiyalakan et al., 2005)

Diverse Customer/Community Partnerships

improved understanding of client and customers needs (Day and Van den Bulte, 2002)
Improved responsiveness and customer loyalty (Rigby, 2006)
Broader perspectives (Lockwood, 2005)
Enhanced public image (Legitimacy) (McEnrue, 1993)
Enhanced ability to deal with changing environments (Lowell and Zanini, 2005)

---

literature makes it clear that these benefits cannot be delivered without an organisational structure that fosters diversity. The form that this could take is the subject of the next section.

Diversity friendly structures

Internal (and external) policy interventions to encourage and foster diversity in organisations require a diversity friendly infrastructure at the organisational level. Stating this another way, single threaded diversity solutions, such as reliance on recruitment, or single-approach management techniques, such as requiring every employee to take diversity training, do not create lasting change or sustainable advantage (Kossak and Lobel, 1996). Golembiewski (1995) concluded, after a comprehensive analysis of several case studies, that interventions that focus in a general sense on 'valuing diversity' are not sufficient to bring about the sustainable benefits from diversity that translate into organisational performance. Similarly, even if some or many individuals develop diversity-friendly relationships in a large system, it is not at all clear that systemic behaviours and attitudes will change sufficiently to make a difference. The obstacles to change can include cultures, structural arrangements, and embedded organisational routines that can blunt diversity-oriented transformations and inhibit their diffusion (Argyris and Schon, 1978). As additional evidence of this, Susan and Allan Mohrman observe (1993), 'Teaching an individual (for example) teamwork skills will not lead to a different way of enacting a role unless the organisation collectively determines that organisational performance is achieved through teamwork and changes the organisational design features to promote it.' An earlier writer Fleishman (1962) reinforces this by making the observation that in organisations with non diversity friendly infrastructure, successful learning by individuals may even be punished because their individual growth curve is ahead of the organisation's.

In fact, the evidence suggests that to achieve sustainable diversity-friendly systems, systemic and structural organisational components need to change in tandem with the introduction of 'diversity policies'. Successful examples of this include the Metropolitan Atlanta Rapid Transit Authority (Golembiewski and Kiepper, 1988) and Avon Products (Thomas, 1991) showing how effective results are only produced where there is close attention to systemic procedures as well as to organisation's structural dimensions.

In order to enrich our analysis of diversity at the organisational level, it is nevertheless important to introduce the important systemic variable of public policy into our framework. As already pointed out, full leveraging of diversity for competitive advantage requires that wider environmental factors are taken into account. A major factor impacting internal diversity policy is wider public policy on this issue. Organisations cannot afford to ignore this since it impacts policy design and, in a similar way, organisational best practice will in turn influence public policy design and debate. In fact, it can be argued that widespread industry-level diffusion requires a two-way flow between organisational and public policy. Examples include the presence of working parental leave policies and benefits for same-sex partners, policies that only began to enter the realm of public policy after they already existed as embedded organisational practice.

In fact, the role of organisations in shaping wider diversity policy and acting as the lead driver in future diversity initiatives in society has been acknowledged by several commentators (Lawler, 1993). We have referred to the importance of structure and we look at this in more detail in the next section.

Diversity, organisational structure, and competitive advantage

Some authors have suggested that bureaucratic organisational structures inhibit an organisation's ability to leverage the diversity, knowledge, and talents of its workforce. While there are many models of diversity management in the literature – Kandola and Fullerton (1998) suggest no fewer than 11 models – few commentators have drawn attention to connections between organisational structure and diversity. As a result, little attention has been given to the need for structural change as a prerequisite for successfully leveraging diversity for competitive advantage. So, although some authors have started to describe these problems (Thomas, 1991; Cox, 1993; Becker *et al.*, 2001; Moss, 2009), this has not been an exclusive concern in their work. For example, the main focus of Cox (1993) was on cultural diversity in organisations, while Becker *et al.* (2001) did attempt to make the link between people, strategy, and performance without a particular focus on structure and diversity. The main focus of Moss (2009) was on the impact of gender in design and marketing.

It should be said that, while it is not the purpose of this chapter to provide an overview of the various models of diversity management in the literature, a new model is introduced (Figure 2.1) that captures the dynamic interaction between structure and diversity density and indicators of performance relating to improvement in strategic resources and competencies within the value chain. Included within structure are information and knowledge management systems, key determinants of an organisation's absorptive capacity, which link to the concept of the 'learning organisation'. A learning organisation may be defined as one capable of transforming 'tacit knowledge' into a hard-to-imitate strategic resource (Barney, 2001), and while the 'learning organisation' can contribute to diversity, so too can diversity contribute to the learning organisation.

The interactive impact of the three factors in the model – structure, diversity density, and the value chain – contribute to 'distinctiveness' in an organisation's competences. Since the literature suggests that the development of competences over time facilitates the accumulation of competitive strategic resources in the value chain (Barney, 2001; Haberberg and Rieple, 2008), the development of these diversity-inclusive competences is a key contributor to absorptive capacity and competitive advantage.

Figure 2.1 shows how diversity can generate tangible benefits that contribute towards competitive advantage. Indeed diversity may be perceived as a potential intangible strategic resource within the value chain. This shows the importance of attaching weight to an organisation's intangible diversity assets, and moving beyond a focus on tangible assets and resources such as, store branches, employee headcount, and distribution depots. The structural aspects such as information system architecture, networking groups, control and reward systems, and corporate governance both influence and are influenced by the 'diversity orientation' (diversity density) in the organisation. For example, the presence of effective networking groups and cross-functional teams will enable effective operational agility and improve product/service development, and investment in information knowledge management systems will help to codify and retrieve appropriate knowledge and thus improve absorptive capacity and improve local responsiveness and market agility.

In the next section, we consider how the intangible benefits that diversity can bring can be measured.

Measuring the benefits of diversity

Calculating the impact of intangible human assets in today's market place has been challenging for a number of reasons. As some authors have pointed out (Becker *et al.*, 2001; Hubbard, 2004), the accounting systems in use today evolved during a time when tangible capital, both financial and physical, constituted the principal source of profits. With today's emphasis on knowledge and intangible assets, however, conventional accounting systems are thought to create information distortions (Becker *et al.*, 2001). As early as 1996, Kaplan and Norton highlighted examples of external investor dissatisfaction with the exclusive focus on financial reporting. They cite, for example, a vice president of US Steel who stated:

> Non-financial performance measures – such as measuring customer satisfaction or speed at which new products move from the development stage – would be very helpful to investors and analysts. Companies should report this type of information to provide a complete picture of their operations.

We will now turn to some of the factors that contribute to an organisation's capacity to utilise diversity in a strategic fashion.

Diversity and the learning organisation

How does an organisation obtain strategic benefits from diversity? We saw earlier, that an important contributory factor in delivering diversity for strategic advantage is becoming a learning organisation. This is defined as one that acquires and transfers knowledge, and modifies its behaviour to reflect new knowledge and insights (Garvin, 1993). The literature on 'diversity' and the 'learning organisation' can be viewed as complimentary since both aim to release the potential of employees for the benefit of the organisation, and both rely on a supportive culture and supportive infrastructure. The learning organisation, in fact, enables the full utilisation of all potential and if the organisation is not diversity-oriented, there is a risk that the available pool of potential will be narrow. The learning organisation therefore needs to ensure that the organisation is successfully managing diversity and Hall and Parker (1993) argue the need for taking a view in which managing diversity and the learning organisation are viewed as complimentary (Figure 2.2). This co-dependence of a diversity-based and learning organisation ensures that more of the available potential within the organisation is realised. How does this co-dependence work? Managing diversity maximises the potential and in doing so increases the available pool of potential for the learning organisation by pushing out the boundaries of the circle. It is this increased pool of potential that is harnessed, resulting in the realisation of all possible potential (the outer circle). Adopting this complimentary approach, as can be seen from Figure 2.2 ensures that all the potential realised is constantly being magnified (Hall and Parker, 1993).

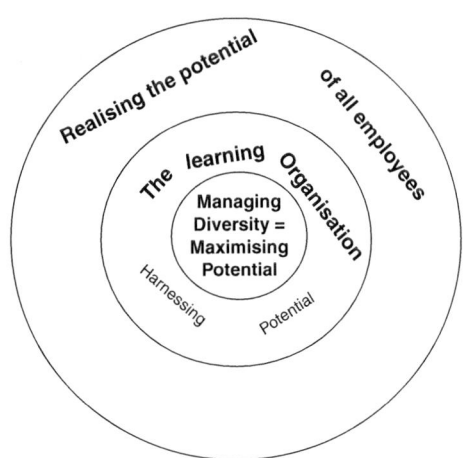

Figure 2.2 Diversity and the 'learning organisation' a complimentary approach. Adapted from Kandola and Fullerton (1998)

The parallels between a diversity and learning organisation approach are important and offer scope to writers on diversity to tackle issues relating to the learning organisation. Managing diversity should not be seen as separate from the learning organisation and should instead be striving to refresh such approaches with principles of diversity by adopting a complimentary approach. Hall and Parker (1993) were the earliest commentators in favour of adopting this complimentary approach.

Having drawn the parallels between these two approaches, it is only fair to point out that some features differentiate them. So, the diversity-oriented organisation, for example, has a more individual focus with specific training targeted at the individual while the learning organisation moves the emphasis from training 'done to you', to learning which is 'learner-led'. Moreover, while both approaches advocate a change in culture, systems, and managerial skills, managing diversity differs in the importance it places on auditing organisational processes with an eye to their objectivity and fairness. The learning organisation, on the other hand, aims to introduce new working methods that enable the organisation to learn more effectively.

Diversity, absorptive capacity, and innovation

As mentioned earlier diversity is a contributor to absorptive capacity, which as we saw earlier describes the extent to which an organisation can absorb scientific or technological information. This notion has been identified and developed by several authors (Cohen and Levinthal, 1990; Zahra and George, 2002) and refers to an organisation's ability to recognise the value, assimilate, and apply new, external knowledge from the environment and make strategic choices that contribute towards competitive advantage.

To relate this to diversity, it can be argued that accumulated prior knowledge increases the ability to put new knowledge into memory and recall it. There may also be a transfer of learning skills across bodies of knowledge, and learning in one task may affect learning in another task. Prior knowledge and heuristics constitute the related problem-solving knowledge that permits individuals to acquire related problem solving capabilities. Learning capabilities involve the development of the capacity to assimilate existing knowledge, while problem-solving skills represent a capacity to create new knowledge. They are not very different. Therefore it can be argued that creative capacity and absorptive capacity are similar.

With regards to the benefits of diversity on learning, the more effort applied to learning the better the subsequent retrieval. A diverse background provides a more robust basis for learning in uncertain situations and stimulates creativity by associating to more linkages. Cohen and Levinthal (1990) also make the point that diversity across individual absorptive capacities connects diverse knowledge structures and elicits the sort of learning and problem solving that yields innovation. It increases the chance for more novel linkages. Critical knowledge is only part of the need for innovation. The ability to know where complementary expertise (who knows what) resides is also crucial and we refer to this in Table 2.2 as 'partnering agility'.

Another study by Nieto and Quevedo (2005) indicated that there was a positive and significant relationship between the variables of absorptive capacity and innovative effort. This led the authors to the view that absorptive capacity was more important in determining the effort put into innovation by organisations than other structural conditions (such as size, coordination between departments, types of diversification strategy, etc) to which organisations were subject.

The concept of absorptive capacity is clearly an important one and we will now discuss how diversity density in an organisation enables the development of 'diversity knowledge' which increases absorptive capacity. One might legitimately ask how absorptive capacity can be developed in an organisation and it is to consideration of this that we now turn.

Several factors have been identified as increasing absorptive capacity. Prior investment in the development of its individual members' capacities is one factor since individual members' prior knowledge base is strongly associated with their capacities to understand new and relevant knowledge. This capacity is, in turn, enhanced when there is familiarity with the knowledge source and this implies that the more novel the external environment, the more difficult it will be to achieve both individual and organisational absorptive capacity.

One study (Hopkins et al., 2008) discussed the importance of external knowledge to organisations involved in markets with a highly diverse customer base, arguing that a firm's 'diversity knowledge' (its familiarity of markets with a highly diverse customer base) is critical to success. Thus they argue that an organisation's diversity knowledge antecedes its ability to recognise the value of this diversity knowledge, assimilate it, and apply it such that profitability is achieved through the development of sales of products and services to those markets. This is also supported by Banks (2007) who suggested that rising immigration in

Table 2.2 Proposed framework by author adapted from Wheeler (1998) and Hubbard (2004)

Stages in the diversity process	Workforce diversity	Cognitive and behavioral diversity	Strategy	Structural diversity
Creating	The recruitment, selection, and retention efforts of the organisation towards diversity that go beyond simple compliance. Flexible and progressive policy on disability. Balanced representation	Diversity awareness initiatives. Control and reward systems to foster diversity. Scenario planning processes and systems to foster diverse thinking (e.g. David et al., 1999). Cognitive 'mental models' in the executive team (Todorova and Durisin, 2007)	Deploying staff in global markets. Strategic alliance creation	Open corporate governance systems in place that reflect diverse stakeholders (Fliaster and Marr, 2001) Fluid and dynamic team/matrix based structures. Control and reward systems to foster diversity
Managing	Succession planning. Performance reviews. Downsizing Litigation. Dual career paths. Cross-functional teams	Job enrichment and rotation. Leadership behaviours and practices. Concept of 'strategic diversity mindset' (Laczniak and Lusch, 1997; Gupta and Govindarajan, 2002; Hopkins et al., 2008; Paul, 2008)	Secondment/rotation to foreign divisions. Flexible corporate parenting styles (Goold and Campbell, 1987)	Flexible corporate parenting styles. Knowledge management systems

Table 2.2 (Continued)

Stages in the diversity process	Workforce diversity	Cognitive and behavioral diversity	Strategy	Structural diversity
Valuing	Work-life benefits Diverse inclusive environment that fosters employee satisfaction and performance	Networking groups Employee aspirations Concept of 'strategic diversity mindset'	Community/corporate image Local responsiveness	Community/corporate Networking groups
Leveraging	Improved 'Absorptive Capacity' Improved employee satisfaction and retention leading to cost savings. Corporate agility: Operational agility (Sambamurthy et al., 2003)	Community/corporate image Improve learning and growth (Senge and Sterman, 1991; Hamel and Prahalad, 1993) Improved innovative capability and product/service development	Corporate agility: customer and partnership agility (Sambamurthy et al., 2003; Mathiyalakan et al., 2005) Dynamic capability Community/corporate image Customer satisfaction and improved CRM (Day and Van den Bulte, 2002)	Improved 'Absorptive capacity' (Cohen and Levinthal, 1990; Zahra and George, 2002) Improved contingency planning capability Improved innovative effort driven by enhanced absorptive capacity (Nieto and Quevedo, 2005)

Note: Measures are not necessarily exclusive to each category, nor is this an exhaustive list.

nations around the world is creating markets with a highly diverse customer base. However, Hopkins *et al.*, stress that the presence of diversity knowledge in an organisation does not, of itself, guarantee that this knowledge will be leveraged by the organisation for competitive advantage. For the absorption process to begin, they argue, the senior executives in an organisation must play a key role in judging the potential of new knowledge. This provides a 'diversity mindset', and they contend that where this is high, diversity knowledge will be more easily recognised and assimilated than where the senior executives' mindset is focused at the operational level.

A word on terms. The concept of diversity density (Hopkins *et al.*, 2008) refers not only to the percentage of racially diverse employees in an organisation's workforce, but also to the extent to which individuals from these diverse groups (including diverse professional groupings) are represented at all levels of the organisation. They derived this concept from the work of Cox and Blake (1991). Where low diversity density would correspond to Cox's concept of a monolithic organisation. Such an organisation would have a low level of racial diversity in its workforce and high levels of occupational segregation. In contrast an organisation with high diversity density is consistent with Cox's concept of a multicultural organisation. In this organisation the work force is both culturally diverse and is also structurally integrated at all management levels and job categories.

The term diversity mindset refers to the extent to which an organisation's senior executives view diversity as a business strategy rather than a management (or HRM department) issue. Several studies (Laczniak and Lusch, 1997; Gupta and Govindarajan, 2002; Paul, 2008) have explored the concept of a global or executive mindset, generally defined as the ability of an organisation's senior executives to demonstrate openness to and awareness of diversity across cultures and markets. These authors also suggest that a global mindset guides senior executives' collection and interpretation of new information about these markets. Hopkins *et al.* (2008) further expand the term diversity mindset to include a component where executives recognise the need to create a 'safe' environment that facilitates knowledge sharing among the firms diverse workforce.

This mindset leads to a better understanding of the needs of markets with a diverse customer base and helps to determine what action is required to influence the buying decisions of customers comprising this market. This leads Hopkins and colleagues (2008) to conclude that the higher the level of diversity density in an organisation, the easier it is for the organisation to assimilate diversity knowledge. They further argue that trans-national organisations using locally informed employees benefit from the country knowledge or 'diversity orientation' perspective introduced. These organisations demonstrate diversity density and can use it to interpret the applicability of diversity knowledge in specific situations.

As indicated earlier, a diversity mindset also includes the motivation to create a diversity climate within the firm. Day and Van den Bulte (2002) further examined this internal 'motivation' process in the domain of customer relationship management. They defined this as a cross-functional process for achieving a continuing dialogue with customers, across all their contact and access points, with personalised treatment of the most valuable customers, to increase customer retention and the effectiveness of marketing initiatives.

Their study is of interest from the point of view of diversity as they point out that an essential ingredient of the dialogue with customers is the ability to integrate information from diverse sources and arrive at a coherent picture of the customer and their needs. They indicate that the heterogeneity of internal resources enriches the 'diversity orientation' of the organisation and enhances the ability to conduct a dialogue across diverse customer contact points. The work of Day and Van den Bulte (2002) provides more evidence of the link between internal 'diversity density' and the ability to manage and make sense of an externally diverse environment in order to obtain competitive advantage.

We have seen how diversity density can help the interpretation of diversity knowledge and a further factor that can support the interpretation is a diversity mindset. Todorova and Durisin (2007) contended that the cognitions of an organisation's executives play a key role in judging the potential and thus value of new knowledge. From a diversity perspective cognitive diversity can be considered to be an element of the 'diversity mindset' explained above but with a particular focus of the perceptions that executives take in from the environment and become part of their cognitive map for making sense of the world.

A useful illustration demonstrating the extent to which cognitive diversity has the potential to enhance organisational learning and absorptive capacity is provided by some earlier research conducted by the author and others (David et al., 1999). The longitudinal study involved exposing senior executives in several companies in the software industry to facilitated scenario planning interventions, and then measuring shifts in cognition using causal mapping techniques developed by Eden et al. (1998) in pre/post intervention interviews.

The conclusions were that actively involving senior executives in scenario planning workshops generated more diverse thinking and provided richer 'mental models' and thus contributed towards a 'diversity mindset'. This, in turn, improved 'absorptive capacity' and the ability to identify, understand, and exploit clues in the external environment. In this particular example, absorptive capacity was demonstrated by increased sensitivity to events that signal the unfolding of a particular 'scenario world' over time. The shared 'mental models' developed in the workshops also facilitated improved interpretation and communication of these events in the executive team. The relationship between diversity knowledge, diversity density, and diversity mindset are captured in Figure 2.3 (adapted by the author from Hopkins *et al.*, 2008).

Of course, the capability to manage diversity strategically is not one that can be acquired instantaneously and it is fruitful, therefore, to focus on the steps in the process by which diversity is achieved. A useful model is provided by Wheeler (1998), shown in Figure 2.4.

The four quadrants of this model identify typical 'steps' or phases that are relevant to all organisations as they go through the process of creating and developing diversity through to fully leveraging diversity

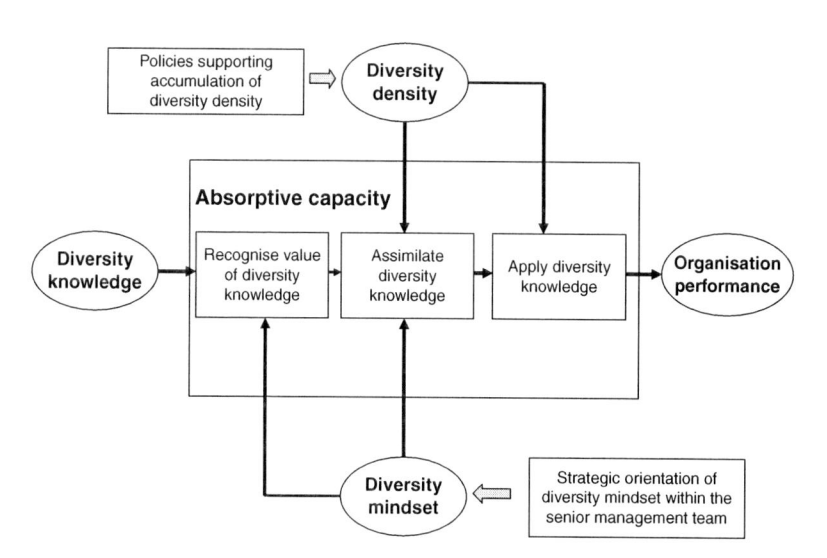

Figure 2.3 Absorptive Capacity within the Context of Diversity. Adapted from Hopkins *et al.* (2008)

Strategic measurement model

Organisational objectives — Processes	Managing	Valuing
Outcomes	Creating	Leveraging
	Compliance	Internalisation/ integration

Diversity objectives

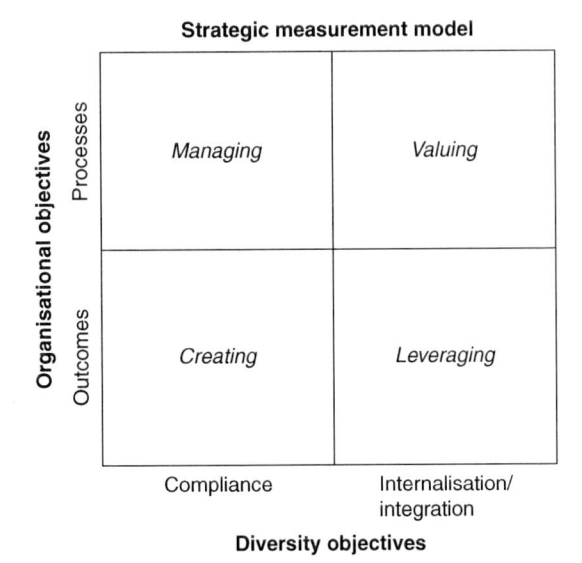

Figure 2.4 Diversity strategic process measurement model
Source: Michael L. Wheeler, 'Measuring diversity: A strategy for organisational effectiveness,' *Employment Relations Today*, 25(1), 1998, 61. Copyright John Wiley & Sons 1998. Reprinted with permission of John Wiley & Sons, Inc.

for competitive advantage. They reflect the stage of 'diversity penetration' in the particular organisation. The ultimate goal, and the theme of this chapter, is to reach a stage in the organisational diversity process where leveraging diversity for competitive advantage is achieved. The model helps remind organisations of the key stages in moving towards this goal.

The first step, Creating, involves the creation of a diverse workforce and infrastructure, with the latter including planning, control, and reward systems. This first step is, in fact, a prerequisite for achieving the other three steps namely, managing, valuing, and leveraging since it should provide organisations with the mix of skills and infrastructure necessary for moving on to the other three stages in the model. Typical measures might include strategic staffing initiatives in global markets, as well as initiating strategic alliances for knowledge transfer, etc.

The creating and managing quadrants might be called compliance-oriented measures in the sense that diversity is often driven by a public policy directive, a legal requirement, or an internal policy initiative. The second quadrant, the Managing diversity quadrant, encompasses measures relating to a variety of management issues and these could include communications issues (collaborative or directive) as well as retention rates of mission critical staff and complaints. It could also include corporate parenting styles in relation to strategic business units (Goold and Campbell, 1987), and 'open' or 'closed' corporate governance models (Fliaster and Marr, 2001).

Both Managing and Valuing diversity components are process-oriented and geared towards ensuring a system supportive of diversity. As mentioned earlier, the strategy and diversity literatures support the view that systemic and structural organisational components need to change in tandem with the introduction of 'diversity policies' in order to achieve sustainable diversity friendly systems. The Valuing component reflects a move from compliance to internalisation/integration with diversity values internalised through employee, manager, and strategic alliance partners attitudes and actions. Measures include, networking groups, leadership 'diversity mind set', culture of organisation, percentage diversity initiatives implemented, and work life benefits utilised.

When a company has reached the fourth and final quadrant, Leveraging, it is actually drawing on the strategic resources and capabilities created within the organisation. These will consist of embedded supportive infrastructure, systems, and procedures and it is the integration of diversity characteristics and infrastructure that will confer competitive advantage through, dynamic capability, improved product development, and understanding customer needs (see Figure 2.1). Measures associated with leveraging diversity would include the relationship with local communities, successes/failures in foreign markets, and the outcomes from strategic partnerships and alliances. Other measures include those associated with measures of agility and dynamic capability (Mathiyalakan et al., 2005), such as time to market.

An understanding of the term agility? Some authors (e.g. Sambamurthy et al., 2003) have argued that agility is comprised of three interrelated capabilities: customer agility, partnering agility, and operational agility. They define customer agility as the ability of the organisation to leverage the voice of the customer to gain market information and detect competitive opportunities. A more diverse marketing department combined with a 'strategic diversity mindset' allows diverse market segments and different cultures to be better understood and responded to.

Partnership agility is the ability to leverage the assets, knowledge, and competencies of suppliers and distributors to form a network to explore opportunities for innovation and competitive action. Amit and Schoemaker (1993) and Day and Van den Bulte (2002), introduced earlier, further explain this type of agility when they point out that differences in firm performance stem from heterogeneity in resources and the existence of these enables a more flexible response to moves by competitors as well as enhancing the ability to have a dialogue with a diverse customer base. Operational agility is the ability of the organisation to redesign existing processes rapidly and create new processes in a timely fashion. Cross-functional teams with diverse skills supported by appropriate infrastructure (e.g. information systems) are better able to take advantage of dynamic market conditions.

The diversity strategic process measurement model (Figure 2.4) is multidimensional and can be a strong tactical tool when looked at from different levels. It can also provide insight into understanding the diffusion of diversity management practice, both within a single organisation and within a particular society over time. In order to illustrate this, the current diffusion of 'diversity management practice' can be compared with the earlier development and growth of the 'total quality movement' as it moved towards 'strategic quality management' (Garvin, 1987). If we do this then we can observe that, in the earlier stages of their development, both initiatives were looked at, as 'problems to be solved' with the emphasis on compliance-oriented responses. In the case of diversity, this may have implied 'equal opportunities' and in the quality area, inspection for compliance. In both cases, the responsibility resided at the functional departmental level and only later, in the development cycle was it apparent that these areas could be leveraged for competitive advantage. In both cases, the critical factor that drove organisations towards a strategic orientation was a change of mindset within senior management. It follows therefore that if senior management want to leverage diversity a prerequisite is 'strategic diversity mindset' within the senior management team.

In order to add further value to this tool the grid in Table 2.2 had been developed by the author combining the different types of diversity with the diversity process stages.

Measuring and leveraging diversity for competitive advantage

In the past few years we have seen an increasing appreciation of the value of the more intangible assets of the business and an associated trend towards strategic performance measurement systems. How can these be measured? One method of measuring these intangible assets is the Diversity Scorecard (Wheeler, 1998; Hubbard, 2004), a tool to assist with the process of creating, managing, valuing, and leveraging organisational diversity for competitive advantage.

The emphasis of this chapter, and indeed the book, is how diversity can impact on organisational performance and so the emphasis in this section will be on why a scorecard approach helps managers better understand the links between diversity, strategic measures of organisational performance and bottom line profitability. The reader is encouraged to look to specific sources such as Hubbard (2004) for extensive guidance on how to introduce the scorecard in an organisation through the development of specific tailored scorecard metrics. This section will draw on the earlier work on scorecard development (Kaplan and Norton, 1996; Wheeler, 1998; Hubbard, 2004) and combine it with the diversity model developed by the author (Figure 2.1) in order to:

- Introduce a strategic measurement model that will assist organisations in creating, managing, valuing, and leveraging organisational diversity for competitive advantage.
- Provide an outline classification of the different types of diversity scorecard measures that can measure the impact of diversity and its contribution to the organisation's performance.

In the next section, we describe a tool for measuring these aspects.

The diversity scorecard: An overview and indicative measures

The 'diversity scorecard' is a tool that assists in creating, managing, valuing, and leveraging all aspects that constitute our wider definition of diversity for competitive advantage (Wheeler, 1998). This scorecard will enable organisations to align diversity initiatives with other critical business initiatives. As a result, organisations will be able to measure and assess diversity management with the same rigour as other operations that are critical in contributing to the 'bottom line'. This approach draws on the original balanced scorecard concept developed by Robert Kaplan and David Norton (1996), and developed to specifically include diversity by Wheeler (1998) and Hubbard (2004).

A brief overview of a generic scorecard structure based on the work of Hubbard (2004) will be presented below for those readers unfamiliar with the scorecard concept.

This scorecard presented in simplified form below should not be confused with the different types of diversity mentioned earlier or the stages in the diversity process in Figure 2.4. The perspectives in Table 2.3 are suggested by Hubbard as a rational basis for grouping of the various metrics that help identify the contribution that diversity makes

Table 2.3 Scorecard perspectives proposed by the author adapted from Hubbard (2004) and Kaplan and Norton (1996)

Diverse customer/community perspective Describes the ways in which value is to be created for diverse customers, how diverse demand for this value is satisfied and operational excellence required to achieve this value. From a community perspective, the scorecard must also reflect the organisation's efforts as a good corporate citizen	Number of staff at client locations Number of staff at client locations Number of countries, cultures, languages by customer vs. your workforce representation Level of access to ethnic group customer information Number of sponsored community events Percentage change in customer demographics
Workforce profile This perspective of the diversity scorecard typically reflects the recruitment, selection, and retention efforts of the organisation beyond the normal affirmative action reporting	Percentage new hires by demographic group Percentage diversity survival and loss rates Percentage turnover by length of service Percentage absenteeism by demographic group
Workforce climate/culture This perspective is structured to provide feedback on the degree to which the organisation has created a diverse, inclusive environment that fosters employee satisfaction and performance	Retention rates of critical human capital Number of lawsuits by demographic group Absence rate Percentage gender-based pay differential Percentage work life benefits utilised Percentage diversity initiatives implemented
Diversity leadership commitment The degree to which the organisations leaders are utilising behaviours that set the vision, direction, policy, and a personal model for the diversity effort through demonstrated actions	Percentage of diversity goals achieved Percentage of diverse employees mentored who are promoted Percentage Board representation by group Diversity mentioned in executive presentations
Learning and growth The degree to which key strategic capabilities are being developed among all segments of the diverse workforce	Employee suggestions. Number of employees with computers Participation in share ownership plans Personal goal achievement Joint ventures and strategic alliances
Financial impact perspective	Appropriate financial measures

to organisational effectiveness. The measures below are only generic examples and typically, each organisation would demonstrate a set of measures that reflected its unique circumstances.

Conclusions

One of the key messages expressed in this chapter is the need for organisations to leverage diversity for competitive advantage. This involves widening the traditional focus of diversity beyond viewing it as 'a problem to be solved', or ethnic representation, or simply another human resource policy. Diversity should instead become an embedded part of the value chain of the organisation, and be viewed as a strategic resource that impacts on the bottom line. In order for this to happen, the (diversity) mindset of senior management needs to change so that they can embrace a strategic view of diversity and develop policies that support the accumulation of diversity characteristics (or 'diversity density') within the organisation. Many organisations think they are embracing diversity when in fact they have only taken a partial journey into three quadrants of Figure 2.3. In other words, they have made compliance-oriented efforts to create diversity measures and introduced management processes to monitor their efforts without taking the final steps towards valuing and ultimately leveraging diversity for competitive advantage. This was pointed out above when the diffusion of 'diversity management' was contrasted and compared with the diffusion of the 'total quality' movement.

Another key theme introduced in this chapter has been the importance of internal (and external) policy interventions to encourage and foster diversity in organisations. These require a diversity-friendly infrastructure at the organisational level as Mohrman (1993), an earlier writer in the field, has pointed out. The successful introduction of diversity cannot be achieved by single-threaded diversity solutions, or by single approach management techniques but, instead, as he says, requires:

> Mission, strategy, and values for overall guidance; objectives and budgets to guide operations; information systems that connect relevant individuals and functions; development career paths that contribute to the ability of individuals to function in integrative organisations; and performance -management practices that encourages the effectiveness of individuals, teams, and systems, as well as facilitating valid and reliable estimates of effectiveness.

In this way, interventions that focus in a general sense on 'valuing diversity' are not sufficient to bring about the sustainable benefits from diversity that will translate into organisational performance. The chapter closed with an overview of a generic 'diversity scorecard' that measures an organisation's ability to align diversity and business initiatives. This helps make the link between diversity management activities and organisational performance explicit, thereby adding credibility to the diversity initiative. This alignment of diversity with business initiatives guarantees a more coherent and integrated approach to diversity, from inception right through to leveraging diversity for competitive advantage.

Acknowledgments

Thanks to Gloria Moss, the editor of this book, for her patience in influencing and encouraging the process of writing this chapter.

Thanks also to Dr Toni Hilton, Associate Dean of Research and Knowledge Transfer at Westminster Business School, for useful and constructive feedback in helping shape the chapter.

References

Amit, Raphael and Schoemaker, Paul J.H., (1993). 'Strategic assets and organisational rent', *Strategic Management Journal*, 14 (January), 33–46.

Argyris, Chris and Schon, Donald, (1978). *Organisational Learning*. Reading, MA: Addison-Wesley.

Baldiga, Nancy R. (2005). 'Opportunity and balance: Is your organization ready to provide both? Which of your valued professionals will be moving up – and which moving out?', *Journal of Accountancy*, 199.

Banks, J.A. (2007). *Diversity and citizenship education: Global perspectives*. Indianapolis, IN: Jossey-Bass.

Barney, J.B. (2001). 'Resource-based theories of competitive advantage: A ten year retrospective on the resource-based view', *Journal of Management*, 27, 643–650.

Becker, B.E., Huselid, M.A., and Ulrich, D. (2001). *The HR Scorecard: Linking People, Strategy, and Performance*. Boston: Harvard Business School Press.

Cohen, W.M. and Levinthal, D.A. (1990). 'Absorptive capacity: A new perspective on learning and innovation', *Administrative Science Quarterly*, 35(1), 128–152.

Cox, Taylor Jr. (1993). *Cultural Diversity in Organisations*. San Francisco: Berret-Kochler.

Cox, Taylor Jr. (2001). *Creating the Multicultural Organisation: A Strategy for Capturing the Power of Diversity*. San Francisco: Jossy-Bass, 77.

Cox, T.H. and Blake, S. (1991) 'Managing cultural diversity: Implications for organisational competitiveness', *Academy of Management Executive*, 5, 45–56.

David, Alan, Brian, Cox, and Adrian, Haberberg (1999) 'Measuring the Impact of Scenario Planning on Organisational Cognition'. *Paper Presented to the 6th*

International Workshop on Managerial and Organisational Cognition, Colchester, UK. Unpublished Working Paper. University of Westminster Press 1999 (ISBN 1 85919 108 8).

Day, George S. and Van den Bulte, Christophe. (2002). 'Superiority in customer relationship management: Consequences for competitive advantage and performance', *The Wharton School: University of Pennsylvania.* Report No. 02-123. Cambridge, MA: Marketing Science Institute.

Eden, C. and Spender, J.C. (eds) (1998). *Managerial and Organisational Cognition: Theory, Methods and Research.* Sage Publications. London.

Fleishman, Edwin A. (1962). 'Patterns of leadership behaviour related to group grievances and turnover', *Personnel Psychology*, 15, 43–56.

Fliaster, A. and Marr, R. (2001). 'Change of the insider-oriented corporate governance in Japan and Germany: Between Americanisation and tradition', *Journal of Change Management*, 1(3), 242–256.

Garvin, D.A. (1987). 'Competing on the eight dimensions of quality', *Harvard Business Review*, 65(6), November–December, 101–109.

Garvin, D.A. (1993). 'Building a learning organisation', *Harvard Business Review*, July–August, 78–91.

Golembiewski, Robert T. (1995). *Managing Diversity in Organisations.* Tuscaloosa and London: University of Alabama Press, p. 13.

Golembiewski, Robert T. and Kiepper, Allan (1988) *High Performance and Human Costs.* New York: Praeger.

Goold, M. and Campbell, A. (1987) *Strategies and Styles: The Role of the Centre in Managing Diversified Corporations.* Oxford: Blackwell.

Gupta, A.K. and Govindarajan, V. (2002). 'Cultivating a global mindset', *Academy of Management Executive*, 16, 116–126.

Haberberg, A. and Rieple, Alison (2008). *Strategic Management: Theory and Application.* Oxford: Oxford University Press.

Hall, D.T. and Parker, V.A. (1993). 'The role of workplace flexibility in managing diversity', *Organisational Dynamics*, 22(1), 4–18.

Hamel, Gary and Prahalad, C.K. (1993). 'Strategy as stretch and leverage', *Harvard Business Review*, March–April, 15–84.

Hopkins, Willie E., Gross, M., and Hopkins, S.A. (2008) 'A Conceptual Assessment of Absorptive Capacity Through the Lens of Diversity'. *Proceedings of the Decision Sciences Institute Annual Meeting*, Baltimore, MD. Unpublished paper. For lead author contact: College of Business, California State University, Chico, Chico, CA 95929 001, 530.898.6272, wehopkins@csuchico.edu

Hubbard, Edward E. (2004). *The Diversity Scorecard.* Elsevier Butterworth-Heinemann. Burlington, MA 01803, USA and Linacre House, Jordan Hill, Oxford OX2 8DP, UK.

Jones, DeEtta (1999). 'The definition of diversity: two views: A more inclusive definition', *Journal of Library Administration*, 27, 5–15.

Kandola, R. and Fullerton, J. (1998). 'Diversity in action: Managing the mosaic', *CIPD, London*, Chartered Institute of Personnel and Development. Cromwell Press. Second edn.

Kaplan, R.S. and Norton, D.P. (1996). *The Balanced Scorecard.* Boston, MA: Harvard Business School Press.

Kossak, Ellen E. and Lobel, Sharon A. (1996). *Managing Diversity: Human Resources for Transforming the Workplace*, Cambridge, MA: Blackwell Business HRM Series.

Laczniak, G.R. and Lusch, R.F. (1997). 'The flexible executive mindset: How top management should look at tomorrow's market', *Journal of Consumer Marketing*, 14, 60–81.

Lawler, Edward E., III (1993). 'Creating the high-involvement organisation', in Jay R. Galbraith, Edward E. Lawler III and Associates, eds, *Organising for the Future*. San Francisco: Jossey-Bass pp. 172–193.

Lockwood, Nancy R. (2005). *HRM Magazine Vil. 50*. June.

Lowell, L, Bryan, and Michele Zanini, (2005). 'Strategy in an Era of Global Giants', *McKinsey Quarterly*, 4, 46–59.

Mathiyalakan, S., Ashrafi, N., Zhang, W., Waage, F., Kuilboer, J.P., and Heinmann, D. (2005). 'Defining Business Agility: An Exploratory Study', 16th Information Resource Management Association International conference, San Diego, CA, May 15–18, 2005.

McEnrue, M.P. (1993). 'Managing diversity: Los Angeles before and after the riots', *Organisational Dynamics*, Winter, 21, 3, 18–29.

Mohrman, Susan (1993). 'Integrating roles and structure in the lateral organisation', In Jay R. Galbraith, Edward E. Lawler III, and Associates eds, *Organising for the Future*. San Francisco: Jossey-Bass pp. 109–141.

Mohrman, Susan A., and Allan M. Mohrman. (1993). 'Organisational Change and Learning.' In Jay R. Galbraith, Edward E. Lawler III, and Associates, *Organising for the Future*, pp. 87–108. San Francisco: Jossey-Bass.

Moss, Gloria. (2009). *Gender, Design and Marketing*, Gower Press. Farnham. Surrey. UK.

Nieto, M. and Quevedo, P. (2005). 'Absorptive capacity, technological opportunity, knowledge spillovers, and innovative effort', *Technovation*, 25, 1141–1157, Elsevier.

Paul, H. (2008). 'Creating a global mindset', *Thunderbird International Business Review*, 42, 187–200.

Rigby, Darell K, Vijay Vishwanath (2006), "Localization - The revolution in Consumer Markets", Harvard Business Review, (April) Vol. 84. No 4, pp. 82–92.

Sambamurthy, V., Bharadwaj, A.S., and Grover, V. (2003). 'Shaping agility through digital options: Reconceptualising the role of IT in contemporary firms', *MIS Quarterly*, 27(2), 237–263.

Senge, P.M. and Sterman, J.D. (1991). *Systems Thinking and Organisational Learning: Acting Locally and Thinking Globally in the Organisation of the Future*, Oxford: University Press.

Thomas, R. Roosevelt Jr. (1991). *Beyond Race and Gender*, New York: AMACON. From (1990) 'From Affirmative Action to Affirming Diversity'. *HBR 68* (March–April): 107–117.

Todorova, G. and Durisin, B. (2007). 'Absorptive capacity: Valuing a reconceptualization', *Academy of Management Review*, 32, 774–786.

Wheeler, Michael L. (1998). 'Measuring diversity: A strategy for organisational effectiveness,' *Employment Relations Today*. Spring 1998. John Wiley and Sons Inc.

Zahra, S.A. and George, G. (2002). 'Absorptive capacity: A review, reconceptualisation, and extension', *Academy of Management Review*, 27(2), 185–203.

3
Eastward Enlargement, Cultural and National Identity, and Diversity in the European Union

Heather Skinner and Krzysztof Kubacki

The European Union consists of a large number of culturally diverse countries and marketers need to be aware of the extent to which each country's culture is homogeneous or heterogeneous. In 1995 Kale argued that 'while economic, political, and legal changes needed to homogenize Europe are daunting, the cultural heterogeneity among member nations will continue to remain the most significant barrier to integration', concluding that culture is one of the most important factors influencing buyer behaviours. This chapter, therefore, contributes to better understanding diversity within the European context by examining eastward enlargement, cultural and national identity, and diversity in the European Union.

A brief history of Europen Union enlargement

The European Economic Community (EEC) was founded by the Treaty of Rome in 1957 with six member nations: Belgium, France, Italy, Luxembourg, the Netherlands and West Germany. These nations were joined, in 1973, by Denmark, Ireland and the UK. Greece joined the EEC in 1981, with Portugal and Spain joining in 1986. The EEC was the forerunner of the entity we now know as the European Union (EU). The EU, formed by the 1993 Maastricht Treaty, extended the scope of the EEC, and established co-operation in common foreign and security policy and justice and home affairs, also establishing the groundwork for a single European currency. At the time of its creation the EU comprised 12 member states. Austria, Finland and Sweden joined the EU in 1995 shortly after its creation, and the 15 member state EU remained stable in composition for almost 10 years. Eastward enlargement of the

European Union (EU) in May 2004 created a domestic European market of over 450 million consumers in 25 member states, the world's largest single market, when the 'A8' nations of the Czech Republic, Estonia, Hungary, Latvia, Lithuania, Poland, Slovakia, Slovenia joined in addition to Cyprus and Malta. The EU further enlarged at the beginning of 2007 when it was joined by Romania and Bulgaria and now currently comprises 27 member states with a population of 493 million. Further enlargement of the EU is likely. Negotiations with Croatia and Turkey started in 2005, and, although an official candidate, a start date for negotiations with Macedonia has not yet been set. If these three candidate countries join the EU it would boost its present population by almost 79 million – an increase of 16 per cent.

The overall objective of the European Union is to create a market in which there are no economic barriers to trade between member countries. However, as the EU enlarges it is becoming increasingly heterogeneous in terms of culture, so while it is the world's largest single market in economic terms, it would be a mistake to assume the market is culturally homogeneous, which fact itself may pose a different type of barrier to trade.

National identity

Many authors believe that a national identity is conferred by where a person is born and where a person lives. However, other cultural markers such as language (Anderson, 1991; Cameron, 1999; Williams, 1999; Laitin, 2002; Mair and Zielonka, 2002) and religion (Laitin, 2002; Mair and Zielonka, 2002) are also very important contributors to a person's feeling of national identity, along with inherited traditions and the cultural values of communal life (Cobban, 1969), and, more recently, the right to hold a passport of that nation (Cameron, 1999).

This wider view of elements contributing to a person's sense of national identity may be accounted for in the various ways that nation states developed and have been perceived over time. Cobban (1969) has traced the growth of the nation state to the middle ages, a time when states were 'political entities and there was no belief in any necessary connection between cultural and political ties'. However, he found that there are opposing views as to what constitutes a nation. One perspective favours definitions based on political unity irrespective of nationality. The opposing conception of the nation is that most favoured by, among others, Herder, the founder of German nationalist thought, who, according to Cobban, was 'almost exclusively concerned with the idea of the nation as a cultural entity'. Cobban notes that 'the modern Western European conception of the nation has largely been a product of the fusion of these two tendencies, combining a measure of free individual choice with a consciousness of the inherited traditions and values of communal life'.

European identity

It was identified by Fuchs and Klingemann (2002) that 'many feel the EU can attain democratic legitimacy only if a European demos with a collective identity takes shape'. However, these authors are concerned that 'in view of the cultural plurality and heterogeneity of European nation states, it is doubtful whether the constitution of a European demos with a tenable collective identity is possible at all'.

Burgoyne and Routh (1999) discuss the findings of the *Eurobarometer* 46 (1997) survey into perceptions of self and national identity in member states, a survey that is periodically undertaken by the European Commission. 'One question asked respondents whether "in the near future" they saw themselves in terms of their "nationality only", as "nationality and European", "European and nationality" or "European only".' Aggregating data in each country, across 'Europe as a whole, 51 per cent saw themselves as "European" to some extent', but 'in all countries, those who felt mainly or wholly European were in the minority'.

Cultural convergence

The creation of a supra-national entity such as the EU has also led to the viewpoint that the concept of the nation state has now moved towards a post-national order where the classic parameters of the nation are rethought, and where the concept of nationhood is superseded by a higher notion of citizenship. This argument is linked to issues of cultural convergence and the belief that 'while societies are steadily moving together [that] the similarities between cultures will become much greater than their differences' (Pugh and Hickson, 2002), diluting distinctive individual national culture (Williams, 1999), and contracting the role of the nation state (Steger, 1998).

Cultural divergence

However, this post-national argument is not unopposed. The alternative argument considers cultural divergence, proposing that nationhood will become more, not less, important to individuals as a reaction to globalisation. Authors such as Zielonka and Mair (2002) believe that an eastwardly enlarged EU becomes much more diverse, citing elements such as political culture, language, religious beliefs and popular culture as revealing both similarities and differences between cultures. Laitin (2002) does not believe that such generalisations can be made across an enlarged EU since he believes that there are fundamental differences between nations from Central and Eastern Europe on the periphery of the European Union, and nations that are closer to the 'continental norm' of the original members.

Eastward enlargement has therefore brought the issue of a single European identity into sharp focus. Mayer and Palmowski (2004) believe that much more scholarly attention needs to be paid to the question of European identities. 'Europe has been described as the birthplace of the concept of the nation-state' (Burgoyne and Routh, 1999) and regardless of the post-national argument 'it is the nation-state that continues...to be the primary frame of reference for the community' (Mayer and Palmowski, 2004). This however makes a single European identity more difficult to achieve, as each nation state strives to maintain its own unique identity in an enlarged EU comprised of many diverse cultures.

Cultural diversity within EU member states has also been affected by the movement of nationals from one EU state to another. In 2007, a study by Sriskandarajah *et al.*, found that it was only as recently as the 1980s that the UK entered a period of net immigration, where more people migrated *to* the UK than *from* it. Since eastward enlargement (in the period from May 2004 to March 2007 when Sriskandarajah *et al.*,'s report was published), 605,375 people from the A8 member states had registered to work in the UK, although fewer than 25 per cent of these migrant workers planned to remain permanently in the UK, a much lower percentage than previous groups of immigrants.

Business and management in an enlarged EU

There are two main approaches to cross-cultural business and comparative management.

- Convergence and etic approaches – the *etic* stance is that management styles should not differ according to culture, especially due to 'technology, structure and global orientation by many firms' (Warner and Joynt, 2002).

- Divergence and emic approaches – the *emic* stance is that management styles should be different *because* cultures differ from each other.

Within the marketing discipline, this can be seen to relate to the standardisation/adaptation debate that has been waging (unresolved) in the literature since Theodore Levitt's seminal paper 'The Globalization of Markets' appeared in the *Harvard Business Review* in 1983.

- Standardisation involves an organisation making no changes to any element of its marketing mix, believing that one universal approach can meet the needs of global consumers in global markets.
- Adaptation involves altering relevant elements of the marketing mix to meet the varying needs of different consumers in different markets. When following an adaptation approach, changes can therefore be made to the product, its packaging and design, the place and method of distribution, pricing strategies, and promotional methods and choice of media.

Levitt claimed evidence for globalisation could be found in three areas:

- Demand (i.e., tastes, preferences, price-mindedness, etc.) is becoming increasingly universal
- Supply (i.e., products, services) tends to become more standardised and competition within industries becomes worldwide
- Marketing policies (i.e., strategies and control systems) managed by multinationals to ensure global competitiveness

Levitt's original (1983) argument seemed to suggest that there was simply no such thing as local markets and that all markets tended towards a universal standard. Therefore organisations indulging themselves in adaptation, producing many variants in overseas markets, were simply wasting resources on a grand scale. Since Levitt has first proposed this idea, a number of articles by various authors have appeared both for and against this basic premise. Levitt himself has stated that total standardisation is not exactly what he meant, and that in some instances 'think global, act local' was the right policy for international marketers.

Globalisation or regionalisation

Levitt's approach also rests on the belief that markets have actually become globalised. This argument is certainly attractive when considering figures such as those noting that over half of all world trade and approximately 80 per cent of all Foreign Direct Investment (FDI) are made by the 500 largest Multi National Enterprises (MNEs) in the world. However, it is difficult to use those figures as real evidence of 'globalisation' when their further examination shows that the largest number of MNEs comes from the core 'triad' of three geographical locations: the USA, the EU and Japan. Moreover, the EU is now in ascendancy within this triad as the collective Gross Domestic Product (GDP) of EU nations is now greater than that of the USA or Japan.

Examined from another angle, while there are notable exceptions, such as Nestle, which sells over 8500 products in over 100 countries and earns over 65 per cent of its revenues outside of its home nation Switzerland, most MNEs still earn the majority of their revenues either within their home country or by selling in neighbouring countries (especially within trading blocs such as the EU and between the triad nations). So, while the EU accounts for more than 36 per cent of all world imports and over 34 per cent of all world exports, 61 per cent of all its imports and exports are accounted for in trade between EU nations. The 2004 figures for Carrefour, for example, show that while the company had 6067 stores in 29 different countries on 4 continents, this company, the world's second largest retailer (Wal-Mart being the largest) made 87 per cent of its sales within Europe. Car manufacturer Volkswagen similarly makes 71 per cent of its sales in Europe, and only 17 per cent in America, its second largest market.

The importance of regional trade means that it may therefore be more effective for MNEs to create strategies that are regional, rather than global, in focus. However, it may also mean that MNEs and other smaller companies entering foreign markets may need to be more responsive to the various diverse cultural sensitivities of the full range of consumers within those markets (following an adaptation approach) as opposed to being global in nature and standardising their business operations.

Segmentation in the EU

Marketers have developed the concept of segmenting the market into groups that an organisation was both *able to* and *wanted to* please, in order to target an appropriate marketing mix to these groups. When conducting international marketing, segmentation has traditionally been undertaken from a geographic basis, segmenting target customers nation by nation. This approach draws on the work of Hofstede (1983) and Trompenaars (1993) both who identified (different) bipolar variables by which a national culture may be understood and assessed.

Hofstede's framework

Hofstede conducted one of the earliest and best-known cultural studies in management on IBM's operations around the world. Using the results of a large-scale survey, he mapped key cultural characteristics of these countries according to four value dimensions: Power Distance; Individualism versus Collectivism; Masculinity versus Femininity; Uncertainty Avoidance. Since his original study, Hofstede has added a fifth dimension, Long Term Orientation (http://www.geert-hofstede.com). Hofstede's work, while important, has also received its share of criticism. Summarised by Holden (2004), these criticisms are that Hofstede's study is of limited value from a marketing point of view since it investigated the cultural values of a company not a 'market'; it is further criticised for not considering employees as 'consumers, negotiators or market intermediaries', and for being conducted in the 1960s, prior to globalisation and the technologies that fuel the knowledge economy. Despite all the criticism, Hofstede's work remains the most often cited source in this field (Braun and Warner, 2002) and can be used as a useful starting point for any investigations into the heterogeneity of national cultures.

Trompenaars' framework

Trompenaars built on Hofstede's work by expanding the framework for stereotyping and comparing different national cultures and by focusing more on the management implications of cultural differences. Key to understanding the dimensions identified by Trompenaars (Universalism versus Particularism; Individualism versus Collectivism; Neutral versus Emotional; Specific versus Diffuse; Achievement versus Ascription; Attitudes towards time – Sequential versus Synchronic; Attitudes towards the environment) is to identify where a country or culture is positioned *relative* to others. So, while Trompenaars' work does consider national culture in relation to each other, his work still assumes that any individual national culture is heterogeneous. The approach that we outline next may offer a more fruitful approach as it better takes into account that any individual nation may include regions within it that are more similar to a neighbouring nation than to other regions within its own national borders.

Segmenting by cross-border clusters

Somewhat of a recent paradigm shift can be seen by those who believe it is more effective to identify clusters of customers who share common characteristics, yet who may not necessarily live in the same country. Van der Merwe and L'Huillier (1989) have identified the following clusters of Euro-Consumers, many of which cross national borders:

Cluster 1: UK and Ireland
Cluster 2: Central and Northern France, Southern Belgium, Central Germany and Luxembourg
Cluster 3: Spain and Portugal
Cluster 4: Southern Germany, Northern Italy, South-eastern France and Austria
Cluster 5: South Italy and Greece
Cluster 6: Northern Germany, the Netherlands, Northern Belgium, Iceland, Norway, Finland and Denmark

Cultural heterogeneity between EU nations

These clusters do not take the newly acceded member states of the EU into account, and it may be tempting for international marketers targeting the A8 nations to group them together. However, Mercado *et al.* (2001) warn that 'despite historical reference to the "Eastern Bloc", Central and Eastern Europe is not a homogeneous area. The countries differ widely with regard to ethnic compositions, languages, historical identities, industrial structures and economies.' Moreover, Kolman *et al.* (2003) argue that although there are significant differences in values between Western and Central Europe, significant differences are also visible between countries like the Czech Republic, Hungary, Poland and Slovakia. An additional and important problem was also identified by Villinger (1996) who found that managers in Central Europe lacked understanding of how to manage in a variety of cultural settings due to their insufficient knowledge of local culture in host nations with which they chose to conduct business. Therefore the danger is that, when attempting to identify clusters of Euro-Consumers in a newly enlarged EU, these countries will be formed into a cluster perceived as homogeneous by marketers and yet remain an area which is highly heterogeneous.

It is claimed that successful organisational exchanges are based upon shared values between parties to the exchange process as well as a stakeholder approach which assumes that there are a 'common set of rules and behavioural expectations' that are 'shared by the majority of members of a stakeholder community' (Maignan and McAlister, 2003, p. 83). When dealing with cross-cultural norms and values in heterogeneous globalised markets, however, it is becoming increasingly difficult to base the exchange process upon shared stakeholder values and norms. It is also increasingly difficult to deal ethically 'in a cross-cultural environment [in which] marketers are exposed to different values and ethical norms' and are less able to rely on 'universally accepted ethical norms' (Nill, 2003, p. 90). Even if Central and Eastern European nations are deemed to be culturally similar, cultural similarity between markets does not always indicate ethical similarity in business relationships.

Ethical issues also arise in relation to contextual differences in levels of economic development. Although many authors believe that in a globalised free market environment it is neither possible nor useful to establish or follow normative ethics, another view (Nill, 2003, p. 92) is that the 'cross-cultural environment where different values clash' is the very reason normative ethics should be sought. One proposal for dealing with the various perspectives on business ethics is 'dialogic idealism', a moral philosophy approach that encourages communication between stakeholders from a variety of cultural backgrounds. This approach is thought to be particularly useful when 'confronted with fundamental questions that have a substantial impact on stakeholders' interests' (Nill, 2003, p. 102).

In a recent five-nation study into national identity, Skinner et al. (2006) found distinct differences, not only between countries close to the so-called 'continental norm' (Laitin, 2002) such as the UK and France and newly acceded EU members formerly from the Eastern Bloc but also between the former Eastern Bloc nations.

Place of birth

A very strong feeling of national identity is gained from being born in a country. For example, in the above-mentioned study (Skinner et al., 2006) nearly 100 per cent of respondents in the Czech Republic, the UK and Poland agreed that this contributed to a feeling of national identity. Although this factor is still very significant for respondents from France (89.5 per cent) and Hungary (85 per cent), lower number of respondents agreed with it.

Parentage

Similar responses were obtained on the questions relating to parentage. In Poland and Hungary, over 90 per cent of respondents agreed that parentage contributed to their sense of national identity and respondents from the Czech Republic and the UK were more similar with over 80 per cent of respondents agreeing this contributed. In France, however, having French parents was agreed to contribute to a sense of national identity by only a little over 70 per cent of those surveyed.

Having a Polish family name and Polish first name was also seen to be a strong contributor to a feeling of national identity by over 80 per cent of Polish respondents. This was agreed to contribute by over 60 per cent of Czechs, but by only over 50 per cent of Hungarians, and over 40 per cent of French respondents. However, in the UK, while having a family name associated with the country of origin was agreed to contribute to a sense of national identity by over 40 per cent of respondents, only 26 per cent felt that having a first name associated with the country of origin was an important contributing factor. The aforementioned differences indicate some strong differences in attitudes across five countries.

Domicile

Another difference is reflected in the understanding of how living in the country of origin contributes to feelings of national identity. It appears to be an important factor for over 90 per cent of all respondents except Hungarians, of whom only 85 per cent agree that this is a contributing factor. This is a particularly interesting finding for historical reasons. Hungary is cited by Cobban (1969) as one of the nations who historically favoured definitions of nationhood based on political unity irrespective of nationality where he gives the example of the Hungarian Law of Nationalities of 1868 stating that 'all citizens of Hungary...form a single nation – the indivisible unitary Magyar nation – to which all citizens of the country, irrespective of nationality, belong'. It is therefore surprising to find that domicile is now seen to contribute less to a feeling of national identity by Hungarians than any of the other nations surveyed.

Language

Both Anderson (1991) and Williams (1999) believe that language is a key indicator of national and cultural identity and over 90 per cent of survey respondents agreed to some extent that this contributed to their feelings of national identity. One could question the validity of these reactions on the basis that one does not become British, Czech, French, Hungarian or Polish simply by speaking the language and being 'invited in to the imagined community' (Anderson, 1991), but this does not make people's feelings any the less real.

Other cultural symbols and traditions

In support of our argument for a consideration of the cultural heterogeneity of newly acceded EU member nations, differences in attitudes towards other determinants of culture observed between respondents in Western and former Eastern Bloc members of the EU were not as significant as were differences between respondents from *within* former Eastern Bloc nations.

Attitudes about the extent to which the national flag contributed towards a sense of national identity varied between the lowest level of agreement from Hungarians (62 per cent) to over 90 per cent of French and UK respondents. The contribution of national colours showed similar variance, between the highest agreement rate of 91 per cent of Polish respondents and the lowest agreement rate of 61 per cent of Hungarians. However, while there were a range of views on the attitudinal impact of the national flag, views concerning the impact of the national anthem were much more uniform across all countries.

Another area with a wide range of opinions was religion. This was agreed to contribute to a sense of national identity by around 23 per cent of respondents in the UK and Hungary, almost 30 per cent of respondents in the Czech Republic, but by 62 per cent of French respondents and almost 80 per cent of Poles. The answer to Michnik's (2003) question 'Who defined the new Poland? Was it the "Catholic Pole", ethnically and religiously defined?' may help understand this last and important finding.

Cultural heterogeneity within EU nations: The marketing opportunity

The above findings offer valuable insights into the cultural heterogeneity that exists *between* EU nations. It is important to realise that this heterogeneity can also, by virtue of the fact that people from a range of countries emigrate to other parts of Europe from their home country, increase levels of cultural heterogeneity *within* EU nations. It would not therefore be prudent for an international marketer to assume that each member state of the EU is itself culturally homogeneous.

It has already been noted that the UK has experienced net immigration since the mid-1980s. Notwithstanding figures for 2008 that are already beginning to show migrant workers retreating from the UK's economic downturn, there is now a large new market within the UK for

56 *Profiting from Diversity*

goods and services aimed at this group of consumers. In particular, there has been an explosion of goods and services targeting Polish workers who make up the largest single nationality of migrants into the UK from the A8 countries, and who are estimated to have around £4bn in disposable income. Indeed, it is estimated that around 2 per cent of the total Polish population now live in the UK, and large UK retailers including Tesco, Sainsbury and ASDA now stock a wide range of Polish food and drink products to serve this group of customers. Other service providers such as pubs and restaurants are re-branding and targeting Polish customers. Along with familiar Polish brands being offered to consumers, food producer Heinz is also launching a range of Polish food products in the UK under the Pudliszki brand name. However, branding experts Brand Republic warn that Polish consumers approach products differently than UK consumers. Areas of difference include attitudes and perceptions to colour which can affect product image; packaging also needs to be clear, direct and informative for Polish customers with the product realistically photographed, a clear brand identity, and all relevant consumer information easily accessible on the front of the package, which could make the product pack appear crowded and unattractive to UK consumers. However, this chapter is not offering an in-depth understanding of consumer attitudes of every cultural group within the enlarged EU. What we are suggesting is that marketers recognise the differences that exist across the EU and conduct their own appropriate research accordingly in order to increase chances of business success.

Conclusions

A homogeneous identity between the A8 nations as Central or Eastern European, post-communist, developing, new EU countries is a generalisation imposed by others on those countries. Despite many similarities, very strong differences exist between these nations in terms of their national and cultural identities. The varying perceptions of importance of cultural determinants in those countries cannot be neglected by marketers when grouping them together into one segment, even if, in order to maintain economies of scale, only minor adaptations are made to the product/service offering that take these cultural differences into account. These changes could be as simple, but as effective, as changing the music on a commercial (Liszt for Hungary, Chopin for Poland, Dvorak for the Czech Republic) or adapting the product in the eyes of local consumers. Cultural diversity within EU nations is also opening up business opportunities as evidenced by the wide range of products and services offered to Polish migrants in the UK shows. Kolman *et al.* (2003) argue that 'it would from a managerial perspective be dangerous to treat the Central European countries as a homogeneous group', even if the temptation is very strong because of the differences between Western and Central European countries. There is also a strong case that grouping these nations together as one homogeneous segment or cluster could lead to questioning the ethics of the companies involved.

In the light of the above, a homogeneous European identity appears to be an impossible dream, probably unachievable, and possibly not even something to which we should aspire given the high levels of cultural diversity within and between EU nations.

References

Anderson, B. (1991) *Imagined Communities: Reflections on the Origin and Spread of Nationalism*, Revised Edition (London and New York: Verso).
Braun, W. and M. Warner (2002) 'The "culture-free" versus "culture-specific" management debate' in M. Warner and P. Joynt (eds) *Managing across Cultures: Issues and Perspectives* (London: Thomson Learning), pp. 13–25.
Burgoyne, C. B. and D. A. Routh (1999) 'National identity, European identity and the Euro' in K. Cameron (ed.) *National Identity* (Exeter: Intellect Books).
Cameron, K. (ed.) (1999) *National Identity* (Exeter: Intellect Books).
Cobban, A. (1969) *The Nation State and Self-Determination* (London: Fontana).
Earley, P. C. and H. Singh (1995) 'International and intercultural management research: What's next?', *Academy of Management Journal*, 38, 2, 327–340.
Ergang, R. R. (1931) *Herder and the Foundations of German Nationalism* (New York: Octagon Books).
Fuchs, D. and H.-D. Klingemann (2002) 'Eastward enlargement of the European Union and the identity of Europe' in P. Mair and J. Zielonka (eds) *The Enlarged European Union: Diversity and Adaptation* (London: Frank Cass Publishers).
Hofstede, G. (1983) 'National cultures in four dimensions: A research theory of cultural differences among nations', *International Studies of Management and Organizations*, 13, 1/2, 46–74.
Holden, N. (2004) 'Why marketers need a new concept of culture for the global knowledge economy', *International Marketing Review*, 21, 6, 563–572.
Kale, S. H. (1995) 'Grouping Euroconsumers: A culture-based clustering approach', *Journal of International Marketing*, 3, 3, 35–48.
Kolman, L., N. G. Noorderhaven, G. Hofstede and E. Dienes (2003) 'Cross-cultural differences in Central Europe', *Journal of Managerial Psychology*, 18, 1, 76–88.
Laitin, D. (2002) 'Culture and national identity: "The East" and European integration' in P. Mair and J. Zielonka (eds) *The Enlarged European Union: Diversity and Adaptation* (London: Frank Cass Publishers).
Levitt, T. (1983) 'The globalization of markets', *Harvard Business Review*, 61, 3, 92–102.

Maignan, I. and D. T. McAlister (2003) 'Socially responsible organizational buying: How can stakeholders dictate purchasing policies?', *Journal of Macromarketing*, 23, 2, 78–89.

Mair, P. and J. Zielonka (eds) (2002) 'The Enlarged European Union: Diversity and adaptation' (London: Frank Cass).

Mayer, F. C. and J. Palmowski (2004) 'European identities and the EU – the ties that bind the peoples of Europe', *Journal of Common Market Studies*, 42, 3, 573–598.

Mercado, S., R. Welford and K. Prescott (2001) *European Business*, 4th Edition (Harlow: Pearson Education).

Michnik, A. (2003) 'What Europe means for Poland', *Journal of Democracy*, 14, 4, 128–136.

Nill, A. (2003) 'Global marketing ethics: A communicative approach', *Journal of Macromarketing*, 23, 2, 90–104.

Pugh, D. S. and D. J. Hickson (2002) 'On organisational convergence' in M. Warner and P. Joynt (eds) *Managing across Cultures: Issues and Perspectives*, Second Edition (London: Thomson Learning).

Skinner, H., K. Kubacki, G. Moss and D. Chelley (2006) 'How understanding nation branding informs the Knowledge economy', *2nd International Colloquium of the Brand, Identity and Corporate Reputation SIG*, Manchester Business School, September.

Sriskandarajah, D., L. Cooley and T. Kornblatt (2007) *Britain's Immigrants: An Economic Profile*, A report for Class Films and Channel 4 Dispatches (London: Institute for Public Policy Research).

Steger, U. (ed.) (1998) *Discovering the New Pattern of Globalization*, Report of the Ladenburg Kolleg Understanding and Shaping Globalization (Ladenburg: Gottlieb Daimler und Karl Benz-Stiftung).

Trompenaars, F. (1993) *Riding the Waves of Culture: Understanding Cultural Diversity in Business* (London: Economist Books).

van der Merwe, S. and M.-A. L'Huillier (1989) 'Euro-Consumers in 1992', *Business Horizons*, 32, 1, 34–40.

Villinger, R. (1996) 'Post-acquisition managerial learning in Central East Europe', *Organization Studies*, 17, 2, 181–206.

Warner, M. and P. Joynt (eds) (2002) *Managing across Cultures: Issues and Perspectives*, Second Edition (London: Thomson Learning).

Williams, L. (1999) 'National identity and the nation state: Construction, reconstruction and contraction' in K. Cameron (ed.) *National Identity* (Exeter: Intellect Books).

Zielonka, J. and P. Mair (2002) 'Introduction: Diversity and adaptation in the enlarged European Union' in P. Mair and J. Zielonka (eds) *The Enlarged European Union: Diversity and Adaptation* (London: Frank Cass Publishers).

4
Knowledge Management and the Positive Impact of a Collectivist Culture

Gloria Moss, Krzysztof Kubacki, Marion Hersh, and Rod Gunn

Introduction

How does cultural diversity affect the development of knowledge? This chapter explores an under-researched issue namely the relationship between individualism and collectivism and knowledge creation and does this through a study of the research process in universities in a collectivist (Slovenia) and individualistic country (Australia). The Higher Education (HE) sector provides a suitable context in which to study this question since it is home to a research community devoted to knowledge creation (KC) and knowledge management (KM), or intellectual capital management (ICM) as it is sometimes known. However, although this chapter focuses on the processes in the HE sector, the conclusions that are reached are relevant to other contexts such as commercial organisations where information and knowledge management are important.

A word on the HE sector before moving on to a discussion of the processes involved in creating new knowledge. A fundamental activity of universities has traditionally been the production (research) and dissemination (through publication and teaching) of knowledge and the importance of these knowledge-based activities has increased in the modern knowledge-based society. In the European Union, universities performed 20.4 per cent of their nations' research effort, while in Australia the proportion of the country's research expenditure allocated to the HE sector increased form 25.5 per cent in 1990 to 29.4 per cent in 1998–99 (Meek, 2003). These numbers are likely to rise as government reporting measures achieve ever greater importance. Examples include the Research Assessment Exercise (RAE) in the UK and the

Research Quantum (RQ) in Australia, both applying quantitative performance measures to research activities. This has produced a research productivity index underpinning the distribution of decreasing research funding and in the UK this pressurised research environment has led to significant structural change (Thomas, 2001) and produced work intensification (Ogbonna and Harris, 2004), elevated stress levels, 'widespread discontent and dissatisfaction' and a lack of team spirit and teamwork (*ibid*).

In fact, a combination of cut-backs in basic funding and research-linked productivity incentives (Hellstrom and Husted, 2004) has introduced market relations into Higher Education Institutions (HEIs) (Shore and Selwyn, 1998). This has led to the commodification of education and knowledge (Willmott, 1995) and pressures to increase knowledge outputs. As it happens, this increased focus on KC, KM and ICM in the HE sector provides a useful setting in which to study the factors that have a positive or negative impact on these processes. The lessons that we can learn from this can then be applied to other contexts and settings.

The chapter starts with an overview of definitions of KC, KM and ICM. It is then followed by a discussion of the influence of organisational and national culture on these activities.

Definitions of KC, KM and IC

It is useful to begin with some of the terms that are used to describe the processes of creating knowledge. The term 'KC' is used primarily to describe the generation of new knowledge, while 'KM' is used to describe 'the availability and use of existing knowledge' (Bajaria, 2000). In fact, the processes of KC and KM describe the steps on the road from tacit knowledge (KC) to explicit knowledge (KM) (Polyani, 1966, 1967; Nonaka and Takeuchi, 1995; Jennex, 2006) to new Intellectual Capital (IC). As many will know, the distinction between tacit and explicit knowledge is between knowledge that can or cannot be formulated directly, whether through rules, data or knowledge representations, and communicated to other people. Tacit knowledge, unlike explicit knowledge, has a personal element which is attached to individual thinking processes (Mooradian, 2005) and while people are generally unaware of the extent of their tacit knowledge, with the knowledge being implicit (*ibid*) or unstructured (Jennex, 2006), there is usually a high level of awareness of explicit knowledge.

In practice, there is in fact overlap between KC and KM /ICM due to the fact that all knowledge has tacit components. Despite this, we can say that the personal element of tacit knowledge, as well as the fact that people are often not aware of their own tacit knowledge, makes it difficult to express it in a form that can be communicated, understood and processed (Leonard and Sensiper, 1998). Indeed, the personal nature of tacit knowledge has made leading commentators suggest that KC requires a willingness on the part of workers with tacit knowledge to share and communicate it (Kim and Mauborgne, 1998; Flood et al., 2001; Jackson et al., 2003). Nonaka and Takeuchi (1995) describe in detail the externalisation process whereby tacit knowledge is converted into explicit knowledge, but disagree with Mooradian (2005) as to whether tacit knowledge can be made explicit without a concomitant loss of precision. Von Krogh et al. (2000) relate the transfer mechanisms to communities of practice and micro communities of knowledge and Dhanaraj et al. (2004) suggest that the abstract nature of tacit knowledge restricts its transfer to those actively involved with it, in contrast to explicit knowledge which does not require the active involvement of another person.

These differences between tacit and explicit knowledge mean that organisations that want to make the most of the tacit knowledge therefore need to involve employees in the KC and KM processes (Jackson et al., 2003). Since scarce knowledge and expertise are embedded in work groups, tacit knowledge cannot be accumulated at the top of an organisation. This leads commentators to emphasise the importance of human capital (Cross et al., 2001; Bartlett and Ghoshal, 2002) with some authors estimating that a significant component of an individual's information environment consists of the relationships he or she can tap into for information (Allen, 1984; Bartlett and Ghoshal, 2002; Cross et al., 2001).

One can see from this how it could be that relationships are viewed as a key element in information gathering and KC with the key role of teamwork, cooperation and collaboration emphasised by several commentators (Collins and Porras, 1994; Moore, 1996; Nonaka and Konno, 1998; Sveiby and Simmons, 2002; Senge, 2006). In fact, the importance of socialisation face-to-face relationships and team interaction is emphasised by Janz and Prasarnphanich (2003) and has led to the realisation that the development of IC is linked to the development of social capital (*ibid* and Jackson et al., 2003).

Much of the discussion in the literature focuses on the elements that facilitate team learning and, from that, KM. Four factors, for example, are isolated by Cross et al., (2001) as distinguishing knowledge-centred relationships. 'Safety in the relationship' is one of them and the behaviours and practices that favour the development of trust are further explored by Abrams *et al.*, (2003). They distinguish between trust in one's own competence and trust based on benevolence and suggest that trust can be enhanced through personal connections and collaborative communications. The importance of sharing of knowledge is further emphasised by Storey and Qunitas (2001).

Culture and knowledge management

We have seen that the literature emphasises the crucial role of teamwork in KC and KM and one might reasonably ask whether different national cultures influence individuals' abilities to create the type of teamwork that is conducive to KC and KM. In fact, the impact of national culture on this process has been overlooked in the literature and this is acknowledged in the view that the 'national view' of IC is still 'in its infancy' (Bontis, 2004a) and has focused on the Western world (*ibid*).

National culture is understood here as the 'shared attitudes, values and understandings in a society which are shaped by common experiences, and result in collective mental programmes' (Clark *et al.*, 1997; Moss and Vinten, 2001). One set of factors that might conceivably influence the propensity to engage in the team-work advocated in the KM literature (referred to in the present chapter as 'team research') is the degree of individualism/collectivism in the national culture, defined by Hofstede as the degree to which people in a culture prefer to act as individuals rather than as members of groups (Hofstede, 1980). It is predicted that there is likely to be a greater incidence of solo-research work in an individualistic national culture than in a collectivist one.

This chapter will draw critically on Hofstede's work on nationality, one of the best known and cited sources in the field (Braun and Warner, 2002; Rowley, 2002). There have been critiques of Hofstede, for example that by McSweeney (2002) which argues that micro-locations such as, individual firms or universities cannot be assumed to be typical of national trends and that organisations have heterogeneous rather than homogeneous cultures. He also argues in favour of the fact that individuals' behaviours may not be fixed on a bi-polar scale but rather may change according to the situation. Despite these criticisms, he argues that Hofstede's dimensions can provide a useful framework for the consideration of national characteristics and it is on this basis that the research behaviour of two countries, Australia and Slovenia, differing on Hofstede's bi-polar scale of individualism / collectivism, are compared here.

Before reporting on the comparison of behaviours in Australia and Slovenia, something will be said about cultures and then about the various pieces of research by the authors of this article that led up to the final comparison of behaviours in Australia and Slovenia. We will begin with a discussion of culture.

Culture

A definition of culture by UNESCO does not underestimate the amount of influence that culture can have. It defines culture as the 'set of distinctive spiritual, material, intellectual and emotional features of society or a social group and...encompasses, in addition to art and literature, lifestyles, ways of living together, value systems, traditions and beliefs' (UNESCO, 2002). This definition shows that culture can operate at both the national and organisational levels (de Long and Fahey, 2000; Hollingsworth and Hollingsworth, 2000), with Janz and Prasarnphanich (2003) concluding that 'organisational culture is believed to be the most significant input to effective knowledge management and organisational learning'. This leads them to suggest that the highest levels of competitiveness can only be achieved through enhancing the knowledge-centred culture of the organisation.

What do we know of the culture of HE? In the UK, a 60-people strong survey by Ogbonna and Harris (2004) elicited comments from an academic working in a new university in which he contrasted the collegial atmosphere of the past ('years ago') with the individualistic culture ('everyone is out for themselves') of the present. A second academic, this time from an old university, reported on the lack of team spirit and the fact that 'people [are] only interested in themselves'. Tellingly, he reported on the fact that he had not spoken to the occupant of the next office for six months.

A similar picture emerges from a study focusing on the experience of new faculty in the UK (Luce and Murray, 1997–98) with reports of isolation, heavy workloads and lack of support from senior colleagues. A further study of HEIs describes high levels of bullying (Lewis, 1999), while a study funded by the Department for Education and Employment in the UK (Davies, 2002) focuses on the lack of encouragement or recognition afforded to academics by their managers, a behaviour linked to the lack of targeted and structured management training.

Further research (Hersh and Moss, 2004) highlighted the extent to which regular or occasional feelings of isolation could affect academics and this emerged from research focusing on indirectly related question namely the degree of interdisciplinarity of most people's research. So, the finding of isolation was incidental to the main theme of the research which concerned propensity for crossing disciplinary boundaries in research, with two groups addressed through questionnaires:

(i) researchers working in the field of assistive technology (these were largely male and from engineering and the sciences),
(ii) researchers visiting the website of the Institute for Feminist Theory and Research (two-thirds of respondents were female).

Although Moss and Hersh's questionnaire did not aim to investigate the effect of human relations on research effectiveness, the answers obtained suggested that this has an important role. Thus, nearly 90 per cent of respondents reporting obstacles in the first group reported feeling isolated either regularly or sometimes. In the second sample, isolation and obstacles and obstruction from colleagues emerged as problems for the majority of respondents with nearly 30 per cent feeling isolated, another third sometimes feeling isolated and the same percentages experiencing obstacles and obstruction from colleagues generally or sometimes. Those surveys suggested that isolation could be perceived as problematic and as an obstacle to KC and KM, highlighting the problematic nature of isolation and individualistic work patterns.

Widespread feelings of isolation

The overwhelming majority of studies of isolation concentrate on the phenomenon but do not explore the relationship between isolation, national culture and knowledge management. A word on this literature is probably appropriate at this point.

There are two types of literature on isolation. The first includes a study by Miller (1975) giving details of the factors that can give rise to or reduce feelings of isolation. Included here is lack of access to those with authority, a factor related to a person's rank and gender, with lower status and the female gender being associated with reduced access. Remedial steps to preventing isolation are considered by Dussault (1996). The second category of studies attempts to map the psychological effect of isolation. For example, Vega and Brennan (2000) examined models of isolation from across the social sciences. However, absent from these studies is any attempt to measure the impact of isolation on KC /KM. In fact, there was precious little consensus as to whether isolation had a negative or positive impact. Some studies associate it with positive feelings (Rousseau, 1995; Pedersen, 1997) and others with negative feelings (Miller, 1975; Seeman, 1975; Taha and Caldwell, 1993; Caldwell, 1997). One study suggests that isolation can have both positive and negative consequences (Diekema, 1992). However, regardless of the nature of the reaction to isolation, very little has been said about the relationship of isolation to productivity.

More recent research by Moss and Kubacki (2007) revealed that two-thirds of a random sample of UK academics experienced negative feelings of isolation, and reported this as having detrimental impact on IC research. They found that isolation in a university setting can be experienced acutely, paralleling the evidence on the debilitating effect of isolation on personal life (Murphy and Kupshik, 1992). Moss and Kubacki asked their respondents to describe their experiences of isolation. These included the fear that lack of contact with colleagues would cause them to spend considerable time carrying out research in directions that later discussions would show to have been a waste of time. This resulted in stress and lack of motivation, making it difficult to switch off from work. The problems created by isolation were perceived as particularly acute when the research was going badly. The isolation could produce the view that management did not care about staff, leading to a loss of commitment to the institution. For people whose self-identification came from their work-based relationships, the experience of isolation could compromise health.

Moss and Kubacki's work also revealed that the causes of isolation could be classified into one of two factors, structural and psychological. Structural aspects included physical elements in the working environment (e.g. the absence of a common room) as well as elements related to the hierarchy, structure and formalised policies and behaviours at work. Underlying psychological factors were implicated at the level of organisational culture as well as at the level of individual psychology. For example, personality was perceived as causing or breaking feelings of isolation. It was apparent that psychological support was perceived as critical to preventing feelings of isolation, and consequently, promoting KC and KM. Since they could be catalysts and motivators, if such support was absent, it was feared that researchers might see no purpose and abandon their work.

In a study conducted in Finland on the student research environment, a model is presented in which high external pressures are alleged to produce a 'degenerative' research climate (Chiang, 2004). Since the HEI sector is characterised by severe market pressures (Shore and Selwyn,

1998), one might expect the sector to be characterised by degenerative research cultures. Unfortunately, although the author refers to an 'individualism/teamwork' continuum, she does not explore the extent to which this might moderate or exacerbate the problem. Early calls for greater investigation of academic labour processes (Oshagbemi, 1996) appear not to have been pursued, possibly on account of the view that 'management practices do not act directly as drivers of intellectual capital' (Castellanos *et al.*, 2004). This appears to contradict the OECD (2001) view that intellectual wealth resides, inter alia, in teamwork and communication skills and the results of research illustrating the impact of social factors (Hersh and Moss, 2004) on the 'transformation process' (Slack *et al.*, 1998), a process model in which inputs are transformed into outputs and which has been applied to the IC process (Bonfour, 2003). As a consequence of this neglect, the potential impact of social factors on research output has been overlooked.

National culture: Collectivism versus individualism

The KM literature advocates a transformation process based on groupwork (Collins and Porras, 1994; Moore, 1996; Nonaka and Konno, 1998; Jackson *et al.*, 2003; Janz and Prasarnphanich, 2003; Senge, 2006). However, the impact of national culture on this transformation process, and through this process on the IC output has been overlooked in the IC, KM and HEI literatures. This is perhaps not so surprising since the 'national view' of IC is still 'in its infancy' (Bontis, 2004a), and has focused on the Western world (Bontis, 2004b).

A recent study (Moss *et al.* 2007) has however explored the extent to which national culture may influence the process of KM. The findings of this study illustrated the debilitating effect that isolation and lack of teamwork can have on people working in an individualistic country while showing the positive impact of a collectivist culture and teamwork. The comparison of the research practices of Australian and Slovenian academics was in part prompted by these two nations standing at opposite ends of the individualistic/collectivistic spectrum, but also by the fact that their economies comparable (ibid.). When it came, however, to relating the extent of someone's feelings of isolation to the *individualism* or *collectivism* in the present, there were no studies. It was this gap that propelled the authors into a new study comparing knowledge-creation in two countries, one individualistic and the other collectivist. The US, the UK and Australia are reported as highly individualistic cultures (Hofstede, 1980, 2001; Trompenaars, 1993) and Slovenia as highly collectivist (Hofstede, 1980, 2001; Globokar, 1996) with values rooted in 'mutual assistance' and the 'collective exchange of skills and work'. In line with expectations, the quantitative results revealed significantly higher levels of teamwork in Slovenia than Australia, and a significant correlation between teamwork and high research output. This confirms the findings of an extensive literature showing that IC and KM is fostered through a transformation process centred on teamwork.

The comparison of the research practices of Australian and Slovenian academics was prompted by the fact that these two nations were at extreme ends of the individualistic /collectivist continuum. Australia, in common with the US and the UK, is reported as being highly individualistic (Hofstede, 1980, 2001, Trompenaars, 1993) while Slovenia is reported as being highly collectivist (Hofstede, 1980, 2001, Globokar, 1996) with values rooted in 'mutual assistance' and the 'collective exchange of skills and work'. The fact that the economies of these two countries were comparable as well made the comparison appropriate (Moss et al., 2007).

The results of the comparison? The quantitative results revealed significantly higher levels of teamwork in Slovenia than in Australia, and a significant correlation between teamwork and high research output. This confirms in dramatic fashion the findings of an extensive literature showing that KM and ICM is fostered through a transformation process centred on teamwork.

The quantitative results from the questionnaires distributed by Moss et al., revealed that significantly more Slovenian academics work with several colleagues or as part of a research team than Australian academics ($p < 0.05$). In terms of research output (journal articles, conference papers and books), Slovenians produced significantly more than Australians ($p < 0.001$). There was also a positive correlation between working with one or more colleagues and increased research output ($p < 0.05$). Those findings were again in line with the researchers' propositions that collaborative work would be associated with increased IC output, and that it would be more prevalent in a collectivist country than in an individualistic one. Analysis of the questionnaire results also revealed that almost half the Australian sample (46 per cent) indicated a preference for working on their own, as compared with 0 per cent of Slovenians. Of those, Australian and Slovenian respondents who conduct research on their own, just over one third (37 per cent) felt isolated. This contrasts with those working in groups where only 9 per cent reported feeling isolated.

The qualitative responses collected by Moss and colleagues threw further light on attitudes to solo and team-research. Only 23 per cent of Australians presented advantages for team-research, as compared with 95 per cent of Slovenians. None of the Slovenian respondents, by contrast, defended a preference for solo-research work. Where team-research was concerned, the arguments fell into four principal categories: increased opportunities for discussion, improved knowledge/information, improved motivation and greater efficiency. Slovenian comments spanned all four categories, whilst Australian comments fell into just three (see Table 4.1). The qualitative responses revealed a stronger focus in Australia than Slovenia on increased output, but a stronger focus in Slovenia on increased knowledge and discussion. This latter point could be linked, the authors argue, to the collectivist nature of the Slovenian culture.

Conclusions

This chapter has explored the latest research on the relationship between cultural diversity and KM. We have seen the positive impact of a collectivist culture and the negative impact of an individualistic culture for Knowledge Management in HEIs. This is an important finding for all organisations in today's Information Society.

The solutions to the problem of isolation experienced by people, particularly in individualistic countries, are beyond the scope of this chapter. However, simple measures to reduce the negative impacts of isolation include the provision of common rooms or other physical spaces in which people could meet (Nonaka and Konno, 1998). This would provide a forum within which relationships could be fostered and knowledge advanced. The evidence presented in this chapter suggests that collectivist culture can enhance both KC and KM. Therefore other measures may include improved communication and mechanisms for regular discussion and clarification of objectives, training, reward systems and organisational structures encouraging collaboration. Where academic work is concerned, a careful balance is required between clarifying research objectives and avoiding narrow prescriptions of the aims or ways of carrying out research, as the latter could lead to a reduction in both academic freedom and creativity. In addition, while supporting and encouraging communication and face-to-face meetings between individual researchers and research groups, it is important to avoid being too prescriptive and recognise that both researchers and research groups generally have their own preferred ways of working. More complex measures would include formal and informal mechanisms of support and changes in the management culture designed to reduce the barriers

Table 4.1 Percentage of Australians and Slovenians citing certain constructs as important in team research

Construct	Citing this factor (%) Australia	Citing this factor (%) Slovenia	Examples Australia	Examples Slovenia
Increased opportunities for discussion	0	20		'Discussion is crucial for me therefore I like to work with a colleague. The institution of mine is small and I do not have colleagues with similar interests. That is why I try to stay in touch with colleagues from other institutions' 'Non-stop brain storming' 'share experiences' 'Like to communicate and share my experiences and knowledge with others' 'Better discussion'
Improved knowledge/ information	29	45	'Different skills' 'Ability to share ideas'	'Compare different solutions' 'Specialised knowledge' 'Exchange of information' 'Diversification of knowledge' 'Different skills and knowledge could be applied' 'Exchange opinions' 'Exchange of ideas' 'Different views, thinking, capabilities' 'Better results'

Table 4.1 (Continued)

Construct	Citing this factor (%)		Examples	
	Australia	Slovenia	Australia	Slovenia
Improved motivation	29	25	'More enjoyable with someone else who can take half the responsibility' 'My work is interdisciplinary'	'I enjoy working with other people' 'Mutual motivation' 'Stimulating environment' 'Shouldering the responsibility' 'Feel a useful member of the group'
Greater efficiency	43	10	'Pleased to see how many outcomes group-research has generated for others as well as myself ' 'Quicker' 'Two heads better than one'	'Division of labour (work), fast search for solutions' 'Sharing the workload'

Source: Moss et al., 2007.

between people (Cross et al., 2001). These are likely to be particularly acute in individualistic cultures (Moss et al., 2007). Crucially, support through periods when researchers are experiencing difficulties in making progress or obtaining negative results could be useful in reducing stress (Yalom, 1991) and helping researchers move foreward. However, such mechanisms would have to be flexible, suited to the particular researcher and voluntary rather than compulsory.

References

Abrams L. C., R. Cross, E. Lesser and D. Z. Levin (2003) 'Nurturing interpersonal trust in knowledge-sharing networks', *Academy of Management Executive*, 17, 64–77.
Allen T. (1984) *Managing the Flow of Technology* (Cambridge: MIT Press).
Bajaria H. J. (2000) 'Knowledge management and creation: Inseparable twins', *Total Quality Management*, 11, 562–73.
Bartlett C. A. and S. Ghoshal (2002) 'Building competitive advantage through people', *MIT Sloan Management Review*, 43, 34–41.
Bonfour A. (2003) 'The IC-dVAL approach', *Journal of Intellectual Capital*, 4, 396–412.
Bontis N. (2004a) 'National intellectual capital index', *Journal of Intellectual Capital*, 5, 13–39.
Bontis N. (2004b) 'Intellectual capitals in Egyptian software firms', *The Learning Organization*, 11, 332–46.
Braun W. and M. Warner (2002) 'The "culture-free" versus "culture-specific" management debate' in M. Warner and P. Joynt (eds) *Managing Across Cultures: Issues and Perspectives* (London: Thomson Learning), pp. 13–25.
Caldwell B. S. (1997) 'Sociotechnical factors affecting communication and isolation in complex environments', *Human-Automation Interaction: Research and Practice* (Lawrence Erlbaum Associates), pp. 298–304.
Castellanos A. R., J. L. Rodriguez and S. Y. Ranguelov (2004) 'University R&D&T capital: What types of knowledge drive it?', *Journal of Intellectual Capital*, 5, 478–99.
Chiang K.-H. (2004) 'Relationship between research and teaching in doctoral education in UK universities', *Higher Education Policy*, 17, 71–88.
Clark T. A. R., D. Ebster-Groz and G. R. Mallory (1997) 'From a universalist to a polycentric approach to organizational research' in T. Clark (ed.) *Advancement in Organizational Behaviours: Essays in Honour of Derek Pugh* (Aldershot: Ashgate).
Collins J. C. and J. I. Porras (1994) *Built to Last* (NewYork: Harper).
Cross B., A. Parker, L. Prusak and S. P. Borgatti (2001) 'Knowing what we know: Supporting knowledge creation and sharing in social networks', *Organizational Dynamics*, 30, 100–20.
Davies J. K. (2002) 'Managing the effect in higher education: Valuing staff to enhance Performance', *HESDA Briefing Paper*, January.
de Long D. and L. Fahey (2000) 'Diagnosing cultural barriers to knowledge management', *Academy of Management Executive*, 14, 113–27.

Dhanaraj C., M. A. Lyles, H. K. Steensma and L. Tihanyi (2004) 'Managing tacit and explicit knowledge transfer in IJCs: The role of relational embeddedness and the impact on performance', *Journal of International Business Studies*, 35, 428–42.

Diekema D. A. (1992) 'Aloneness and social form', *Symbolic Interaction*, 15, 4, 481–500.

Dussault C. (1996) 'Behavioural feedback to risk variation ensues from unsatisfied appetency', *Accident Analysis and Prevention*, 28, 4, 477–86.

Flood P., T. Turner, N. Ramamoorthy and J. Pearson (2001) 'Causes and consequences of psychological contracts among knowledge workers in the high technology and financial services industry', *International Journal of Human Resource Management*, 12, 1152–61.

Globokar T. (1996) 'Intercultural management in Eastern Europe', *International Studies of Management and Organization*, 26, 47–60.

Hellstrom T. and K. Husted (2004) 'Mapping knowledge and intellectual capital in academic environments', *Journal of Intellectual Capital*, 5, 1, 165–80.

Hersh M. and G. Moss (2004) 'Heresy and orthodoxy: Challenging established paradigms and disciplines', *Journal of International Women's Studies*, 5, 6–21.

Hofstede G. (1980) *Culture's Consequences: International Differences in Work-related Values* (Beverly Hills, CA: Sage Publications).

Hofstede G. (2001) *Culture's Consequences: Comparing Values, Behaviours, Institutions, and Organizations across Nations* (London: Sage Publications).

Hollingsworth J. and E. Hollingsworth (2000) 'Radikale Innovationen und Forschungsorganisation: eine Annaherung' ['Radical innovation and a research organisation: An approach'], *Osterreichische Zeitschrift fur Geschichtswissenschaften* [*Austrian Journal of Historical Studies*], 11, 1, 31–66.

Jackson S. E., M. A. Hitt and A. S. DeNisi (eds) (2003) *Managing Knowledge for Sustained Competitive Advantage* (San Francisco: Jossey-Bass).

Janz B. D. and P. Prasarnphanich (2003) 'Understanding the antecedents of effective knowledge management: The importance of a knowledge-centred culture', *Decision Sciences*, 34, 351–84.

Jennex M. (2006) 'Culture, context, and knowledge management', *International Journal of Knowledge Management*, 2.

Kim W. and R. Mauborgne (1998) 'Procedural justice, strategic decision making, and the knowledge economy', *Strategic Management Journal*, 19, 323–38.

Leonard D. and S. Sensiper (1998) 'The role of tacit knowledge in group innovation', *California Management Review*, 40, 112–32.

Lewis D. (1999) 'Workplace bullying – interim findings of a study in further and higher education in Wales', *International Journal of Manpower*, 20.

Luce J. A. and J. P. Murray (1997–8) 'New faculty's perceptions of the academic work life', *Journal of Staff, Programme and Organisation Development*, 15, 103–10.

McSweeney B. (2002) 'Hofstede's model of national cultural differences and consequences: A triumph of faith – a failure of analysis', *Human Relations*, 55, 89–118.

Meek V. (2003) 'Market coordination, research management and the future of higher education in the post-industrial era', Paper produced for the *UNESCO Forum Regional Committee for Asia and the Pacific*, Paris, September.

Miller J. (1975) 'Isolation in organizations: Alienation from authority, control, and expressive relations', *Administrative Science Quarterly*, 20, 260–71.

Mooradian N. (2005) 'Tacit knowledge: Philosophic roots and role in KM', *Journal of Knowledge Management*, 9, 104–13.

Moore J. (1996) *The Death of Competition* (NewYork: Harper Collins).

Moss G. and K. Kubacki (2007) 'Researchers in higher education: A neglected focus of study?', *Journal of Further and Higher Education*, 31, 3, 297–310.

Moss G. and G. Vinten (2001) 'Choice and preferences: Testing the effect of nationality', *Journal of Consumer Behaviour*, 3, 198–208.

Moss G., K. Kubacki, M. Hersh and R. Gunn (2007) 'Knowledge management in higher education: A comparison of individualistic and collectivist cultures', *European Journal of Education*, 42, 3, 377–94.

Murphy P. M. and G. A. Kupshik (1992) *Loneliness, Stress and Well-Being* (London: Routledge).

Nonaka I. and N. Konno (1998) 'The concept of "ba": Building a foundation for knowledge creation', *California Management Review*, 40, 40–54.

Nonaka I. and H. Takeuchi (1995) *The Knowledge-Creating Company* (New York: Oxford University Press).

OECD (2001) *The Wellbeing of Nations: The Role of Human and Social Capital* (Paris: OECD).

Ogbonna E. and L. Harris (2004) 'Work intensification and emotional labour among UK university lecturers: An exploratory study', *Organization Studies*, 25, 1185–1203.

Oshagbemi T. (1996) 'Job satisfaction of UK academics', *Educational Management and Administration*, 24, 4, 389–400.

Pedersen D. M. (1997) 'Psychological functions of privacy', *Journal of Environmental Psychology*, 17, 147–56.

Polyani M. (1966) *Personal Knowledge: Towards a Post-Critical Philosophy* (Chicago: University of Chicago Press).

Polyani M. (1967) *The Tacit Dimension* (London: Routledge and Keoan Paul).

Rousseau D. (1995) *Psychological Contracts in Organizations* (Thousand Oaks, CA: Sage).

Rowley C. (2002) 'Review of Hofstede culture's consequences', *Asia Pacific Business Review*, 9, 115–16.

Seeman M. (1975) 'Alienation studies', *Annual Review of Sociology*, 1, 9, 91–123.

Senge P. (2006) *The Fifth Discipline: The Art and Practice of the Learning Organization* (New York, NY: Doubleday).

Shore C. and T. Selwyn (1998) 'The marketisation of higher education: Management discourse and the politics of performance' in D. Jary and M. Parker (eds) *The New Higher Education: Issues and Directions for the Post-Dearing University* (Stoke-on-Trent: Staffordshire University Press), pp. 153–72.

Slack N., S. Chambers, C. Harland, A. Harrison and R. Johnston (1998) *Operations Management*, 2nd ed. (London: Pitman).

Storey J. and P. Quintas (2001) 'Knowledge management and HRM' in J. Storey (ed.) *Human Resource Management: A Critical Text* (London: Thomson Learning).

Sveiby K. and R. Simons (2002) 'Collaborative climate and effectiveness of knowledge work: An empirical study', *Journal of Knowledge Management*, 6, 420–33.

Taha L. H. and B. S. Caldwell (1993) *Behaviour and Information Technology*, 12, 5, 276–83.

Thomas H. (2001) 'Funding mechanism or quality assessment: Responses to the Research Assessment Exercise in English institutions', *Journal of Higher Education Policy and Management*, 23.

Trompenaars F. (1993) *Riding the Waves of Cultures: Understanding Cultural Diversity in Business* (London: Nicholas Brealey Publishing).

UNESCO (2002) http://www.unesco.org/iycp/uk/uk_tb_national_articles.asp?Code Contact524857, date accessed 11 June 2007.

Vega G. and L. Brennan (2000) 'Isolation and technology: The human disconnect', *Journal of Organizational Change Management*, 13, 5, 468–81.

von Krogh G., K. Ichijo and I. Nonaka (2000) *Enabling Knowledge: How to Unlock the Mystery of Tacit Knowledge and Release the Power of Innovation* (New York: Oxford University Press).

Willmott H. (1995) 'Managing the academics: Commodification and control in the development of university education in the UK', *Human Relations*, 48, 9.

Yalom I. D. (1991) *Love's Executioner and Other Tales of Psychotherapy* (London: Penguin).

5
Gender-Based Motives for Purchasing Fair Trade Products in France

Florence de Ferran

The last few years have witnessed an upsurge of fair trade throughout the world and particularly in Europe. In 2004 fair trade represented a global market of over €446m, three-quarters of which covered Europe and the remaining quarter the United States (Herth, 2005). This accounted for 0.1 per cent of the value of European trade and 0.01 per cent of that of international trade. By 2007 this buoyant market had swelled to over €2.3bn (FLO International, 2008).

In most European countries the fair trade market has an annual growth rate of 10 to 25 per cent (Sterns, 2000). In 2007 the countries with the highest turnover of fair trade products were: the US with €730m, the UK with €704m, and France with €210m. The countries with the steepest increase in turnover in this respect were Sweden (166 per cent), Norway (110 per cent) and Spain (105 per cent) – all countries that still have low fair trade turnovers (less than €45m). In terms of annual per capita expenditure on fair trade products, Switzerland unquestionably leads the way, with €20.8, compared to the European average of under €5 (FLO International, 2008).

The French fair trade market has a high growth rate that can be linked to active communication on the subject. The turnover of fair trade products rose from €12m in 2001 to €210m in 2007 – a tendency confirmed by the increasing fair trade recognition, which rose from 24 per cent in 2001 to 81 per cent in 2007 (Ipsos, 2001, 2007). The products with the highest sales are:

- coffee, which accounts for 36 per cent of sales (growth of 8 per cent), the uncontested leader and emblematic product of fair trade;

- cotton, with 18 per cent of sales in just 3 years, owing to the development of the fair trade textile sector;
- cocoa, which accounts for 10 per cent of sales (47 per cent growth) (Max Havelaar, 2008).

Half of the organisations commercialising these products were founded less than five years ago, and a quarter of them less than two years ago (Altervia Consulting, 2005). In view of the development potential of this market, these organisations and all those that would like to start commercialising this type of product need to have a better understanding of their buyers. Despite research on the subject, knowledge of fair trade consumers is still limited.

All these data point to a steady growth of the fair trade market. This trend will probably result in a differentiation of behaviours that is likely to increase, in view of the consumer's versatility (Marion, 2004; Lipovetsky, 2006). Today, no brand has really embarked on a market segmentation with a positioning that matches the target. Only one type of positioning is used, related to the nature of the retail store chosen (de Ferran and Grunert, 2007) because the market is divided into two types of networks that represent different ideals: the integrated one represented by world shops and the labelled one. Generally, firms engaged in an alternative market or in the non-profit sector use specialised stores, such as *Artisans du Monde* which is like an *Oxfam* shop, representing alternative and activist distribution networks, whereas more conventional firms – whether they sell fair trade or not – cater for sales networks more largely integrated into the market economy such as supermarkets.

It therefore seems important to take this phenomenon of diversification of behaviours into account, as it allows for a differentiation of the offer, with the aim of optimising firms' targeting and positioning. The fact that over 50 per cent of the population is aware of this alternative type of trade (Ipsos, 2005), even if the idea of buying such products does not particularly appeal to everyone, is evidence of that. The power of appeal of communication may be a key factor of success in such cases.

In view of the development of this type of consumption, questions arise on the relevant criteria for segmentation of this market. We have chosen to focus on the purchaser's gender because the food market – of interest to us here – has been affected for several years by *gendered marketing*. More and more products are developed specifically for men or women, from yoghurt to biscuits or sodas. This new type of marketing is perceived differently, depending on the consumer's age. A recent study by Ipsos Marketing (2008) shows a generational effect in this type of segmentation: whereas 48 per cent of the youth consider that the products meet real needs, only 32 per cent of the older generations think so. Half the respondents say they buy products because they are suited to their lifestyle and consumption habits, whereas only 17 per cent say they do so to affirm their femininity or masculinity. It therefore seems that *gendered marketing* is closer to the lifestyles adopted by men and women than to the consumer's claim to a masculine or feminine identity. As individuals' values are indicators of their lifestyle, it seems relevant to examine the differences in values between men and women, in relation to their purchasing habits, if we wish to define the categories of products for which this type of marketing can be applied. In this chapter we therefore examine the extent to which men and women are driven by different values when purchasing fair trade products. To that end, we focus on the motives behind their behaviour.

This investigation is important because the fair trade market is not really segmented yet, whereas the increasing number of actors involved requires more segmentation so that everyone can develop their activity. A difference in the motivations for making this kind of purchase can serve as a basis for a gendered segmentation of the market.

Before presenting the methodology and results of this study, we consider buyers' motives, as well as the values that are the main drivers of behaviour and can reveal individuals' motives. We then consider the influence of gender on behaviours.

Motives for buying fair trade products

Purchasers of fair trade products can be described as socially responsible consumers because they attest to a concern for society as a whole. The scale of socially responsible consumption developed in a French context by François-Lecompte (2005) confirms this. The purchasing of fair trade products is associated with one of the five dimensions of this scale, which is the purchasing of products with an ethical side called '*produits-partage*'.

Various studies have sought to further our understanding of the factors triggering the purchase of fair trade products. Some have defined consumer typologies (Bird and Hughes, 1997; Ozcaglar, 2003, 2005; de Pelsmacker *et al.*, 2004; Sirieix *et al.*, 2004; de Ferran and Grunert, 2007) while others have identified the factors determining such purchases (Shaw *et al.*, 2000; Shaw and Shui, 2001; Sirieix and Tagbata, 2004; Ozcaglar *et al.*, 2006; Vantomme *et al.*, 2006). The first type of research reveals purchasers' motives. The findings are based on frequency of purchases, purchasing intentions, or the factors determining choice. French purchasers of fair trade products seem to be sensitive to economic imbalances between the North and the South, and to believe that their purchases enable them to influence the system. They feel that they have a moral obligation to buy this type of product, and express their sensitivity to causes in the form of boycotts or militant action (Ozcaglar, 2003). A study of Belgian consumers (de Pelsmacker *et al.*, 2004) has shown that this type of purchasing is driven more by an ideal than by a civic spirit. Finally, an inductive study based on the life history of French consumers (Ozcaglar, 2005) highlights various dimensions of the consumption of fair trade products, through which an identity is built. While some associate it with a consumerist act, others see it as an act freeing them from a lifestyle imposed by our society. In these cases, buying fair trade products is prompted by the suffering caused by the consumer society and its negative externalities, and by individuals' search for authenticity and control over their environment and needs.

More generally, fair trade products purchasers seem to be individuals of average age with a high level of education. They are sensitive to North/South imbalances, and the nature of their purchasing motivations is both social and individual. They are moreover perceived as responsible, open-minded, honest and intelligent consumers.

These researches are interesting but they have methodological limits that complicate the use of their results. To characterise purchasers, most studies use a measurement of the intention to buy which hardly seems appropriate, considering the gap between intention and actual purchase of products with an ethical and symbolic dimension (Roberts, 1995). Moreover, some studies use non-qualified or very small samples (of about 20 individuals) which limit their scope. Apart from these limits, these studies have failed to consider the influence of situational factors on behaviour. Yet the diversity of behaviours and perceptions can be shown only in relation to situations, which can be defined by a multitude of elements such as culture, the context of the purchase and the purchaser's characteristics. The underlying motivations of a behaviour are determined by the elements involved in its implementation (Pitts *et al.*, 1991) and consequently depend on a set of factors both internal and external to the individual. In other words, behaviours are based on elements peculiar to the individual, his or her needs, value system, attitudes and so on, as well as on external elements which influence him or her, such as the situation of the purchase, the type of products bought and so on.

In this study we endeavour to enrich knowledge on the fair trade products purchasers by considering situational factors. Apart from behavioural factors (such as socially responsible consumption) or attitudinal factors (such as involvement or sensitivity to price), analysed in a broader study (de Ferran, 2006a), we consider socio-demographic factors, usually known to firms. In particular, we focus on gender because of its use as a segmentation variable.

The impact of gender on behaviour

Many studies have shown the significant impact of gender on behaviour in various fields. For example, in the field of consumption, perceived benefits and the value attributed to a product are influenced by the purchaser's characteristics (Lai, 1995).

As regards the concepts that reveal motives, such as values or cognitive structures, many studies show the moderating role of gender and other socio-demographic variables. For example, research on socially responsible purchasing behaviours has shown that age is a factor differentiating cognitive structures (Kréziak, 1995; McEachern and McClean, 2002).

The personal values that bear witness to motives vary, depending on gender, age, income, level of education and social class (Rokeach, 1973) or gender, age, level of education and profession (Schwartz, 1992) or gender and place of residence (Kahle, 1996).

Where differences pertaining to the values held by men and women are concerned, sociological as well as biological factors are believed to be the cause. From a sociological point of view, these differences are said to be related to the learning of distinctly different roles during the process of socialisation (Rokeach, 1973). Research on this subject is based on two theoretical typologies on the orientations of masculine and feminine values, by Parsons and Bales (1955) and Bakan (1966), respectively. The latter typology distinguishes an agentic orientation, typical of men, and a communal orientation, characteristic of women. Men are characterised by self-protection and assertion, solitude and the repression of their emotions, whereas women favour relationships with others, mutual help, broad-mindedness and the fact of caring for others. As for biological or genetic factors, they relate to all the dispositions that humans have at birth and that they have not learnt. Men and women are therefore believed to have different instincts (Geary, 1998). The expression of these biological factors could be said to be strongly influenced by sociological factors and so the focus in this chapter is on sociological factors.

Various studies using the Rokeach typology of values reveal a tendency towards gendered values (Rokeach, 1973; Feather, 1984; Di Dio *et al.*, 1996). A study by Rokeach (1973) shows that men are more hedonistic, materialistic and success-oriented than women, who are motivated more by internal happiness, love, respect for themselves and an absence of conflict. A study by Feather (1984) on Australian students and their families, and another by Di Dio *et al.* (1996) in Canada, confirm the agentic orientation of men and the communal orientation of women.

Other research has, in contrast, suggested that the difference in values between men and women may be influenced by generational factors and that today's gender roles are less differentiated than before. A study by Lyons (2005) is an example since five values described there – hedonism, stimulation, kindness, conformism and security – cannot be used to characterise men or women and appear to be linked to a particular generation. Lyons (2005) explains this by the fact that post-baby boom generations attach greater importance to hedonism and less to conformity, security and conservation than do baby boomers.

Research carried out in 1998 nevertheless shows that perceptions of gender differences remain stable even if society has evolved (Putrevu, 2002). One approach to interpreting these facts has been to cite the importance of sociological data showing that even if women work full-time away from the home, they remain responsible for most domestic chores (grocery shopping, preparing meals, cleaning, etc.). In other words, irrespective of changes in society, domestic life has not changed much with time (Kurdek, 1993) and gender role differences offer one explanation – a sociological one – for the origins of gender differences in values. Following this logic, it could be said that women will always be more concerned about others due to their role within the family, whereas men may place a higher value on power. Women, on the other hand, may ascribe greater importance to self-fulfilment than men.

These differences in values could be expected to arise in relation to perceptions of the benefits associated with fair trade products. Motives and above all the content of cognitive structures, that is, the nature of the elements that trigger a purchase, are therefore likely to differ according to the purchaser's gender.

Methodology

We have chosen to use the theory of means-end chains as the main underlying theory and methodology for this research since it enables us to determine motives and, more particularly, the role of values in a judgement, through the choice of product attributes. This theory explains the most abstract motives in terms of values, and the most concrete ones in terms of the benefits associated with the purchasing of a product.

The means-end chain approach goes back to the psychology of personal constructs by Kelly (1955), who argued that people make sense of the world by categorising its elements into a set of hierarchically ordered categories, of which the most abstract ones motivate behaviour and the more concrete ones correspond to behavioural alternatives. The concept was introduced into consumer research by Gutman (1982) where the hierarchical levels were defined as attributes, consequences and values, and where the perceived links between them determine the selection of attributes when making purchases. In its empirical application, it is usually coupled with a method of personal interviews called laddering (Reynolds and Gutman, 1988; Grunert and Grunert, 1995) that aims at eliciting respondents' means-end structures by probing for a number of ladders, that is, answers with an increasing level of abstraction, by the repeated question 'why is this important to you...?'.

Ladders are usually conceived as linking product attributes to consequences to life values. A product's attributes are related to its consequences, that is, to the benefits derived from it, as consumers choose those products that enable them to obtain the desired benefits from their behaviour (Gutman, 1982). The degree and desirability of these consequences vary. As products are evaluated on the basis of their capacities to generate consequences relevant to the individual, consumers assess which attributes of a product meet those criteria, and base their choice on the presence of those attributes. To facilitate their choice, they group them into functional categories, according to whether they have the attributes or not to generate the desired effects in a particular situation.

The consequences correspond to a state resulting from an action, but are not ends in themselves. They simply make it possible to bring the individual closer to a desired final state. The individual's values thus determine the size of the benefits. Thus, the means-end chain approach and the laddering technique appear suitable for investigating how consumers link the fair trade attribute to underlying motives and values.

Not all consumers share the same values and base their choices on the same attributes. Different means-end chains exist for the same behaviour. In this respect, we determine whether the nature of the elements constituting the ladders underlying the purchasing of fair trade products varies, that is, whether the attributes, benefits and values depend on the buyer's gender.

In terms of respondents, 174 purchasers of fair trade coffee were questioned since coffee is the fair trade product with the largest market share (Herth, 2005). They were recruited as they made their purchase in general stores, and this methodology was adopted both to ensure that respondents really were consumers of fair trade coffee, and that they were buyers sensitive to marketing techniques, rather than simply purchasers buying from specialised stores.

The ladders were collected using hard-laddering technique (Walker and Olson, 1991) with a list of items (de Ferran, 2006b) which was formalized from a content analysis on the results of 20 interviews using soft-laddering technique (Reynolds and Gutman, 1988). Considering the diversity of values evoked, we decided to classify them according to Rokeach's typology of values (1973).

The answers collected from 154 buyers were then analysed by the generation of a hierarchical value map in order to determine the nature of the buyers' motives. These maps were based on the implication matrices derived from each distribution network's ladders, and the cut-off level was chosen based on heuristics proposed by Reynolds and Gutman (1988).

Results

Our sample has an over-representation of women: 107 women and 47 men. 79 per cent of the respondents are greater than 25 years old and 63 per cent are married or live with somebody.

To determine whether the content of the means-end chains peculiar to the purchasing of fair trade coffee varies according to the buyer's gender, we compare the hierarchical value maps of men and women. They are presented in Figure 5.1 with (a) the hierarchical value map of men who mentioned 180 chains and (b) the hierarchical value map of women who evoked 400 chains.

The contents of means-end chains differ, depending on the buyer's gender and in relation to several factors:

- Certain attributes and consequences are peculiar to each of the groups:

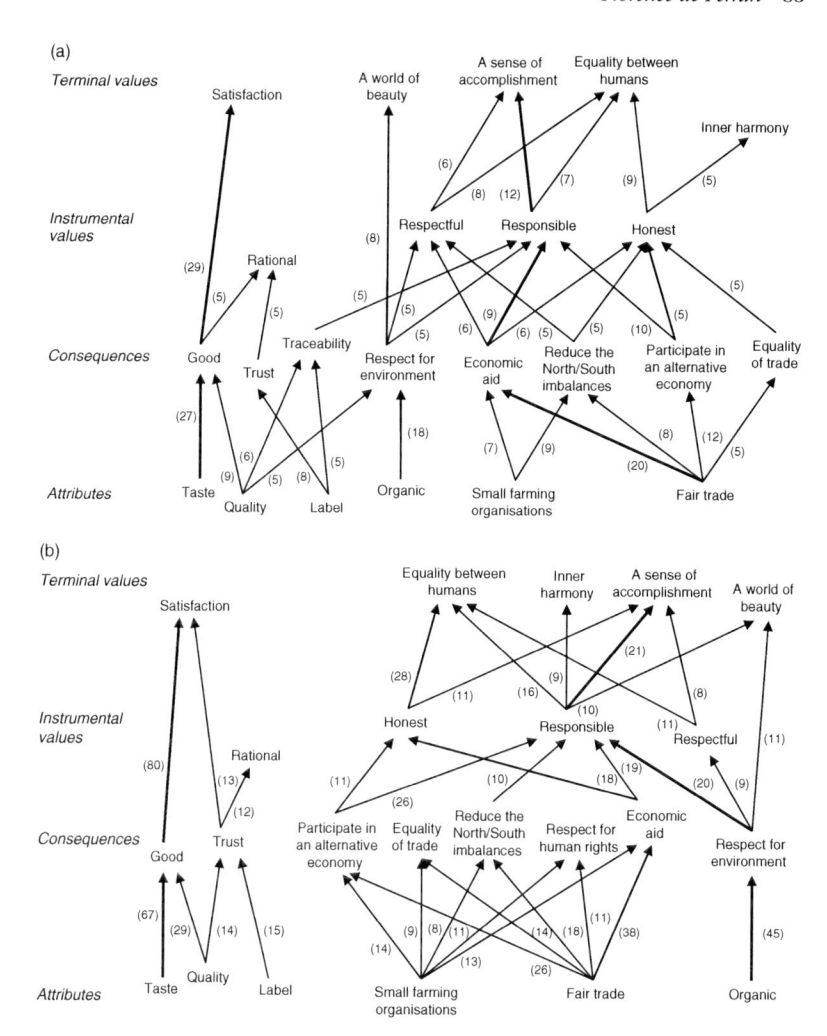

Figure 5.1 (a) Hierachical value map of fair trade coffee purchase by men (*n* = 180/ threshold = 5) and (b) hierarchical value map of fair trade coffee purchase by women (*n* = 400/ threshold = 8)[1]

- women mention purchasing *fair trade* coffee and coffee in which *small farmers* have participated as a form of *respect for human rights*;
- men mention the *traceability* provided by a fair trade *label* and a *quality* product. The *quality* of the product is also linked to *respect for the environment*.

- As regards the main dimensions of the two hierarchical value maps, we note that
  - women mostly have individual motives such as *satisfaction* and are more sensitive to the *organic* nature of the product than to the fact of it being *fair trade*;
  - men have as many individual motives, such as *satisfaction*, but also have social motives, such as the *sense of accomplishment* provided by a *fair trade* product purchase.
- As you can notice above on the figure, the women's hierarchical value map is more complex than the men's in regard to values, with a larger number of relations between instrumental and terminal values. On the other hand, men's hierarchical value map is more complex when it comes to relations between consequences and values. So, men's behaviour is based on more functional elements.
- Moreover, all the attributes described by men have a multiplicity of links with the benefits, whereas for the women this diversity of links is valid only for the attributes of *fair trade* and *small farmers*. This shows that women have more expertise in this field because they associate more elements to fair trade and small farmers than men.

The hierarchical value maps can also be studied from a quantitative point of view via the coefficients of centrality and prestige (Pieters *et al.*, 1995). The coefficients of centrality of the two groups are comparable (Pearson's coefficient of correlation = 0.95 with $p < 0.000$). As regards attributes, *fair trade* has the highest coefficient of centrality, irrespective of gender (0.11 in both groups), and the other attributes have similar coefficients. As regards the consequences, *good* is the most central (0.20 (women) and 0.16 (men)). For instrumental values, that is, preferable modes of behaviour, *responsible* is the most central (0.16 (women) and 0.14 (men)). When it comes to terminal values that refer to desirable end-states of existence, we observe a difference between the two groups: *satisfaction* for the women (0.11) and *equality between humans* for the men (0.09). Then, the terminal values central to all the meanings evoked by men and women differ according to gender.

Although the coefficients of centrality of all the items are comparable with coefficients of correlation between the two groups greater than 0.90, some differences between the groups are apparent in the hierarchy of coefficients of centrality, which differs from one group to the next. For example, for men, the most central attributes are *fair trade* and then *taste* and *small farmers*, whereas for women they are *fair trade* and *taste*.

For men the most important terminal values are *equality between humans, satisfaction* and *a sense of accomplishment*, whereas for women they are *satisfaction, equality between humans* and *a sense of accomplishment*.

Coefficients of prestige are comparable between the two groups (Pearson's coefficient of correlation = 0.96 with $p < 0.000$), that is, in the ladders evoked, the same elements are the destination of others elements. Irrespective of the purchaser's gender, *good* and *responsible* are the strongest coefficients. With regard to terminal values, we find the same difference between the two groups as with the coefficient of centrality: women aim more to be *satisfied* whereas men are more interested in an ideal of *equality between humans*.

On the whole, women's and men's cognitive structures are similar, with high coefficients of correlation. They are not however identical, and have specific characteristics as regards the elements mentioned, the hierarchy of the most central elements, the main dimensions of the hierarchical value maps and the complexity of means-end chains. It will be important to consider these particularities in the definition of differentiated marketing.

Discussion

Considering the amount of data in our results, we will limit the discussion to the differences identified in the main dimensions of the hierarchical value maps.

Men's and women's motivations are characterised by duality:

- A hedonistic and universalistic – as defined by Schwartz and Bilsky (1987) – dimension in the case of men. This dimension was expressed through a wish for quality and taste (the hedonistic element), followed by a drive for equality between humans (the universalistic element), with fair trade perceived as the means of providing that.
- A hedonistic, then transcendental – as defined by Schwartz and Bilsky (1987) – dimension in the case of women. This was expressed through a drive for quality and taste (the hedonistic element), followed by a drive to influence the social context through the purchase of a product which is organic in nature.

Hence, men and women do not have fundamentally the same motives for buying fair trade coffee. They do not ascribe the same importance to the social dimension of this purchase (as opposed to the individual one, i.e. the individual outcomes of the purchase). This difference can be related to the social role learnt by each of the two sexes: whereas women tend to want to satisfy their families with their purchases, men are more idealistic. Women influence 75 per cent of the household's purchases and buy for themselves and/or their family, whereas men generally buy exclusively for themselves and these differences are consistent with gender-based stereotypes. They help explain women's concern about the satisfaction that their family will derive from consuming the products purchased, and help explain a lesser focus on the purchase as a means of engagement through an individual act. They offer one explanation also, for the transcendental dimension to women's purchase of fair trade products since organic products can help preserve the health of their families and themselves.

In fact, the findings of gender differences in motives are consistent with many studies which continue to highlight the presence of gender differences, or as some commentators would say, 'gender stereotypes'. For example, our findings are consistent with the agentic and communal orientations defined by Bakan (1966), and confirm the conclusions of Lyons (2005) that women grant more importance to their family and the world in general whereas men seek power which can be expressed through the purchase of a product that conveys a meaning. They thus seem to position themselves as important actors of change since they claim their power through the purchasing act.

Men moreover show more diverse motivations than do women and there are a number of possible explanations for this. One is a lower degree of expertise or knowledge on the part of men concerning the consumption of fair trade coffee and the other is greater diversity in their perceptions. In order to test the importance and validity of these two possible explanations, a more precise measurement of expertise or involvement would be necessary.

It is important to note that while there may be differences in some of men's and women's motives to buy fair trade coffee, there are also similarities in terms of purchasing motives for this product. Individuals make this purchase for the pleasure, to derive satisfaction from consuming a good product with a good taste. This motivation is consistent with the aims of consumption in general. Strong (1997) contends that individuals always see their own satisfaction before that of others or that of the Third World's needs. They consume above all to satisfy their primary needs, irrespective of the altruistic part of their consumption. Hedonism is therefore a value sought by both sexes and no longer only a value prevalent among men, as Lyons (2005) established. The fact that the product studied is a food probably largely explains this common point.

From a managerial point of view, the results of this research have improved our understanding of the fair trade purchasers' motives. Several positions can be envisaged in the different perceptions identified by the means-end chains. These positions allow for the formalisation of communication axes adapted to what the buyer seeks.

Depending on the consumer's profile, specific messages can be devised. Men buy fair trade coffee for the sustainable social contribution that it provides and for its taste, whereas women are more sensitive to the quality of the product and the fact that it is organic, thus helping to maintain a sustainable environment. Communication intended for men therefore has to be more idealised and focused on the fair trade nature of the product, whereas that intended for women must have tangible elements of personal satisfaction, as well as reference to the environmental protection afforded by the purchase of an organic product. These recommendations can serve in the implementation of targeted communication with the aim of increasing behaviours.

It is important not to underestimate a primary axis of communication for both sexes, namely the satisfaction derived from purchasing a product that tastes good. At the same time, secondary communication axes can be developed that relate to the fact that the fair trade product makes it possible to preserve the environment and provide a sense of accomplishment. It should be noted that the main axis will be the core of the communication, whereas the secondary axes can have a less central position or be scattered on other communication media such as product packaging, to highlight information that interests some buyers only. In this respect, the choice of an eco-design packaging may be relevant, especially for women, for whom respecting the environment appears to be important. Firms could opt for an eco-design approach, from which many benefits can be derived in terms of image, positioning, and especially cost reduction. Eco-design, which corresponds to a responsible approach such as fair trade, requires that the entire life-cycle of the product be taken into account and that the ecological nuisances that it could cause be reduced, from the extraction of the raw materials to the end of the product's life. Although it requires an investment in terms of expertise, analysis and R&D, eco-design corresponds perfectly to a responsible approach and could thus be a *plus* for fair trade products.

Irrespective of the solution adopted – targeted or general public communication – packaging is highly important for this new product category because fair trade is a complex system for most individuals to understand. It is therefore necessary to use the packaging to give buyers the maximum information possible, as concisely as possible, in order to make this approach convincing. Reference to other sources of information such as a website or newsletters is also appropriate so that the buyer has a better understanding of fair trade, and from this can build up knowledge of all aspects of this market and its trade.

The results of this research can be qualified with regard to a number of limits of a methodological nature. First, the external validity could have been improved by expanding this research to encompass other fair trade products and by subjecting it to a larger representative sample. Moreover, it is probable that the purchasing motives for non-food fair trade products such as clothes are different from the ones presented here.

Irrespective of the type of product, this research has nevertheless shown the necessity of segmenting the fair trade market since an analysis of men's and women's motives has revealed differing expectations.

Note

1. All the direct relations that are greater than or equal to the threshold have been formalised. The numbers mentioned on the figures correspond to the number of direct relations between the attributes, consequences and/or values. The dominant orientations are represented in bold type.

References

Altervia Consulting (2005) *Mise en place d'un état des lieux économique sur le commerce équitable en France en 2004*, Rapport de synthèse pour le Ministère des Affaires Etrangères et la Plateforme du Commerce Equitable, Avril.

Bakan D. (1966) *The duality of human existence*. Chicago: Rand McNally.

Bird K. and Hughes D.R. (1997) 'Ethical consumerism: The case of "fairly-traded" coffee', *Business ethics: A European review*, 6, 3, 159–67.

de Ferran F. (2006a) *Les déterminants à l'achat de produits issus du commerce équitable: une approche par les chaînages cognitifs*, Thèse de doctorat, IAE Aix en Provence, 8 Décembre.

de Ferran F. (2006b) 'A comparison of three laddering techniques applied to a socially desirable product, the fair trade coffee', *Proceedings of the 35th EMAC conference*, May, Athens, Greece (CD-Rom).

de Ferran F. and Grunert K. (2007) 'French fair trade coffee buyers' purchasing motives: An exploratory study using means-end chains analysis', *Food quality & preference*, 18, 2, 218–29.

de Pelsmacker P., Driesen L. and Rayp G. (2004) 'Are faire trade labels good business? Ethics and coffee buying intentions', *Proceedings of the 33rd EMAC conference*, May, Murcia, Spain.

Di Dio L., Saragovi C., Koestner R. and Aube J. (1996) 'Linking personal values to gender', *Sex roles*, 34, 621–36.

Feather N.T. (1984) 'Masculinity, feminity, psychological androgyny, and the structure of values', *Journal of personality and social psychology*, 47, 604–20.

FLO International (2008) Global Fair trade sales increase by 47%, http://www.fairtrade.net/news.html, date accessed May 2008.
François-Lecompte A. (2005) *La consommation socialement responsable: proposition et validation d'un cadre conceptuel intégrateur*, Thèse de doctorat, Université Pierre Mendès-France.
Geary D.C. (1998) *Male, female: The evolution of human sex differences*. Washington, DC: American Psychological Association.
Grunert K.G. and Grunert S.C. (1995) 'Measuring subjective meaning structures by the laddering method: Theoretical considerations and methodological problems', *International journal of research in marketing*, 12, 209–25.
Gutman J. (1982) 'A means-end chain model based on consumer categorization processes', *Journal of marketing*, 46, Spring, 60–72.
Herth A. (2005) *Le commerce équitable: 40 propositions pour soutenir son développement*, Rapport au premier ministre J.P. Raffarin, Mission parlementaire auprès de Christian Jacob, Mai.
Ipsos (2001) *Le commerce équitable*, Etude pour la Plate-forme du commerce équitable, Octobre.
Ipsos (2005) *Baromètre: les français et le commerce équitable*, Enquête Ipsos-Max Havelaar France, Mai.
Ipsos (2007) *Baromètre: les français et le commerce équitable*, Enquête Ipsos-Max Havelaar France, Mai.
Ipsos Marketing (2008) *Enquête pour Marketing Magazine*, Mars.
Kahle L.R. (1996) 'Social values and consumer behavior: Research from the LOV', in Seligman C., Olson J.M., Zanna M.P. (eds), *The psychology of values*, The Ontario Symposium, 8, chap.6, 135–51.
Kelly G.A. (1955) *The psychology of personal constructs*. New York: Norton.
Kréziak D. (1995) 'Comportement des consommateurs et environnement: une approche exploratoire', *Actes du 11ème Congrès de l'AFM*, Reims, Tome 2, 1110–35.
Kurdek L.A. (1993) 'The allocation of household labor in gay, lesbian, and heterosexual married couples', *Journal of social issues*, 49, 3, 127–39.
Lai A.W. (1995) 'Consumer values, product benefits and consumer value: A consumption behavior approach', *Advances in consumer research*, 22, 381–7.
Lipovetsky G. (2006) *Le bonheur paradoxal, Essai sur la société d'hyperconsommation*. Paris: Gallimard.
Lyons S. (2005) 'Are gender differences in basic human values a generational phenomenon?', *Sex roles: A journal of research*, 53, October.
Marion G. (2004) *Idéologie marketing*. Paris: Eyrolles.
McEachern M.G. and McClean P. (2002) 'Organic purchasing motivations and attitudes: Are they ethical?', *International journal of consumer studies*, 26, 2, 85–92.
Max Havelaar (2008) http://www.maxhavelaarfrance.org, July 2008.
Ozcaglar N. (2003) 'Le commerce équitable: Consommation à la mode ou nouveau mode de consommation?', *Conférence L'Entreprise Citoyenne*, 23 Octobre, Nanterre.
Ozcaglar N. (2005) *Apport du concept d'identité à la compréhension du comportement du consommateur responsable: une application à la consommation de produits issus du commerce équitable*, Thèse de doctorat, Université Lille 2, ESA.

Ozcaglar-Toulouse N., Shui E. and Shaw D. (2006) 'In search of fair trade: Ethical consumer decision-making in France', *International journal of consumer studies*, special issue: Promoting and Debating Political and Ethical Consumerism around the World, 30, 5, 502–14.

Parsons T. and Bales R.F. (1955) *Family, socialization, and interaction process*. Glencoe: Free Press.

Pieters R., Baumgartner H. and Allen D. (1995) 'A means-end chain approach to consumer goal structures', *International journal of research in marketing*, 12, 227–44.

Pitts R.E., Wong J.K. and Whalen D.J. (1991) 'Consumers' evaluative structures in two ethical situations: A means-end approach', *Journal of business research*, 22, 2, 119–30.

Putrevu S. (2002) 'Exploring the origins and information processing differences between men and women: Implications for advertisers', *Academy of marketing science review*, 6, 1.

Reynolds T.J. and Gutman J. (1988) 'Laddering theory, method, analysis, and interpretation', *Journal of advertising research*, 28, 11–31.

Roberts J.A. (1995) 'Profiling levels of socially responsible consumer behaviour: A cluster analytic approach and its implications for marketing', *Journal of marketing theory and practice*, 3, 4, 97–117.

Rokeach M. (1973) *The nature of human values*. New York: The Free Press.

Schwartz S.H. (1992) 'Universals in the content and structure of values: Theoretical advances and empirical tests in 20 countries', *Advances in experimental social psychology*, 25, 1–65.

Schwartz S.H. and Bilsky W. (1987) 'Toward a universal psychological structure of human values', *Journal of personality and social psychology*, 55, 3, 550–62.

Shaw D. and Shui E. (2001) 'Ethics in consumer choice: A multivariate modelling approach', *European journal of marketing*, 37, 10, 1485–98.

Shaw D., Shui E. and Clarke I. (2000) 'The contribution of ethical obligation and self-identity to the theory of planned behaviour: An exploration of ethical consumers', *Journal of marketing management*, 16, 879–94.

Sirieix L. and Tagbata D. (2004) 'Quelle valorisation par le consommateur de la dimension éthique des produits? Le cas du commerce équitable', *Colloque de l'AIEA2*, Laval, Québec.

Sirieix L., Meunier A. and Schaer B. (2004) 'Les consommateurs et le commerce équitable: scepticisme, confiance accordée et disposition à s'engager', *Economie et Sociétés*, 38, 3, 571–90.

Sterns P.A. (2000) 'Yes! We have fair trade Bananas', *IAMA World food and agribusiness congress*. Chicago, Illinois, USA, March.

Strong C. (1997) 'The problems of translating fair trade principles into consumer purchase behaviour', *Marketing intelligence & planning*, 15, 1, 32–7.

Vantomme D., Geuens M., de Houwer J. and de Pelsmacker P. (2006) 'Explicit and implicit determinants of fair trade buying behavior', *Advances in consumer research*, 33, 699–703.

Walker B.A. and Olson J.C. (1991) 'Means-end chains: Connecting products with self', *Journal of business research*, 22, 2, 111–18.

6
Women Managers in Latvia: A Universal Footprint for the Future?

Gloria Moss, David Farnham, and Caryn Cook

In 2006, close on 41 per cent of managers in Latvia were female (Eurostat, 2006). This was the highest proportion of women managers anywhere in the European Union (EU), exceeding the proportion of female managers in the UK and by some 6 per cent, and exceeding the proportion of female managers in Sweden, Ireland and Germany by 9, 11 and 14 per cent respectively. The divergence between the proportion of male and female managers in Latvia, and elsewhere in the EU, poses the question as to the factors that have created this situation and whether they are unique. At the same time, this critical mass of female managers in Latvia provides a window of opportunity for the authors of this chapter to interview managers in Latvia and study perceptions of the impact of female managers on organisations.

Given the strategic significance of female managers in Latvia, this chapter has three main aims. First, it provides a summary background to the post-communist, Latvian economy. Second, it outlines women's role in the 'new' Latvian economy, especially at managerial level and, third, it reports on the findings of in-depth, semi-structured interviews with 27 female and male, middle and senior managers in the Latvian services sector. All interviews were conducted in English and as the reader will see, the dominant view is that women import something different to management and the working environment from men. Many of the respondents considered women to have management characteristics not commonly found in Latvian male managers and considered that these qualities offered a source of competitive advantage. This provides an instance of the way diversity can profit an organisation.

A word of caution is called for. We need to remember that the views reported here are specific to the managers interviewed, and since these are not a representative group, cannot be taken as more than a conspectus of opinion of a group of middle and senior managers in Latvia. However, a comparison of these views with recent research findings on gender and leadership reveals significant parallels and this gives the views greater construct validity.

In the information that unfolds, we sketch some details of historical and contemporary Latvia before reporting on the views of respondents as to whether men and women work and manage in similar or different ways. We then set these views alongside research findings concerning male and female management styles, before presenting respondents' views as to the factors that have given rise to the high proportion of female managers in Latvia. Some concluding remarks then follow.

Women and the changing Latvian labour market

Latvia occupies a strategic geographical location with a border to Russia and a coastal front on the Baltic Sea, due south of Sweden. This situation has defined the fate of Latvia since its early history. Its capital city, Riga, was founded by the Germans in 1207 and in 1621 the country came under Swedish rule. By the end of the eighteenth century, Latvia had passed to Russian rule and there were just a couple of decades between 1918 and 1940 when Latvia attained its independence. During this period, the country experienced rapid economic growth and achieved one of the highest living standards in Europe.

This independence was short-lived. In 1940, the Russians re-occupied the country, and the following year planned the mass deportation of anti-Soviet elements mainly to camps in Siberia. The roll call of Latvians amounted to 15,424 inhabitants and the problems were compounded by the occupation of Riga by Nazi troops in 1941. Following the war, a further 120,000 Latvians were imprisoned or deported to Soviet concentration camps while, in Latvia itself, the Russians imposed Soviet farming methods as well as some of the Soviet Union's most advanced manufacturing industries. This led to the establishment of electro-technical factories that used the educated specialists found in Latvia.

A break with Soviet rule came in 1990 with Latvia's declaration of independence. This was followed in 2004, under the popular Presidency of Vaira Vike-Freiberga, Latvia's twice elected female President, by early accession to the EU and NATO membership. Since independence, its economy has, as in its earlier experience of independence in the 1930s, thrived with annual growth in GDP in 2004–2008 at slightly over 10 per cent per year. This rate was more than four times the EU average

(LIAA, 2008), with a national debt among the lowest in the EU (ibid.). Latvia's population is just 2.3 million.

How has this growth been achieved? Like other ex-Soviet states, Latvia has experienced radical political and economic restructuring and has had to face uncertainties as it moved away from a centrally controlled Soviet economy to market-based systems of work and organisations (Alas and Rees, 2005). These changes have demanded that workers develop market-based skills and flexible patterns of work if they wish to be competitive. The biggest contribution to growth has come from the services sector as can be seen from Table 6.1:

Table 6.1 Percentage of the Latvian working population employed in different sectors, 1997 and 2000

Sector	1997	2000
Agriculture and fishery	22.5	14
Industry	25	27
Services	52.5	59

Source: Ramina *et al.* (2001).

In terms of women in the labour force, four issues stand out. First, in terms of the labour market activity rate, the rate for women in Latvia in 2003 was 64.7 per cent which is high by European standards (Vanags, 2004). As regards employment (i.e. those with employed status), the rate for women stood at 57.9 per cent of economically active women in 2003, a figure that compares with an EU-15 average of 56 per cent and an EU-25 average of 55.1 per cent. In terms of unemployment, female unemployment has, until 2003, been consistently lower than male unemployment and in 2003, male and female unemployment fell sharply in response to the buoyant economy.

As regards pay, the extent to which male hourly earnings exceeded female earnings in 2003 was 16 per cent – exactly the same as the estimated EU-15 average (ibid.). According to Vanags (ibid., p. 3), these figures support 'what would probably be the typical view' among Latvian inhabitants that 'Latvia does not have a significant gender equality problem'. A similar view emerges from a study by Raita Karnite (2007) which claims that 'gender discrimination in careers is not a problem in Latvia' and that 'gender segregation is not a topical problem in Latvia' (http//:www.eurofound.europa.eu/eiro/studies/tn0612019s/lv0612019q.htm pp.5 and 6, accessed on 11 April 2009).

In terms of a comparison of men's and women's educational background, Karnite (ibid.) also cites statistics showing that 63.2 per cent of students of universities and colleges are female and that in 2005, 18 per cent of the male labour force and 29.2 per cent of the female labour force had a university-level education. This picture of a highly educated female population is found also in earlier figures from the Council of Higher Education of Latvia (date unspecified), cited in a report for the Higher Education Research Network (HERN) by Rivza (2003). These figures show that in the period prior to 2003, 63 per cent of those with degrees or an equivalent qualification were female.

As regards the proportion of male and female managers in Latvia, Eurostat statistics compiled by the European Commission in March 2006 showed that Latvia had the highest proportion of female managers in any member state at 41 per cent. In terms of women's representation at the highest decision-making bodies in management, against a European average in 2005 of 10 per cent, Latvia had (with Slovenia) the highest proportion at 22 per cent (Holst, 2005).

This high level of economic and management participation by women in Latvia makes it possible to do what is not so easy to do in other European member states, namely study the perceived impact and style of women in management when they constitute a near-majority of managers. The fact that they have reached near parity with men is significant since the contrasting situation of being in a minority position is claimed to lead women to mould their management style on that of the male majority (Gardiner and Tiggerman, 1999) and to display a more stereotypically masculine style than males (Eagly and Johnson, 1990; Ferrario and Davidson, 1991) in order to decrease visibility and lessen perceived differences and stereotyping by men (Kanter, 1977; Davidson and Burke, 2004).

Clearly, a situation such as that in Latvia, in which women have achieved near-parity with men in terms of representation in management, affords a rare glimpse of how women manage when freed of the constraints of being a minority.

The research interviews

In undertaking their study of women holding managerial posts in the Latvian services sector, the authors of this chapter identified four major research questions:

1. What, if anything, distinguishes male and female management styles?

2. What is the impact of having female managers in Latvian organisations?
3. What factors have led Latvia to have a high proportion of women in managerial jobs?
4. What obstacles are there to the appointment of female managers in Latvia?

The selection of respondents was made in three ways. First, one of the authors had gathered business cards from an earlier presentation on Management to managers in Latvia and those based in Riga were approached to see if they wanted to participate in the interviews. In a second phase, approaches were made to organisations that had a presence on the British Chamber of Commerce (BCC) website. In a third phase, one of the organisations on the BCC website, an international executive recruitment agency, Talentor, sought interviewees from amongst their network of contacts. This three-pronged approach produced 27 respondents from a cross-section of sectors (service and industry), disciplines (general management, finance, HR, education, management consultancy and journalism), management levels (middle to senior to top management), ages (from late 20s to 50s), and employment status (entrepreneurs and employees). Five respondents (just under 20 per cent) were male, and whilst the respondent population could not be said to be representative of the management population of Latvia, it did offer a broad cross-section of opinion.

The wide cross-section of opinion accessed is significant. Given the need to understand the context of the research, non-probability sampling was deemed appropriate (Glaser and Strauss, 1967; Lincoln and Guba, 1986) and a key issue within the judgement-quota, non-probability sampling employed is identifying and gaining access to key informants whose insight on the issues of research is required (Crimp and Wright, 1995). In this project, this necessitated access to a cross-section of middle to top level management personnel in Latvia. Moreover, while quantitative sampling is driven by the imperative of *representativeness*, qualitative sampling is concerned with *depth* and *richness* of data. The potential richness of qualitative data leads Gummerson (1991) to argue that representativeness can be of secondary importance over the achievement of quality data: in this way, the remarks individuals make about a subject can have content validity and the occasional use of verbatim quotations from interviewees can also bring the reader into the reality of the issue under investigation.

How were the interviews conducted? Following an introduction to the project ('we are conducting a study into women in management in Latvia') and confidentiality assurances, respondents were asked in semi-structured interviews about the four research questions. Where applicable, interesting lines of enquiry were followed up to facilitate unbroken discussion. All interviews followed the same schedule and lasted an average of 45 minutes. At the end of the interview, participants were encouraged to express feelings and opinions that were related to the subject but not touched on during the interview, making the conversation informal and relaxed and encouraging comments (Coolican, 1999). In most cases, two interviewers were present.

In terms of coding respondents' comments, two concurrent methods were adopted. First, answers were noted against the structured questions provided in the interview and, in doing this, the pattern described by Mariampolski (2001) with analysis occurring 'at the same time as data collection' was followed. In this way, analysis occurred with the first interview and finished after the last sentence of the report, with the researchers looking out for patterns of attitudes during the discussions. The analysis was 'a continuous and evolving process rather than one which takes place entirely at the conclusion of data collection' (ibid.). Moreover, order can be introduced into qualitative data by adopting systems of categorisation, enabling the frequency of categories to be quantified (Moss and Daunton, 2006).

Our focus in this chapter will be on answers to the first two questions since these have a direct bearing on the theme of this book, namely the contribution that diversity (in this case, gender) may bring to organisations. Since people's observations concerning the first were frequently bound up with remarks on the impact of these styles on organisations, responses to the first two questions will be rolled together. Later on in the chapter, we will also report on the last two questions, since these have a bearing on the factors that can give rise or block gender diversity.

Differences/similarities between male and female styles of management and impact on organisations

Respondents were asked as to whether, based on their experience in the workplace, men and women managed in similar or different ways. The overwhelming proportion of respondents spoke of differences with only 1 of the 27 respondents considering that there was no difference in management style. This view came from a female respondent aged 42 who said: 'I don't see a difference. It's mostly a personality thing'. The remaining 26 respondents spoke of differences in men's and women's style of management, with their views coalescing around 9 themes.

Emotionality

Seven respondents (men and women) expressed the view that women were more emotional, whether in their attitudes to projects and behaviours or in their way of dealing with people. One man in his early 30s with a PhD in chemistry from an American university and now running his own company focused on women's emotional investment with work:

> Women are more emotionally attached to their job. For men, if something fails it is a problem but they can go home and forget about it. For women, they take the ups and downs very emotionally. For other people in the team, they feel it. They probably become more emotionally involved in the project and probably feel upset if it doesn't work.

This respondent spoke of the positive impact that this emotional engagement could have on productivity saying: 'If you feel that this is not something you do just to get paid, then you try harder I think. This attitude would make people work harder.' He cited an instance of this behaviour from his employment in all-female laboratory and how, when problems arose, the 'women took it very emotionally. They stayed longer and worked harder. They really wanted to do the job.' He went on to describe the impact he thought this emotionality could have on other people, with women finding it easier to raise up 'positive or negative emotions so that the person a women talks to better understands what they need to do'. He contrasted this with men's interactive style: 'He is more stiff and more rude and how a manager would communicate with workers about the need to clean the floor.' The female manager might tell the shift manager: 'Do you want to live like pigs? We want to be a good company' – thus making the man feel guilty, whilst a male manager might say, 'idiot, clean up the floor'.

The notion that women's behaviours can stir up positive and negative emotions was echoed by a 40-year-old female respondent who spoke of the skills normally found in a male company head she had observed. Of him, she commented:

> He is always very strong and lacks emotional leadership skills. If a man leads, he doesn't have this emotion. Instead, he uses a control system which permits him to ask why someone is not doing something.

She added that 'Women are nice diplomats. They say "well done" from the heart and offer flowers and chocolate if there's a good idea, maybe once a month. The man's thank you is formal – it's not emotional'. On this theme of women's greater emotionality, another female respondent in her late 20s described men as 'prepar[ing] content and females think[ing] how to package it. Women are more emotional, they'll think how another person will accept it.' A very senior woman in her late 40s said of women's more emotional approach: 'Men shake hands. I never shake hands – I kiss people who I worked with and who I see again (use arms to embrace).You have a feeling that you went through something interesting and exciting.'

Decision-making

Two male respondents and one female respondent raised the issue of men and women adopting diverse approaches to decision-making. One, an academic at the Stockholm School of Economics, spoke of women's strategic approach to negotiations:

> For women, it may be more like chess playing. In negotiations, women are more prepared to have lengthy negotiations, agreeing on nitty-gritty details and adopting a more holistic approach. Men, by contrast, have a more straightforward, aggressive approach to settling things. Women use more softening tactics than men – for me this is a very clear approach. I have never seen men do this. Men ignore the whole spectrum of possibilities and may lose out on the subtleties of negotiation.

Another male manager spoke of women being less predictable than men: 'Men are more predictable in their reactions. With men, you say A and you get B. With women, you say A and you get A, B, C or S.' When pressed, for an example, this respondent cited the case of a female supplier who, sooner than reduce prices, added additional services for their customers. The male respondent took the view that 'men would say either we can or cannot but would not look at the whole picture. We are talking about extremes to better understand the tendencies.'

A senior female manager in her late 40s described men as overplaying positive features, with women taking a more balanced approach to evaluating outcomes. In her view, 'women will take a wider view of the project, see the negatives and see things for real'.

Focus on results

Around 25 per cent of the respondents, of both sexes, volunteered the view that women were strongly results-orientated. Typical of these views were those of a young male chemist whose professional experience was gained in the US as well as Latvia. His view is that results and targets are all-important in operational and management issues. In his view, this is 'why women are more suitable at this'.

Four female respondents had made similar observations. According to the managing director of one of the country's top media outlets, 'If you want a doer, get a woman...ladies are like producers – put down the idea, the terms'. Another very senior woman in charge of her own publishing company and advisor to the government volunteered the view that 'If we compare lot of companies in Latvia, women are always thinking about results not power. Latvian women managers like their work: the position is not as important to them as their work.' A head of human resource development for a foreign-owned company, with an MSc in Human Resources, said that in her view, 'Women are more goal-oriented than men.'

Men, on the other hand, were thought to have a rather greater focus on processes. According to the male PhD chemist and entrepreneur, if women are results-focused, men are more process-oriented. As he put it, 'Men are more enjoying the process than the result.' An interesting analogy was provided by the female head of the media outlet who likened men to actors. 'If you look for a good speaker, then find a man. Men like to be on the stage – they are more like actors. Their talk is more important than the job, so if you want a talker, find a man.' Talk of different priorities also came from the female executive director of cross-cultural institution with an MSc from the London School of Economics. She expressed the view that 'Men tend to focus directly on profit, while women tend to focus more on the big picture, employee satisfaction. I think that women just view other things as being important, such as a happy workforce.'

Long-term/short-term focus

Another theme, the focus of the thinking of the female managing director of a large media organisation concerned the relative focus of men and women on the short and long term. In her opinion,

> Women are really long-term thinkers and workers. I have had the situation where I had hard negotiations with men who have forced me to do drastic things to improve current results. In doing this, they could sacrifice what happens in five years time. Women, by contrast, have a more long-term focus – they're growing this tree because they know that after three years it will be up to the ceiling...Men are more short-term – they can sell all the leaves even though the tree may crash down.

This respondent went on to observe that 'the male manager will be keen to do anything to grasp success in this year to say "I am a hero". ' Men are the gender constantly needing to be flattered. 'Without it, they're like plants without water. Women have higher self-esteem and do not need other people to flatter them.'

Consensual/oppositional approach to management

Six respondents, three males and three females, referred to women's greater use of a participative management style compared with men. One of these, a 40-year old male academic at the Stockholm School of Economics, thought that the difference in management style was linked to 'different concepts of what it is to be a leader. For males, the concept of a leader may be for immediate and visible domination.' A similar thought came from another male respondent, a serial entrepreneur with an MBA track record of several successful start-ups behind him. He spoke of men having a male style of management 'which is more suited to the army and women a creative style, a more participative style which is better in the service sector. Women are more towards the coaching style, less yelling. These are the so-called X and Y of management theory.'

The association between women and a participative style of management was made by three other respondents. One, a female finance manager with an MSc from Stockholm School of Management expressed the view that 'women are more talkative evaluating, describing and sharing information'. Another respondent, the female director of a non-governmental organisation, with a PhD from an American university, said that 'women involve people more in decision-making than men'. She described the companies run by women as having flatter structures than other comparably sized institutions. 'Flatter structures produce better accessibility to the top and more involvement in decision-making.'

A third respondent, working for a non-governmental organisation, said, in her view,

> It's more natural for women to accept a democratic model of business management than men. Unavoidably, you have to come to a democratic style if you want to embrace diversity. Women act more as moderators whereas men keep the last word as managers.

She contrasted men's approach to management with that of women who, in her experience, 'are more relational and also more likely to welcome a bottom-up approach to a top-down one'. She had observed differences across culture. 'Businesses with branches in Scandinavia tend to be more advanced in the way they deal with employees', whilst those from Russia are more authoritarian. She had noticed, in general, that 'there's an assumed way of how a manager should act – cold and inaccessible; you feel more powerful when you're distant but it's deceptive. People think that this will make them more respected.'

According to the male serial entrepreneur, women's preference for exercising power democratically makes it easier for them to work in a non-hierarchical organisation. This offers more freedom. In his view, 'this style of management is more likely to be found in the service than other sectors'.

Focus on teamwork

A related theme concerned men's and women's relative preference for teamwork. The female founder of a successful publishing house had noticed that, in interviews, high level female interviewees usually used the 'we' rather than the 'I' form of address. The finance manager of a publishing house expressed the view that 'women are generally considered better at people management skills'.

These thoughts were echoed in the views of a woman working for a non-governmental organisation, with a PhD from an American university. According to her, 'women are more relational. By nature, they are more caring, they spend time as a manager paying attention to employees, contacting them and communicating with them, spending any time possible to keep the personal connection going with them. This empathy, caring, comes more naturally to women than men.' These descriptions of women's priorities were mirrored in the management priorities described by the female director of a large media organisation in Latvia, with 1000 staff:

> Women may have a more open style. I usually like to delegate to other people and usually trust that they can do it. Usually we have an open discussion. If people feel good in a company, they can do more, their results will be better and sometimes they will create new ideas. If people feel good in a job with colleagues in an atmosphere or culture they enjoy, they have more initiative to offer new ideas.

The way men communicated with staff was described in contrasting terms both in relation to their preferred mode and content of communications. Where the first is concerned, the female founder of a flourishing publishing house and advisor to the government said that 'women want to communicate face to face but men prefer to communicate through e-mail – it's faster. They don't like face-to-face communications. For us women, it's genetic – we like face to face communications. Men and women are not similar.'

This interest in people was corroborated by a female managing director of a large media organisation who spoke of women managers' efforts on behalf of their employees:

> female managers fight until the last battle for their employees. If one has an employee who is lazy, a female manager will put a big effort into how to solve their professional and psychological problems. Only if the person fails for the second or third time will she fire the person. Male managers, in the same case, would say 'bye bye', I need a strong worker without personal problems.

Interestingly, a very senior female, a former MD in finance, spoke of women's willingness to acknowledge their ignorance. She recalled how happy she was to say 'don't ask me about it because I don't know anything about it' and then 'let's talk it out', 'let's work on it together'. This whole idea of consensus building was, in her view, more familiar to women than men, an idea that chimed with the views of a young female manager with a PhD from America. She said that in her experience, 'men's approach was to say "let's offer a solution" rather than "let's think about it out loud"'.

Risk

Five respondents raised issues relating to men's and women's relative propensity to risk. According to a very senior managing director in finance, 'women are reluctant to take risks'. Another female manager in a market research firm expressed the view that 'men are risk takers, they are more daring'. According to a male serial entrepreneur, 'women are less prone to take risks – this is bad for them since they need to take risks to succeed. If you do not take risks then you lose opportunities.' This attitude to risk may underline the observation by a female finance manager in a publishing company that 'men tend to overplay the positive features of a project while women take a more balanced approach in the evaluation process'.

Respondents were also asked about the factors that led Latvia to have a high proportion of female managers. Responses are summarised in the next section.

Factors promoting the employment of female managers in Latvia

What are the factors promoting the high incidence of female managers in Latvia? According to one respondent, a male entrepreneur and managing director, this was not a pan-Baltic phenomenon, but one specific to Latvia. In his words, 'If you went to Lithuania, you wouldn't find it. They still have a very strong tradition of men leading everything. Somehow, Latvia has passed this.'

In the course of the interviews, a large number of factors were identified as contributing to women's presence as managers in the workplace. These are listed below with respondents' comments noted against each point.

History and social traditions

One factor identified by several respondents concerned Latvia's history and social traditions. In this way, a manager in a market research company referred to the country's legacy of strong women, living in families in which men and women served as equal partners. Reflections of these family traditions were preserved in Latvia's folklore and folksongs which featured powerful women and families in which men were not at the apex. This particular manager volunteered the view that 'the country does not have a long experience of patriarchy' and, in her view, an explanation is to be found in the fact that 'patriarchy has its origins in the south east, in Russia, and is rooted in Catholic belief'. This manager went on to express the view that 'some historians claim that Latvian society was not really patriarchal and not matriarchal but with a tendency to matriarchy'.

A second factor, highlighted by an entrepreneur with a PhD in Chemistry but instanced by several respondents, related to the Second World War and the impact this had on men and women. In the words of this respondent, 'a lot of good men were killed or deported to concentration camps, and during and after the war, few were available to work. Women stepped forward with the realisation that they could run farms and other enterprises, which left them strong after the war. Even when men returned, the existence of strong women, and the premium placed on men socially, meant that men became lazy and drank vodka.'

A third factor related to the conscription of Latvian men into foreign armies, a factor respondents again described as invoked in Latvian folksong. According to one manager, around one hundred years of folksong describe men's conscription into the army and the way that this left women with responsible jobs and responsibilities in the men's absence. According to one female respondent, women in the nineteenth century could own their own livestock, responsibilities women did not have in other countries, and was of the view that 'past history forced women to be strong'.

A fourth factor related to the influence of the Soviet occupation. According to one female manager, during this period 'men's initiative was kept down' while, in conformity with Soviet tradition (she referred to a long-standing tradition in the Soviet Union of employing women on a par with men, offering them posts heads of municipalities, factories and other organisations), women became more equal than in many parts of the Western world. In her view, the Soviet period encouraged the notion that 'we are all workers fighting for the communist state' and this added to the image of the strong woman.

Respondents also talked of the influence exercised by Scandinavia with one male academic expressing the view that 'if you're a Scandinavian firm, it's very unlikely that you'd follow gender inequality in any area of management. This filters through to Latvia since Scandinavians are heavily present in the country.' This academic went on to suggest that the Swedish presence in the country through Swedish banks, design firms, and the influence of 'Swenglish', had made Swedish influence on the country more important than that of Russia.

A final historical factor related to the demise of technologically based industry after the demise of the Soviet Union. Just one technology-based factory alone employed 18,000 people and the people working in this sector suffered disproportionately during the breakdown of the Soviet Union. The specialist labour employed, largely men, had difficulty finding new work and many were not able to handle the consequent stress, turning to drink for solace. According to a female respondent working for a charitable organisation, women are better able to cope with long-term stress than men, and this made them a more dependable resource. Moreover, according to another respondent, the majority of Latvian women do not drink and these combined factors increased women's attractions to employers. Interestingly, one reason advanced for women's greater resilience was having 'the main responsibility for children and not having the opportunity to slack off'.

Absence of an aristocracy

One respondent referred to the lack, historically, of a Latvian gentry and the fact that unlike the UK, there were no men's clubs from which women could be excluded. 'Consequently, there was never a Nora (Ibsen Doll's House) – a "fluttering bird" – there was never such a situation in Latvia.'

Female characteristics

In the course of discussions, several respondents expressed views concerning the attributes they associated with men and women. A first characteristic that was spoken of by some respondents concerned 'the high degree of responsibility and diligence exercised by women'. For example, one male manager mentioned that 'women are more responsible – if you're asked to complete this or that, with a lady you can expect a more accurate result. She will do all she can to get the result.' Echoing this sentiment, a female director of an important media outlet cited the fact that

> Women have a high level of responsibility. I can trust them more – they are neat, not lazy, they work hard to give the impression of being good employees. Many times, I have had the situation where women, in a hard situation, would say that they need to learn about it and ask a colleague about it. They are more cooperative in this sense. It's not only 'bla, bla, bla just give me the opportunity' (typically, a man's response). A lady's response might be 'it's too big a project for me' – her self-assessment is not as high as a man's – but I know she can do the job.

This director went on to suggest that, in her experience, women with kids 'are extremely responsible. They are very stable, do not waver in their moods and know that when there's a conflict, they need to solve it.' This links, perhaps, with the views of a male serial entrepreneur who commented on women's resilience:

> In the 1990s upheaval when the economy collapsed, women were better at coping with this; they were more resilient, they are mothers – have family obligations and they cannot let themselves down. Men got depressed; they lost social status and income because the changes were so rapid. They could not adapt – they basically went out of the working circuit and women replaced these places.

A second theme, expressed by five respondents, concerned women's long-term career focus and the fact that they were happy to defer earning until the completion of their studies. One of these respondents, the director of a large media organisation, said that 'men want to do business and achieve the money but not the long-term plans'. These thoughts were echoed by a female head of HR development who said: 'It's not popular for men to go step by step. They prefer to jump and immediate benefits. Women are just more qualified because of this factor.'

A third theme, referred to by other respondents, concerned the fact that women might be better able than men to withstand long-term stress. A contributory was suggested to be the fact that women have the main responsibility for children and therefore do not have the opportunity to slack off. Moreover, according to a female respondent, if women are not successful, it is not the biggest goal in their life so they can compensate with other interests such as children, friends and hobbies.

Some male characteristics

Some respondents referred to the disadvantage of employing males, given the huge problem of alcoholism in Latvia, especially in rural areas. This problem had its origins in the post-Soviet period when men had difficulty dealing with the transition to a market economy and a new political system. Several respondents instanced the fact that many men would turn to drink if they were unsuccessful or had a problem. In terms of the scale of the problem it was estimated that a large proportion of Latvian men, perhaps 15 per cent, mostly Russians, had a substance abuse problem, whether drink or drug-related. A female management consultant with an MSc in Psychology referred to the lack of fortitude of some men and the fact that Latvia had 'a women-type culture which puts women in a strong position in society. If you ask Latvian women about Latvian men they would say they are weak and they look to other countries for husbands.'

Of course, this problem was not universal and according to a male head of administration of a large bank, there was a 'big gap' between those men who had a problem and the Russians in the country who founded new companies. This gap led him to speak of Russian men in Latvia going 'fast up or down', with substance abuse being 'a way of hiding from society'. According to the male head of administration of a large bank, there appear to be two types of males: '(a) low level males (b) people who want to be in charge. There is nothing in between these two types.' This was partially confirmed by a female head of production who spoke of the desire amongst men with education to establish their own business. 'At the top, the management is often men...Men tend to work for themselves and not for a team. If the man doesn't succeed, he starts drinking and will never become a manager.'

Pay

Several respondents referred to the fact that women managers were paid less than men, earning on average 15 per cent less pay than men, with the only exception being women working in Scandinavian companies. One female head of HR development said that if a male and female candidate of comparable quality presented themselves for a job, lower pay would be a factor in the employer's decision to choose the woman.

Societal pressures to be multi-tasking

Another factor credited with assisting women up the management ladder is, according to one male manager, the 'invisible push in society for women to be nice looking, excellent mothers and successful in their job life. There's a kind of pressure on women to be successful in all aspects of life.'

Support

In terms of support mechanisms, respondents spoke positively about the support provided by the state which included free kindergarten place for ages 3–6. They also referred to national legislation that provided for a year and a half's maternity leave. In terms of other sources of support, a male manager mentioned that there were several women entrepreneurs with multi-million pound turnovers who received their initial funding from their husbands. This source of funding gave easier access to funds than might otherwise have been the case. The female manager of a market research company, in turn, expressed the contrary view saying, 'when I speak with my friends we say wouldn't it be good if men were strong and were able to support us, then we could do pretty jobs like teaching but we have no choice'.

Role models

Several respondents mentioned the positive impact of positive female role models in Latvia, with frequent reference to the ex-President of Latvia and the former Managing Director of the Hansa bank, the largest bank in Latvia.

Obstacles to the appointment of female managers

The final question posed related to the obstacles that respondents thought existed to the appointment of female managers. It should be pointed out at the outset that two respondents, one a self-employed entrepreneur (male) and the other a management consultant (male), did not perceive obstacles to women's advancement. According to the male entrepreneur with a PhD from the US where he spent eight years, American women 'have to fight for their rights to go to work'. In his view, in the US more than in Latvia 'there's the attitude that women cannot do serious jobs, a view shared by men and women'. He contrasted this situation to that of Latvia where 'they don't have to fight for their right to work. Nobody told them they couldn't do it and it is amazing what you can do if you don't know what you can't do. If you don't know that, you can do amazing things.' He went on to say that 'there is not much to stop women being promoted. There may be organisations where they would not – in construction for example – but females are not choosing this profession.'

The second respondent was equally sure that no barriers existed:

> There are no factors that discourage women. I haven't noticed any discrimination in terms of sexual discrimination. It is different with regards to racial, Russian and Latvian speaking, but in terms of gender, everyone is given the same opportunities – no borders. There are no problems in getting into higher education or getting into management positions in Latvian companies.

Despite the perceived lack of obstacles on the part of these two respondents, five factors were identified by other respondents as holding women back. These are described below.

Not suited to sales jobs

A young PhD chemist with his own business took the view that women 'don't have that salesmen in them'. A serial entrepreneur, however, volunteered that he gets repeated calls from female sales people and that although men will often call once, 'they rarely, unlike women, call again'. According to the director of a non-governmental organisation, 'women are better able to cope with long-term stress than men', one factor in this possibly being the fact that women have 'the main responsibility for children and not having the opportunity for slackening off'.

Children

According to several respondents, women's responsibility for children represents the main impediment to women's advancement in the workplace. One male entrepreneur with a PhD in chemistry summed up this way of thinking when saying that the 'the main obstacle is children'. This accords with the view of a female director of a non-governmental organisation who singled out the burden that family life places on working women: 'Family commitments – women still work two jobs – work, clean, raise kids and go to work. 80 per cent of women at least do two jobs. The expectation is that it's the women who do it.' A female director of production expressed similar thoughts when she said that 'Women are devoted to families, they have responsibilities at home that they are not ready or prepared to sacrifice. Women will put the family first and want maternity leave – I have heard it explained to me that this is why I get less money.'

According to some respondents, the pressure on women is leading more people in upper-class families (but not middle- or lower-class families) to consider employing a housekeeper, although 'there's not a lot of live-in child care'.

According to a male academic at the Stockholm School of Economics, childcare is still viewed 'as the prime duty of women'. He said,

> It is expected that you would spend a year or two with your kid and this means that you have challenged or damaged your career prospects since a career break is not easily accommodated. Formally, after a year and a half, you should be offered the same position

and although you may be given a position which is formally and hierarchically the same as your previous post, it may be a different post from previously.

This academic offered the example of a woman who had held a major position as editor of a TV culture programme and then, on her return from maternity leave, was offered a job on a political programme. She disliked this new field and moved jobs to work for an advertising agency producing video clips. This change of employer marked a move from middle-level management to the bottom of the ladder and, as the academic said, 'there's something about the return to work that may damage the woman's career position'.

In addition to these practical difficulties, a female director of a non-governmental organisation referred to a general perception that being a good mother was at odds with being 'a big shot manager'. According to her, there is a perception that working women are 'neglecting their kids while visible women are typically people with grown-up kids or people who've never had children'. In terms of women of child-bearing age who have not yet had children, the perception is that they 'will leave, have children and go on maternity leave. In this way, mothers can be advantaged.'

Old boy network

Another perceived obstacle was the old-boy school network. The male academic from the Stockholm School of Economics referred to a 'quasi old-boy school network that would not allow women to get to the top' and he spoke of its influence in state-owned companies such as Latvian Electricity, Latvian Rail and Latvian Post. He described these as post-Soviet organisations which would not allow women to enter the male realm since they had yet to be transformed into a new model of organisation.

Gender expectations

A female director of production quoted her father as having repeatedly conveyed the message to her that 'girls are not people'. When asked for an example, she cited the occasion when she was going through border controls with her father, mother, brother and two other older girls in the car. Her father, on being asked how many people there were in the car, said 'one'. The authorities questioned this and he said 'Can't you see that I am only one – one boy and one kid and just women.'

This respondent was quick to point out that her father does not treat women disrespectfully and that he was brought up by his mother in the absence of a father. Nevertheless, she was brought up to believe that 'although women are strong, loyal, persistent, enduring, men were still considered the strong gender. It is not fair but it is *socially* accepted' (authors' italics).

In terms of job expectations, the female director of a non-governmental organisation described gender expectations as a 'huge obstacle'. She believed that these expectations were responsible for the fact that 99 per cent of teachers and nurses are female with salaries that are lower than in other professions. She also spoke of a widely held perception that women were better at people management than men and 'so the only male usually in a school will be a principal or a sports teacher. They get on the admin track and keep getting promoted.'

Discussion of gender expectations led her to describe men 'as figure heads'. She cited the case of a dean at the University of Latvia who 'didn't do anything but had ten females running round him. This is often the situation. The figure head is a male and there's no reason to promote the female.' According to a female finance manager employed by a large publishing company, 'there is a culture of preference for male leaders. In companies, men show a preference for dealing with men.' A director of production volunteered a similar comment independently and offered the analogy of a chicken farm:

> There is the cock and there are the chickens. This may be sarcastic but it is accepted and the average Latvian person would understand. I have a cousin, one of the first to graduate from a private law school, and she was always annoyed that her colleagues (male) worked much less but earned more. She now has her own law company.

In terms of the factors that lead to men's appointment, a female director in a large bank referred to the opportunities afforded to men by networking: 'Men know more men (pubs, drinking beer, golf)'. She volunteered that she personally had 'never been in a women's professional network and was never thinking about this top post until it arose'.

Lack of confidence

Another factor quoted as preventing women from entering management was a perceived lack of confidence. According to the female founder and creative director of a publishing house, a typical female response from a woman informed of a new job is to say that 'maybe my competence is not so good', while a man might say 'Me of course'. The main obstacle for women is lack of confidence. 'Women think that maybe in one or two years they can get this position.'

Discussion

The respondents' replies in the study described above are rich and appear to show male and female managers adopting different approaches to management. This is in line with the literature on leadership which suggests that women manage through a reliance on transformational leadership (coupled with the contingent reward aspect of transactional leadership) while men are said to rely more exclusively on the exercise of transactional leadership.

Having said this, several studies highlight the fact that when women constitute a minority of managers, they are under pressure to replicate the management style of the majority so as not to isolate themselves (Kanter, 1977; Eagly and Johnson, 1990; Ferrario and Davidson, 1991; Gardiner and Tiggerman, 1999; Davidson and Burke, 2004). This would suggest that in situations where women constitute a minority of managers, they are likely to adopt the transactional style associated with male managers. In situations, however, where women are not in this minority position, one might expect that they would not be under pressure to replicate the style of the male majority.

The position of women in Latvia is a distinct one insofar as women represent a critical mass of managers and a study of their style of management affords a rare opportunity to examine how women manage when they are not in a minority and under pressure to replicate the dominant style of management. The respondents indicate that the management style of female managers in Latvia corresponds to the elements attributed to women in the leadership literature (see Table 6.2 for a list of these features).

The research literature describes transformational leadership as producing superior long-term results for organisations across a wider range of sectors and continents than the non-contingent reward aspects of transactional leadership (Ferrario and Davidson, 1991; Bass and Avolio, 1994; Lowe and Kroeck, 1996; Bass, 1997b, 1998; Sarros *et al.*, 2002; Alban-Metcalfe and Alimo-Metcalfe, 2003a; Eagly *et al.*, 2003; Eagly, 2004) with outcome variables including enhanced organisational productivity, greater job satisfaction and commitment, and lower levels of stress (Ferrario and Davidson, 1991; Bass and Avolio, 1994; Lowe and Kroeck, 1996; Bass, 1997b, 1998; Alimo-Metcalfe and Alban-Metcalfe,

Table 6.2 Comparison of the attributes of men's and women's leadership styles noted in the literature, with the corresponding features of Latvian men's and women's management noted by the respondents

Leadership styles associated with *men* in the literature on leadership	Corresponding elements highlighted by respondents	Leadership styles associated with *women* in the literature on leadership	Corresponding elements highlighted by respondents
Management by exception	*Male managers said not to concentrate much on attention to staff since they lack 'emotional leadership skills'*	Charisma	*Several people spoke in awed terms of the charismatic qualities of very senior women in Latvia*
Monitoring followers' performance and correcting mistakes	*Example of the male manager who rebuked an employee who had not cleaned the floor*	Inspirational motivation	*Respondents said that 'women find it easier to raise up positive emotions'; another spoke of the fact that women's emotional involvement in the work makes people work harder*
Hard skills of information command and control	*One particular man is said to use a control system; management by men is said to be for 'domination' and involves a straightforward, aggressive approach to settling things*	Intellectual stimulation	*Women are said to motivate others by involving them in projects*
		Individual consideration	*Women are said to spend time paying attention to employees, contacting and communicating with them, and showing empathy and caring*

Table 6.2 (Continued)

Leadership styles associated with *men* in the literature on leadership	Corresponding elements highlighted by respondents	Leadership styles associated with *women* in the literature on leadership	Corresponding elements highlighted by respondents
Contingent reward	*The man's 'thank you' is formal and staff are motivated by being promised bonuses or penalties*	Contingent reward	*One respondent commented that 'women say "well done" from the heart'*
		Leading by example	*No relevant comments noted.*
		Empowerment	*Women are said to operate a more participative, coaching style and that women involve people more in decision-making than do men*
		Using interactive skills	*One respondent noted that 'women are more relational than men'; another noted that 'women prefer face-to-face communication than men'*

2003b). Other studies have produced the 'augmentation hypothesis' according to which the contingent reward aspect of transactional leadership is complementary to transformational leadership, with the former assisting followers to meet expectations (Bass, 1995, 1999) and the latter assisting followers to move beyond expectations (Bass, 1998; Judge and Piccolo, 2004). Interestingly, respondents attributed similar benefits to the management style adopted by women in Latvia and Table 6.3 contains a comparison of the benefits listed in the literature on leadership with the benefits women managers are said to bring to organisations in Latvia.

Many of the benefits ascribed to transformational leadership are attributed also to women managers in Latvia. This suggests that Latvian

Table 6.3 Comparison of the benefits the literature ascribes to transformational leadership and the benefits respondents attribute to women managers

Benefits of transformational leadership together with the contingent reward element of transactional leadership	Benefits of the management style ascribed by respondents to women managers in Latvia
Better long-term results	*'Women have a more long-term focus.'*
Include enhanced organisational productivity	*'If people feel good in a company, they can do more.'*
Greater job satisfaction and commitment	Emotional engagement makes *'people work harder.... they (the employees) really wanted to do the job'.* *'Women view other things as being important such as a happy workforce.'*
Lower levels of stress	*'Problems are solved faster and without stress';* the case of a large Bank showed how a woman at the helm could produce *'a happy workforce'.*
Helps followers meet expectations	Raises up *'positive or negative emotions so that the person a women talks to better understands what they need to do'.* *'Women are more goal-oriented than men.'*
Helps followers exceed expectations	*'If people feel good in a job with colleagues in an atmosphere or culture they enjoy, they have more initiative to offer new ideas.'*

organisations can gain a competitive advantage by employing women. It also indicates the extent to which gender diversity can bring benefits to organisations. A key question in women's appointment as managers remains the obstacles they may face in achieving these positions. Perhaps, it is relevant that the two respondents who took the view that women did not face obstacles in the workplace were both men and it is conceivable that their gender shields them from some of the problems facing women in the workplace.

In-depth interviews with male and female managers in Latvia have highlighted the extent to which men and women may adopt different styles of management there. This finding is in line with earlier findings on leadership style and suggests, given women's adoption of a predominantly transformational style, that organisations may gain competitive advantage by employing women in management. It is appreciated that the respondents interviewed did not constitute a representative sample of managers but they originated from a wide variety of organisations and the cohesiveness of their views adds credibility to their accounts. To what extent this evidence provides a 'universal footprint for the future' is yet to be demonstrated.

Acknowledgement

The authors would like to acknowledge the support of Baiba Jasuna at the Talentor Recruitment Agency in Riga. She organised a large proportion of the interviews that are described in this chapter and without her help, the authors would not have had the quality of respondents that she brought to the project.

References

Alas, R. and Rees, C.J. (2005), Estonia in transition: Exploring the impact of change on women managers, *Women in Management Review*, Vol. 20, No. 6, pp. 446–60.

Alban-Metcalfe, J. and Alimo-Metcalfe, B. (2003a), Leadership culture and change inventory – an organisational 360 feedback instrument, *Selection & Development Review*, Vol. 19, pp. 7–10.

Alban-Metcalfe, J. and Alimo-Metcalfe, B. (2003b), Leadership: A masculine past, but a feminine future?, paper presented at the BPS Occupational Psychology Conference, Bournemouth, 8–10 January.

Bass, B. (1997a), Personal selling and transactional/transformational leadership, *Journal of Personal Selling and Sales Management*, Vol. 17, No. 3, pp. 19–28.

Bass, B. (1997b), Does the transactional-transformational leadership paradigm transcend organizational and national boundaries, *American Psychologist*, Vol. 52, No. 2, pp. 130–9.

Bass, B. (1998), Current developments in transformational leadership: Research and applications, invited address to the American Psychological Association, San Francisco, CA, August.

Bass, B.M. (1995), Theory of transformational redux, *Leadership Quarterly*, Vol. 6, pp. 463–78.

Bass, B.M. (1999), Two decades of research and development in transformational leadership, *European Journal of Work and Organizational Psychology*, Vol. 8, pp. 9–32.

Bass, B. and Avolio, B. (1994), *Improving Organizational Performance through Transformational Leadership*, Sage, London.

Coolican, H. (1999), *Research Methods and Statistics in Psychology*, 3rd ed., Hodder & Stoughton, London.

Crimp, M. and Wright, L. (1995), *The Market Research Process*, Prentice Hall, London.

Davidson, M. and Burke, R.J. (2004), Women in management worldwide: Facts, figures and analysis, an overview, in Davidson, M.J. and Burke, R.J. (eds),

Women in Management Worldwide: Facts, Figures and Analysis, Ashgate Publishing Ltd, London, pp. 1–15.

Eagly, A. (2004), Few women at the top: How role incongruity produces prejudice and the glass ceiling, in van Knippenberg, D. and Hogg, M.A. (eds), *Identity, Leadership, and Power*, Sage Publications, London.

Eagly, A. and Johnson, M. (1990), The leadership styles of women and men, *Journal of Social Issues*, Vol. 57, No. 4, pp. 781–97.

Eagly, A., Johannesen-Schmidt, M. and van Engen, M. (2003), Transformational, transactional, and laissez-faire leadership styles: A meta-analysis comparing women and men, *Psychological Bulletin*, Vol. 129, No. 4, pp. 569–92.

Eurostat (2006), http://209.85.229.132/search?q=cache:c_IcI8ueFgwJ:epp.eurostat.ec.europa.eu/pls/portal/docs/PAGE/PGP_PRD_CAT_PREREL/PGE_CAT_PREREL_YEAR_2008/PGE_CAT_PREREL_YEAR_2008_MONTH_03/1-06032008-EN-AP.PDF+eurostat+-+female+managers+%2B+2006+%2B+latvia&cd=1&hl=en&ct=clnk&gl=uk, Accessed on 11 April 2009.

Ferrario, M. and Davidson, M. (1991), Gender and management style: A comparative study, paper presented at the British Academy of Management Conference, University of Bath, Bath, September.

Gardiner, M. and Tiggerman, M. (1999), Gender differences in leadership styles, job stress, and mental health in male- and female-dominated industries. *Journal of Occupational and Organizational Psychology*, Vol. 72, pp. 301–15.

Glaser, B. and Strauss, A. (1967), *The Discovery of Grounded Theory: Strategies for Qualitative Research*, Aldine, Chicago.

Gummerson, E. (1991), *Qualitative Methods in Management Research*, Sage, London.

Holst, E. (2005), Women managers: Enormous deficit in large companies and employer's associations, Weekly Report, *Econ papers*, Vol. 1, No. 4, pp. 57–67, http://econpapers.repec.org/article/diwdiwwrp/wr1-4.htm, Accessed on 11 April 2009.

Judge, T. and Piccolo, R. (2004), Transformational and transactional leadership: A meta-analytic test of their relative reliability, *Journal of Applied Psychology*, Vol. 89, No. 5, pp. 755–68.

Kanter, R. (1977), *Men and Women of the Corporation*, Basic Books, New York, NY.

Karnite, R. (2007), Gender and career development – Latvia, http:www.eurofound.europa.eu/eiro/studies/tn0612019s/lv0612019q.htm, 18 May.

LIAA (2008), mhtml:file://F:\Latvia\LatviaGrowth.mht, Accessed on 11 April 2009.

Lincoln, Y. and Guba, E. (1986), *Naturalistic Inquiry*, Sage, Beverly Hills, California.

Lowe, K. and Kroeck, K. (1996), Effectiveness correlates of transformational and transactional leadership: A meta analytic review of the MLQ literature, *Leadership Quarterly*, Vol. 7, No. 3, pp. 385–426.

Mariampolski, H. (2001), *Qualitative Market Research: A Comprehensive Guide*, Sage Publications, London.

Moss, G. and Daunton, L. (2006), The discriminatory impact of non-adherence to leadership selection criteria: The case of higher education, *Career Development International*, Vol. 11, No. 6, pp. 504–21.

Ramina, B., Hodireva, V., Martuzans, B., Cvetkova, I. and Silina, S. (2001), Vocational education and training and the labour market in Latvia, Latvian national observatory, http://www.aic.lv/Obs_2002/pi_dt_en/empl_lv.htm, Accessed on 11 April 2009.

Rivza, B. (2003), The impact of the fundamental goals for higher education on the roles of women in Latvia, Higher Education Research Network, 5th seminar and steering group meeting, 13–15 March.

Sarros, J., Gray, J. and Densten, I. (2002), Leadership and its impact on organisational culture, *International Journal of Business Studies*, Vol. 10, No. 2, pp. 1–26, http://www.li.lv/index.php?option=com_content&task=view&id=119&Itemid=474

Vanags, A. (2004), Gender mainstreaming in the public employment service, http://209.85.229.132/search?q=cache:cgBRLaCE9K8J:biceps.org/files/LV_Vanags.pdf+Vanags,+A+(2004),+Gender+mainstreaming+in+the+public+employment+service,&cd=1&hl=en&ct=clnk&gl=uk, Accessed on 23 April 2009.

7
Variety is the Spice of Life: How Design Diversity Can Enhance Profitability

Gloria Moss

The congruity principle

Some farsighted individuals have pointed to the importance of delivering products that match consumer preferences. A case in point is the business guru, Michael Hammer, who spoke of the need for products to be shaped around the 'unique and particular needs' of the customer (Hammer 1995, 21) and for products and services to be 'configured to' the needs of customers (ibid., 21). In the field of branding, similarly, an academic, Karande, has similarly made a case for congruence between the brand personality and the consumer's self-concept on the basis that purchases offer a vehicle for self-expression (Karande *et al.* 1997).

The focus on shaping products around customer preferences has led to a search for the factors that influence congruence. This is a prize worth fighting for. Much retailing research is driven by the notion that the physical form of a product is an important element in its design and it has, indeed, been found that the perception of beauty correlates highly with the rating of a product as 'interesting', of 'good design' and 'imaginative' (Lindgaard *et al.* 2006). Moreover, where correlations with perceptions of usability are concerned, a preliminary study found that 53 per cent of participants (with a sample base of 100) 'showed a significant positive relation between beauty and their assessment of usability' (Hassenzahl 2007, 293). This led to speculation that beauty and usability may correlate as a consequence of a 'halo' effect, leading to a tendency to infer a higher quality of the product from its beauty (ibid., 294).

What is this perceived higher quality worth? In one study (Bloch *et al.* 2003), participants saw and rated pictures of two different toasters which, while equal in terms of function, differed in terms of beauty. Participants were asked to state their willingness to pay for both toasters, and their answers demonstrated a willingness to pay a premium of around 55 per cent for the toaster perceived to be beautiful. In further studies, the premium individuals have been prepared to pay was found to be influenced by individual and situational aspects. Where individual aspects are concerned, it has been found that the so-called *centrality of visual product aesthetics* (CVPA) is an important moderator of beauty's value and affects the premium that individuals are prepared to pay for beauty. In the toaster study, high CVPA individuals were willing to pay a premium of 66 per cent for the beautiful toaster while low CVPA individuals were prepared to pay a premium of only 40 per cent (Hassenzahl 2007).

Where situational aspects are concerned, it was found that the value of beauty was dependent on the context in which the product was used. Where the product has high task-related context, beauty played only a minor role; by contrast, where the context emphasised self-presentation or personal identity, beauty assumed greater. Moreover, it was found that the perception of beauty, in the right context and presumably with the appropriate CVPA, was mediated by greater attention. This latter finding emerged from an interesting study conducted by researchers at a market research organisation, Bunnyfoot. Using eye-tracking to monitor responses, they noted the fixations of respondents to bus shelter advertisements and recorded the relationship between fixations and whether the stimulus was liked or not. According to the study:

> The most significant finding, from a marketing perspective was the discovery of a robust correlation between the number/duration of fixations a person makes while looking at an advertisement and whether or not they liked the advertisement.
>
> (Maughan *et al.* 2007, 341)

In this way, of the participants who were neutral about an advertisement or disliked it, only 20–24 per cent fixated 15–20 times, whereas 60–67 per cent of those who liked the advertisement fixated 15–20 times. As we can see, not only do products that are liked receive greater attention, but those that are perceived as pleasurable are used more frequently than those not so perceived, leading to enhanced purchasing. As we shall see later, what people like is often a mirror image of what they actually produce themselves. This brings us back to the notion of congruity, one which finds parallels in other fields. In the field of communications, for example, it translates into the notion that persuasiveness can be enhanced by similarity between source and receiver (Brock 1965). In social psychology, it translates into the 'matching hypothesis' or 'similarity-attraction' paradigm according to which increased similarity leads to increased attention and attraction (Byrne and Nelson 1965; Berscied and Walster 1978). In other words, the person you like is the person who mirrors your own thoughts and views, and may possibly even mirror your looks and behaviour.

Findings continue to emerge about the importance of congruence (or 'rapport' or 'mirroring' as it is sometimes called). At California State University, Sacramento, a study of psychotherapists' successes with their clients showed that therapists who got the best results had the most emotional congruence with their patients at meaningful junctures in the therapy. These mirroring behaviours showed up as the therapists comfortably settled into the climate of the clients' worlds by establishing good rapport (Brizendine 2006). Likewise, the need to shape products or services around the 'unique and particular needs' of the customer (Hammer 1995) places a premium on what one might call an interactionist as against a universalistic approach. This means that instead of seeking solutions or laws that will apply to *all* situations, we should seek out solutions that work in *particular* instances (Porteous 1996). This perspective inspires the search for segmented values and links, in turn, with the 'empathy principle' according to which aesthetic value does not inhere in objects but is the product of empathy between object, perceiver and artist (Diploye and Macan 1988).

The importance of achieving congruence between the product and customer preferences cannot be underestimated. A failure to achieve this match will be that design and marketing activities are sub-optimised. By way of example, Vibrandt, a UK-based design consultancy, conducted research on the Kotex brand, discovering that women across Europe perceived brands in the sector to be 'designed and marketed by men' (Lorenz 2005). In a case such as this in which a product with a clearly female market is branded in largely male terms, the model would alert one to the possibility that the brand would be suboptimal in impact. By contrast, the assumed benefits of getting it right (Brock 1965; Crozier and Greenhalgh 1992; Hammer 1995; Karande *et al.* 1997; De Chernatoney *et al.* 2004) include enhanced customer pleasure and purchasing (Groppel 1993; Donovan *et al.* 1994; Yahomoto and Lambert 1994). These benefits are too important for organisations to ignore.

The interactionist perspective

The interactionist perspective, unlike the universalistic one, seeks to segment preferences according to individual variables. In this way, one could seek to discover how *preferences* correlate with variables such as gender, personality and nationality. An interactionist perspective could also seek to discern the link between these variables and the artefacts that people produce. It would then be possible to discern the relationship between independent variables such as gender, personality and nationality, and dependent variables such as *preferences* and *productions*.

How broadly can the net be cast in an effort to understand these links? An immediate issue is the extent to which the field of design is a discipline on its own rather than allied to cognate disciplines such as Fine Art. This is an important issue since the answer will contain pointers as to which literatures can be drawn on in discussing the link between creator and created work and between preferences and individual variables. If, for example, there is strong evidence pointing to the unity of graphic expression across varied fields, from Design to Fine Art to doodles, then the literatures from *all* these fields can be used to inform our discussions. The next section looks at the evidence for the unity of graphic expression across a variety of fields.

In the section that follows this one, we will show how personality and gender are reflected in the graphic work that people produce and, then, how these variables influence preferences.

The inter-connectedness of art and design

A theoretical debate on the inter-connectedness of art and design has been pursued since Antiquity, but taken up again by Read (1953) in his book *Art and Industry*. Read argues that any distinction is largely the creation of the machine age and that in the pre-Renaissance period, the so-called fine arts (architecture, sculpture, painting, music and poetry) were not explicitly named nor distinctly recognised as separate classes of disciplines with some more applied than others. He cites also the fact that in classical Greece, there was a single word, *techne*, that was used to cover the utilitarian as well as the non-utilitarian genres. He concludes that the utilitarian arts (i.e. objects designed primarily for use) appeal to the aesthetic sensibilities as abstract art and that there is an intuitive as well as rational element in their design that means that they satisfy the canons of beauty.

The debate has been taken up by more recent commentators. One pair (Buchanan and Margolin 1995) refer to Read's work as being a standard text in the US and Britain, and also as being an exceptionally influential introductory work on design for general readers. Buchanan is Professor of design and head of the department of design at Carnegie Mellon University. He considers that there is no contradiction between the notion of design as a cognitive skill and one involving expression and emotion, quoting approvingly George Nelson's vision of design as communication and of the designer as artist.

This train of thought leads him to make a persuasive case for design as an expressive skill, arguing that Leonardo da Vinci's speculations on mechanical devices were simply another expression of his poetic and visual imagination. In the same way, he argues that Walter Gropius's goal was to provide a concrete connection between artistic exploration and practical action. This leads him to write eloquently about the role of expression in the designer's work:

> Most designers recognise that the appearance and expressive quality of products is critically important not only in marketing but in the substantive contribution of design to daily living...Expression does not clothe design thinking; it *is* design thinking in its most immediate manifestation, providing the integrative aesthetic experience which incorporates the array of technical decisions contained in any product.
>
> (p. 46)

Read and Buchanan's sentiments show that there is nothing in the finished work of 'design' that intrinsically sets it apart from the work of 'fine art'. Modern thinking supports this insofar as it has defined a new discipline of *visual culture* which blurs the boundaries between different visual disciplines. Rogoff (Mirzoeff 1998) makes a strong case for this, arguing that images do not stay within discrete disciplinary fields such as 'documentary film' or 'Renaissance painting' since neither the eye nor the psyche operates along or recognises such divisions.

We can see that the differences between fine art and design, insofar as they concern degrees of functionality and freedom of expression, are issues of degree rather than issues of fundamental difference. This means that although limits may be placed on the designer by the demands of the brief, he or she will always be left with the possibility of self-expression.

Some might further object that design work, unlike paintings and drawings, is often produced as part of a team effort, rather than an individual one. This is, indeed, often the case. However, the feature which distinguishes fine art from design is, in this case, a practical one – concerning the way the work task is organised – and does not say anything about fundamental differences between the two disciplines. In fact, there have been periods in the history of fine art when *objets d'art* were produced by a team, and this continues to be the case in some instances.

The relatedness of art and design, argued at a theoretical level, is supported by empirical research examining the connections between graphic expression and its creators. In the limited space of this chapter, we will touch on some of the landmark pieces of work, many stretching back a goodly number of years.

Amongst the earliest examples of empirical research is work by Preyer (1895) who postulated that should the writer lose his writing arm, as Nelson did for example, and have to use the opposite hand, or even the mouth or foot as in the case of paralysis, the same basic tendencies would appear in the script, although obviously not executed with the same fluency. The confluence of styles led Preyer to postulate the concept of *brainwriting*, a concept that was later corroborated in empirical work by Pophal (1985).

The consistency of different forms of graphic expression postulated by Preyer was also found by Allport, better known for his influential personality theory (Fancher 1996). With fellow researcher, Vernon, he examined the extent to which features of different motor acts intercorrelated. A total of 25 male subjects (of whom no details are provided) took part in experiments in which subjects were asked to draw a number of different shapes using either (alternatively) right or left hands and feet. Measurement of the figures was then made, and a comparison made of the average area of figures, the total areas occupied by the figures, and the proportion of unoccupied space. The results showed high correlations (greatly in excess of what you could expect from chance alone) between the varied creations of each individual whether in respect of the average area occupied by figures or the proportion of the space left unoccupied.

The intercorrelations between the different forms were in excess of 0.5, the minimum level for this number of subjects at which the results are significant at the 0.01 level, and the results therefore successfully demonstrate the presence of similarities between the different forms of graphic expression of a single person.

Having established the consistency of graphic expression, whether paintings, drawings or designs, the next question concerns the impact of individual variables such as gender and personality on what people produce as well as like. As will be seen, these variables can have a significant impact on *productions* as well as *preferences* and understanding the nature of this diversity assists greatly in understanding how best organisations can achieve the congruity between product and customer preferences recommended in the marketing literature.

The impact of individual variables on productions and preferences

Productions

As anyone will know who has glanced at a magazine stand, the obsession with celebrities is widespread. If you are a well-known actor, designer, writer or architect, the media will be on your back, hacking into bits of your life, and assembling a makeshift collage on how this relates back to your work. Celebrity culture is now such a well-established concept that there is a bibliography on the phenomenon (http://blake.intrasun.tcnj.edu/celebrityculture/Celebrity%20Bibliography.htm).

Much of the celebrity culture is flippant, but one serious issue it raises concerns the extent to which artists and designers leave footprints of themselves in the work they create. Does a piece of design or art leave a more permanent footprint of the person who has created it than the part played by an actor? Does it tell us something about their character and their gender?

If we put the issue of gender to one side for a moment, there is a body of research exploring the ties binding art and design works to their creators. This work is nicely summed up by Alfred Tunnelle who is quoted as declaring the artist to be someone who sees things not as they are but as he is (Hammer 1980). Tunnelle's thoughts appear in a book on projective drawings and this is no accident since there is a body of research (much of it now quite old but no less valid for that) that views the process of drawing or designing as a process of projection. According to this way of thinking, the drawing or design serves as an X-ray image of its creator and this is one reason for the inter-connectiveness of different forms of graphic expression.

Related to this is the fact that all forms of expression, whether sketches or models, are directed by motor movements in the brain. According to psychologists, Allport and Vernon (1967), the brain directs the hand of the writer and the artist and the handwriting or paintings that they produce will reflect aspects of the creator. As they write 'motor acts... must reflect to a large degree the organisation of the total brain field' (Allport and Vernon 1967). This is similar to Preyer's earlier use of the term 'brainwriting' (1895).

Much research in the field of Art Therapy (Hammer 1980) inevitably demonstrates this connection between the creator and graphic expression and Table 7.1 presents a snapshot of the way previous commentators have linked graphic expression to particular aspects of personality. Where reference to gender occurred in the research, Table 7.1 also shows the extent to which these researchers associate particular graphic traits with either men or women.

As we can see from this table, researches over several decades have linked features of graphic expression to particular personality types as well as to gender. Where the latter is concerned, some argue against

Table 7.1 Summary of the views of researchers as to ways in which personality is manifested in graphic expression, and the gender with which a particular form of graphic expression is associated

Personality trait	Manifestation in graphic expression	Author giving this interpretation	Where mentioned by the author, the gender of person with this form of graphic expression
Aggressiveness	Straight line	Waehner (1946)	–
Aggressiveness, outgoing behaviour and assertiveness	Straight line	Alschuler and Hattwick (1969)	Males
Assertiveness	Straight line	Hammer (1980)	–
N-Ach, non-conforming, energetic	Straight line	Aronson (1958)	–
Aggressiveness and preoccupation with conflict and power	Violent themes	McNiff (1982)	Males
Creativity, restraint, self-centredness	Rounded forms	Waehner (1946)	Females

Dependence, compliance, affection, fanciful imagination	Rounded forms	Alschuler and Hattwick (1969)	–
Femininity	Rounded forms	Hammer (1980)	–
Non-aggressiveness, concern with people and animals connected with environment	Life themes	McNiff (1982)	Females

a specific 'feminine sensibility' (Harris and Nochlin 1976) while others agree with Erik Erikson in speaking of a 'profound difference in the sense of space in the two sexes' (1973). One factor which can make discussions of such gender differences problematic is the fact that not all commentators agree on the importance or meaning of gender as a variable (Caterall and Maclaran 2002).

In terms of interpretations of gender, these can range from the postmodern view that gender is an unproductive dichotomy (Firat 1994), to the evolutionary psychological perspective that plays down the influence of sociocultural factors (Jackson 2001), emphasising instead the operation of innate factors (Lupotow et al. 1995). This latter approach is gaining in popularity in several disciplines and, according to recent commentators, should not be overlooked by those researching consumer behaviour, even if this approach restricts the possibilities of social and cultural change (Caterall and Maclaran 2002). The position adopted in this chapter allows of the possibility that gender is a productive dichotomy, all the while allowing for the eventuality that differences are the product of sociocultural or innate differences.

In seeking to identify the extent to which there may be separate male and female design styles, one is standing outside the patriarchal system in which 'Art by women is judged according to norms and expert constraints that are not their own' (Heide 1991). The approach adopted here is philosophically coherent with a Diversity approach which acknowledges the co-existence of a wide range of realities and in which differences are viewed as strengths, not a weakness (White 1995). It has to be acknowledged that, aside from the authors' work (Moss 1995, 1999; Moss et al. 2006), and work comparing the

Table 7.2 The sex with which various graphic features are associated

Graphic characteristic	Sex with which graphic trait is associated	Researchers giving this interpretation
Straight line	Male	Alschuler and Hattwick (1969), Franck and Rosen (1949), Majewski (1978), McNiff (1982), Moss (1995, 1996, 2001)
Rounded line	Female	Waehner (1946), Hammer (1980), Alschuler and Hatwick (1969), Franck and Rosen (1949), Majewski (1978), Moss (1995, 1996, 2001), Stilma and Vos (2009)

three-dimensional products produced by men and women (Stilma and Vos, 2009), work comparing the graphic expression of males and females is scattered and not brought together as a coherent body of work, and there is also more recent work. Much of this scattered work compared the drawings and paintings of males and females, whether in terms of the shapes and colours or themes employed, and I have summarised it elsewhere (Moss 1996, 2009). One example is offered below to give the reader a flavour of this work.

A PhD study by Majewski (1978) compared the male and female drawings from a sample of 121 drawings. These were rated on 31 characteristics and statistically significant differences emerged on nine of these. These included a greater tendency on the part of the females to employ circular as against rectilinear shapes, to depict the environment, happy faces as well as females. These are not isolated findings. Where depiction of ones own gender is concerned, an earlier study by Levy (reported later by Hammer in 1980) found that in a sample of 5,500 adults, 89 percent drew their own sex first. Levy's sample included college students, high school students and psychiatric patients, and if the latter group is excluded, a total of 72 percent drew their own sex first. Many other studies have highlighted the tendency for people to depict others of the same gender (Stilma and Vos 2009; Moss 2009).

Where form is concerned, many researchers have observed the extent to which males have a tendency to use straight lines, and females rounded lines (Moss 2009) as shown in Table 7.2.

In terms of other differences emerging from the literature, whether from studies of drawings, paintings or design, these are summarised in Table 7.3:

Table 7.3 Differences in male and female graphic expression over a number of studies (Moss 2009)

	Male productions	Female productions
Visual elements	Straight lines and shapes	Rounded lines and shapes
	Use of few and darker colours	Use of many and brighter colours
	Regular typography	Irregular typography
	3-D images	2-D images
	Lack of detail	Detail
	Images of men	Images of women
	Moving objects	Stationery objects

Preferences

In terms of preferences, research I have conducted reveals a consistent tendency for people's preferences to be for visual artefacts that contain features typical of their personality or gender. The conclusion relating to personality was obtained by examining the results of studies presenting the painterly preferences of people with a given personality. If the type of paintings produced by people of a particular personality was compared with the type of paintings liked by people by that personality, it appears that people like paintings produced by people of a similar personality type to their own (Moss 2009). By way of example, a study by Knapp and Wolff (1963) found that *preferences* for abstract art were associated with intuitive types while preferences for representational art were associated with sensing types. Since two researchers (Read 1958; Burt 1968) had associated the *production* of abstract art with the intuitive maker and the production of representational art with the sensing maker, the *preferences* of people of a particular personality type match the *productions* of people of a similar personality type.

When it comes to the effects of gender, we find something similar. Preference tests using graphic, product and web designs show that the tendency for men and women to prefer designs produced by people of the same gender as themselves and therefore displaying a production aesthetic typical of their gender are statistically highly significant (Moss 1995, 1996; Moss and Colman 2001; Moss and Gunn, 2009). Detailed results for web design show that each sex has a highly significant tendency to prefer designs produced by people of their own gender and displaying a same-sex production aesthetic. However, as the following

Table 7.4 The strength of male and female preferences for websites and elements of websites produced by people of the same gender as themselves (Moss and Gunn 2009)

	Male preferences for male-produced designs	Female preferences for female-produced designs
Overall preference for own-sex website	0.01	0.01
Language	0.01	0.01
Pictures	Prefer the female Production aesthetic	0.01
Shapes	No significant preference as between the male and the female-produced shapes	0.01
Layout	0.01	0.01

results show (see Table 7.4) the tendency for women to prefer a same-sex production aesthetic is more pronounced than in the case of men.

In terms of explanatory factors, those most commonly advanced relate to socio-cultural and biological variables (Lupotow *et al.* 1995; Moss 2009). Either or both could inform the designs produced by men and women, ensuring that men and women leave their footprints in the designs they produce. The same could apply to preferences with the factors producing strong evidence of own-sex preference rooted in sociological and biological factors.

Implications

We have seen that there are a number of statistically significant differences in the extent to which male and female-produced graphic design displays certain features. These differences relate to subject matter as well as to features such as shape, colour, detailing and in some cases extend to three-dimensionality. We have also seen that in the main, preferences mirror productions with males preferring visual work produced by men and displaying the male production aesthetic and women preferring visual work produced by women and displaying the female production aesthetic (Moss 1995, 1996, 2001). This tendency to own-sex preference holds true across numerous experiments with one recent study of webdesign preferences showing men preferring the male-produced websites on most measures but preferring the female aesthetic where pictures were concerned and showing equanimity as between the male and female production aesthetic where shapes are concerned (Moss and Gunn, 2009).

The implications for achieving the congruity principle? The congruity principle held that people should be offered products that appeal to people's self-concept and shaped around the 'unique and particular needs' of the customer (Hammer 1995, 21). We have seen that the 'unique and particular needs' or *preferences* of the customer can be shaped by their personality and by their gender and this suggests that one way of satisfying the congruity principle is to provide customers with products matched to the production aesthetic of that group. In other words, if the customers consist of male extroverts (as might be the case with football fans), the designs most likely to appeal to them would be those typically produced by extrovert men. Conversely, if the customers consist of female introverts (as might be the case with embroidery hobbyists), then these could best be appealed to with the type of design produced by introverted women. A model showing the importance of this mirroring principle is shown in Figure 7.1 (see below).

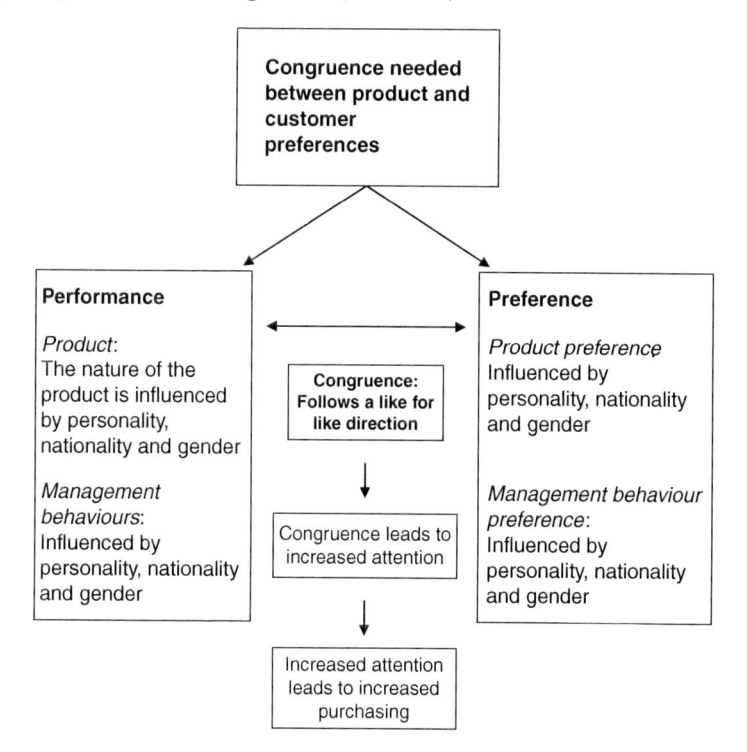

```
                    ┌─────────────────────┐
                    │ Congruence needed   │
                    │ between product and │
                    │ customer            │
                    │ preferences         │
                    └─────────────────────┘
                          ↙        ↘
┌───────────────────────┐           ┌───────────────────────┐
│ Performance           │           │ Preference            │
│                       │           │                       │
│ Product:              │ ┌───────┐ │ Product preference    │
│ The nature of the     │ │Congru-│ │ Influenced by         │
│ product is influenced │←│ence:  │→│ personality, national-│
│ by personality,       │ │Follows│ │ ity and gender        │
│ nationality and gender│ │a like │ │                       │
│                       │ │for    │ │                       │
│                       │ │like   │ │                       │
│                       │ │direc- │ │                       │
│                       │ │tion   │ │                       │
│                       │ └───────┘ │                       │
│ Management            │     ↓     │ Management behaviour  │
│ behaviours:           │ ┌───────┐ │ preference:           │
│ Influenced by         │ │Congru-│ │ Influenced by         │
│ personality,          │ │ence   │ │ personality, national-│
│ nationality           │ │leads  │ │ ity and gender        │
│ and gender            │ │to     │ │                       │
│                       │ │increa-│ │                       │
│                       │ │sed    │ │                       │
│                       │ │atten- │ │                       │
│                       │ │tion   │ │                       │
│                       │ └───────┘ │                       │
└───────────────────────┘     ↓     └───────────────────────┘
                        ┌───────────┐
                        │ Increased │
                        │ attention │
                        │ leads to  │
                        │ increased │
                        │ purchasing│
                        └───────────┘
```

Figure 7.1 Model showing the links needed between performance and preference in order to create congruence (Moss, 2007)

Conclusion

A great deal of empirical work supports the notion that design is likely to have most appeal where it employs the production aesthetic associated with the groups it is appealing to. What these studies have done is highlight the diversity of design productions and preferences and in so doing increase our awareness of the extent to which design can be targeted at consumer demographics. Given the premium prices that people are prepared to pay for products with visual appeal (Bloch *et al.* 2003; Hassenzahl 2007), an enhanced understanding of the part that design diversity plays in the congruity principle will increase the profitability of design.

In a subsequent chapter, we will explore some of the practical steps which need to be taken in order to introduce design diversity into an organisation. Since many of these may encounter obstacles, these issues will be taken up in a subsequent chapter in this book.

References

Allport, G.W. and Vernon, P.E. (1967), *Studies in Expressive Movement*, New York: Macmillan.
Alschuler, R.H. and Hattwick, W. (1969), *Painting and Personality*, Chicago, University of Chicago Press.
Aronson, E. (1958), 'The need for achievement as measured by graphic expression', in Atkinson, J.W. (ed.), *Motives in Fantasy, Action and Society*, Princeton: Van Nostrand Press.
Berscied, E. and Walster, E. (1978), *Interpersonal Attraction*, Cambridge, MA: Addison-Wesley.
Bloch, P.H. *et al.* (2003), 'Individual differences in the centrality of visual product asesthetics: Concept and measurement', *Journal of Personality and Social Psychology* 71, 665–79.
Brizendine, L. (2006), *The Female Brain*, New York: Morgan Road Books.
Brock, T.C. (1965), 'Communicator-recipient similarity and decision change', *Journal of Personality and Social Psychology* 1, 650–4.
Buchanan, R. and Margolin, V. (eds.) (1995), *Discovering Design*, Chicago: University of Chicago Press.
Burt, R.B. (1968), *An Exploratory Study of Personality Manifestations in Paintings*. Doctoral dissertation, Duke University (Dissertation Abstracts International 29, 1493-B Order number 68–14, 298).
Byrne, D. and Nelson, D. (1965), 'Attraction as a linear function of positive reinforcement', *Journal of Personality and Social Psychology* 1, 659–63.
Caterall, M. and Maclaran, P. (2002), 'Gender perspectives in consumer behaviour: An overview of future directions', *The Marketing Review* 2, 405–25.
Crozier, W. and Greenhalgh, P. (1992), 'The empathy principle: Towards a model for the psychology of art', *Journal for the Theory of Social Behaviour* 22, 63–79.

De Chernatoney, L. et al. (2004), 'Identifying and sustaining services brands values', *Journal of Marketing Communications* 10, 73–94.
Diploye, R. and Macan, T. (1988), 'A process view of the selection/recruitment interview', in Schuler, R. et al. (eds.), *Readings in Personnel and Human Resource Management*, St Paul, MN: West.
Donovan, R.J. et al. (1994), 'Store atmosphere and purchasing behaviour', *Journal of Retailing* 70(3), 283–94.
Erikson, E.H. (1973), *Childhood and Society*, London: Pelican.
Fancher, R.E. (1996), *Pioneers of Psychology* (3rd Ed.). New York: Norton.
Firat, F.A. (1994), 'Gender and consumption: Transcending the feminine?', in Costa, J. (ed.), *Gender Issues and Consumer Behaviour*, Thousand Oaks, CA: Sage, 205–28.
Franck, K. and Rosen, E. (1949), 'A projective test of masculinity-femininity', *Journal of Consulting Psychology*, 247–56.
Groppel, A. (1993), 'Store design and experience orientated consumers in retailing: comparison between the United States and Germany', in Van Raaij, W.F. and Bassomy, G.J. (eds.), *European Advances in Consumer Research*, Amsterdam: Association for Consumer Research.
Hammer, E.F. (1980), *The Clinical Application of Projective Drawings*, Springfield: Charles C Thomas.
Hammer, M. (1995), *Reengineering the Corporation*, London: Nicholas Brearley Corporation.
Harris, A. and Nochlin, L. (1976), *Women Artists*, California: Los Angeles County Museum of Art.
Hassenzahl, M. (2007), 'Aesthetics in interactive products: Correlates and consequences of beauty', in Schifferstein, H.N.J. and Hekkert, P. (eds.), *Product Experience*, Amsterdam: Elsevier.
Heide, G. (1991), *The Dancing Goddess: Principles of a Matriarchal Aesthetic*, Boston: MA: Beacon Press.
Igbaria, M. and Parasuraman, S. (1997), 'Status report on women and men in the IT workplace', *Information Systems Management* 14(3), 44–54.
Jackson, S. (2001), 'Why a materialist feminism is (still) possible – and necessary', *Women's Studies International Forum* 24(3/4), 280–93.
Karande, K. et al. (1997), 'Brand personality and self concept: A replication and extension', *American Marketing Association, Summer Conference* 165–71.
Knapp, R.H. and Wolff, A. (1963), 'Preferences for abstract and representational art', *Journal of Social Psychology* 60, 255–62.
Lindgaard, G. et al. (2006), 'Attention web designers: You have 50 milliseconds to make a good impression', *Behaviour and Information Technology* 25, 115–26.
Lorenz, T. (2005), 'Soft sell', *Design Week* 20(29), (7 November), 18–19.
Lupotow, L., Garovich, L. and Lupetow, M. (1995), The persistence of gender stereotypes in the face of changing sex roles: Evidence contrary to the sociocultural model, *Ethology and Sociobiology* 16, 509–30.
Majewski, M. (1978), *The Relationship between the Drawing Characteristics of Children and Their Sex*, unpublished doctoral dissertation, Illinois State University.
Maughan, L. et al. (2007), 'Like more, look more: Look more, like more: The evidence from eye-tracking', *Journal of Brand Management* 14(4), 336–43.

McNiff, K. (1982), Sex differences in children's art, *Journal of Education* 164, 271–89.

Mirzoeff, N. (ed.) (1998), *The Visual Culture Reader*, London: Routledge.

Moss, G. (1995), Differences in the design aesthetic of men and women: Implications for product branding, *Journal of Brand Management* 3(3), 51–61.

Moss, G. (1996), Sex: The misunderstood variable, *Journal of Brand Management* 3(5), 296–305.

Moss, G. (1999), Gender and consumer behaviour: Further explorations, *Journal of Brand Management*, 7, 2, 88–100.

Moss, G. (2007), 'Psychology of performance and preference: Advantages, disadvantages, drivers and obstacles to the achievement of congruence', *Journal of Brand Management*, 14(4), 343–58.

Moss, G. (2009), *Gender, Design and Marketing*, Gower: Surrey.

Moss, G. and Colman, A. (2001), *Journal of Brand Management* 9(2), 89–99.

Moss, G. and Gunn, R. (2009), 'Gender differences in website production and preference aesthetics: Preliminary implications for ICT in education and beyond', *Behaviour and Information Technology*, DOI 1080/0144929080.

Moss, G., Gunn, R. and Heller, J. (2006), 'Some men like it black, some women like it pink: Consumer implications of differences in male and female website design', *Journal of Consumer behaviour* 5, 328–41.

Pophal, R. (1985), *Handwriting–brainwriting*, New York: Bernard.

Porteous, J.D. (1996), *Environmental Aesthetics: Ideas, Politics and Planning*, London: Routledge.

Preyer, W. (1895), *On the Physiology of Handwriting*, Hamburg.

Read, H. (1953), *Art and Industry*, London: Faber and Faber.

Stilma, M. and Vos, O. (2009), 'Gender based product design research: Is there an indicating difference in product design made by male and female design graduates', *Design Principles and Practices: An International Journal*, 3, www.design-journal.com

Waehner, T.S. (1946), 'Interpretations of spontaneous drawings and paintings', *Genetic Psychology Monograph* 33, 3–70.

White, J. (1995), 'Leading in their own ways: Women chief executives in local government', in Itzin, C. and Newman, J. (eds.), *Gender, Culture and Organizational Change*, London: Routledge.

Yahomoto, M. and Lambert, D.R. (1994), 'The impact of product aesthetics on the evaluation of industrial products', *Journal of Product Innovation Management* 11, 309–24.

Part III
Obstacles to Diversity Initiatives

8
Embedding Diversity: The Obstacles Faced by Equality and Diversity Specialists

Alison Preece

> Well, I think that people tolerate minorities... It's like a rainy day: it's boring but you must live with it.
>
> (Barbosa and Cabral-Cardosa, 2007)

The above quote, attributed to a European academic, neatly summarises the attitude faced by many equality specialists who have the responsibility of embedding diversity within an organisation. Over the last 30 years, employers in both private and public sectors have adopted a plethora of policies and initiatives to promote equality of opportunity and more recently, diversity, within both their operations and their workforce. In addition, many organisations have developed specific posts with the responsibility for co-ordinating the implementation of such policies. Increasing the diversity of the workforce, enabling disabled people, addressing gender imbalance, and promoting awareness and tolerance for people of different faiths, sexual orientation and ages are all generally accepted as 'a good thing' by both those with a social conscience and by others arguing the economic business case. So why do the statistics show a different story, and what are the realities and practicalities faced by equality specialists attempting to embed equality and diversity within an organisation?

Equality specialists and their role

Equality and diversity specialists come to the role through a variety of routes; many have a general human resources background, some have worked actively in one or more of the equality strands in a range of capacities, whilst others come to the post with personal experiences of being marginalised by society. As Lawrence (2000) states, whatever their background:

> As equal opportunities officers they are often engaged in attempting to introduce and manage significant organizational changes. The job of equal opportunities officers requires the mobilization of considerable professional (and political) skills in introducing organizational changes and responding to the demands of various constituencies, who may have different agendas for change, in terms of both timescale and ultimate objectives.

The level at which such posts sit within organisations varies considerably, with many located within the human resources department. Only the largest of organisations have stand alone teams devoted to equality issues and some employees have the responsibility for equality as only one part of their role. Few are set within the most senior levels of management. The very fact that the role of an equality specialist exists can in itself cause a problem for embedding diversity. Unconsciously, or consciously, people will assume that they do not have to think about equality or diversity issues as there is a specific role within their organisation to deal with this. The title that these posts hold varies a great deal and for the sake of clarity, the term 'equality specialist' will be used throughout this chapter to encompass all those working in the field of equality and diversity.

The arguments for promoting equality and diversity from both the social justice view, which rests on innate fairness, and from the business case, which emphasises the economic benefits, are well documented. Whichever angle an equality specialist chooses as a starting point, it is also worth considering the confusion that the development of the concepts of equality and diversity brings to the role. At its simplest, a common perception of equality is that we should value all people equally and treat everyone the same, whereas the concept of diversity asks us to consider that there are different ways of behaving, thinking, living and that we should make adjustments for these differences, admitting that we are not all the same and that therefore there can never be a 'level-playing field'. It is interesting to consider further the backgrounds of the two viewpoints. The equality movements grew out of the injustice of a situation where some sections of society were not considered equal to others. The strength of the campaigns for equal rights, by whichever group, has been the ability to draw support from large numbers of people who identified with a cause, many of whom felt that they had experiences in common due to shared attributes/values. One voice would not have been so powerful. However, in an era in which individuality is often highly valued, we are now frequently considering the needs of the individual and many of us do not identify with a large group movement. It may be worth asking whether, by concentrating on the needs of the individual, we weaken the case for making changes by losing the critical mass of support of people who identify closely as a group. Stereotype has become a word associated with the negative aspects of large group characteristics where, in reality, there may still be some value in considering the needs of the majority of people who belong to a certain group. We may not be willing to change society for one person but pressure from large numbers can make a more powerful argument which may achieve results.

Whilst recognising this, we also need to recognise the diversity of human nature; we rarely fit into any one group. Our identities have many layers and it is the intersectionality of these characteristics that is the reason for our individual specific needs.

The complexities of this argument can create problems for equality specialists but within an organisation, it can be argued that their role is to ensure that the diversity of people's needs is recognised and considered, in order to achieve a more equitable society thus satisfying all needs. As Liff and Wajcman argue, 'Sometimes minorities are disadvantaged not because they are treated differently but because they are treated equally... If their particular needs are to be taken into account, different procedures rather then the same procedures should apply' (1996, cited in Barbosa and Cabral-Cardosa, 2007).

The impact of human nature

If the argument for equality of opportunity and for the valuing of diversity is so strong, why do we need specialists to work within organisations to enforce it? One view is that equality specialists are dealing with difference and since humans are programmed to regard anything that is different as suspicious, specialists are needed to break this natural programming. For primitive humans, anything unknown signalled risk or danger, or alternatively was seen as inferior or a weakness. It could be argued that, over time, this reaction has been embedded within society and translated into prejudice against those who are different from the majority. Within an organisation this may be one of the reasons for the development of cultures that value uniformity and conformity to the norm (or dominant culture) in both behaviour and attitude. The view of diversity as an organisational asset worth valuing seems to contradict the traditional preference for strong organisational cultures that encourage uniformity in thinking patterns and behaviours (Cornelius *et al.*, 2000; Granrose, 1997, cited in Barbosa and Cabral-Cardosa, 2007).

In considering the case for speaking of resistance to difference as a programmed response, it is interesting to reflect on work on the physiological response of humans to diversity and an interesting case in point is the work of neuroscientist Antonio Damasio. He has examined the connections between emotions and the workings of the brain and in his book, *Looking for Spinoza*, he considers how some emotions and reactions may have been useful in tribal society but are no longer appropriate.

> reactions that lead to racial and cultural prejudices are based in part on the automatic deployment of social emotions evolutionarily meant to detect difference in others because difference may signal risk or danger, and promote withdrawal or aggression... We can be wise to the fact that our brain still carries the machinery to react in the way it did in a very different context ages ago. And we can learn to disregard such reactions and persuade others to do the same.
>
> (2003, p. 40)

But can we? How easy is it to disregard instinctive reactions? In order to confront behaviours, equality specialists first have to enable people to identify their own prejudices and stereotypes, and those prevalent in society – both negative and positive. Here again we come up against the intricacies of the human brain which, in order to make sense of the huge amount of information it receives, is very efficient at categorising objects with similar characteristics. Unfortunately, this sorting and categorising also works well with people so that anyone, for example, who dresses in a particular way or speaks with a certain accent, is instantly and often unconsciously classified according to previous experience or popular stereotype.

These physiological arguments combined with a possible conscious, or unconscious, desire to preserve the status quo present equality specialists with a difficult task. Many equality specialists who are involved in delivering awareness training are often met with the attitude that equality or diversity theories are nothing new, that we all treat everyone the same now, and 'I'm not prejudiced'. One role of an equality specialist is therefore to encourage people to see behind these statements and to consider that stereotypes and prejudice are alive in all of us, precisely because we are humans. In theory this should help each of us to confront our natural reactions in the way that Damsio hopes.

This message, however, must be delivered in such a way as to avoid accusations of telling people how to think. People will be less inclined to embrace the concepts of equality and diversity if they are presented with a list of rules of what they should not do, than if the arguments are presented for the positive aspects of a policy in which they have a chance to contribute and from which they can expect to derive benefit. For any organisation that is serious in the consideration of embedding diversity issues, such training becomes mandatory and ongoing for all members of staff. The commitment of the leaders and senior managers within an organisation is crucial in supporting this activity and if such leaders do not lend their support to awareness raising activities, the role of the equality specialist is that much harder.

The impact of legislation

In recognition of human nature, it can be argued that society has attempted to impose equality on itself through the introduction of legislation. For many equality specialists, dealing with the details of what this legislation has meant for employers has become the basis for their work. The need to pass laws illustrates the reluctance of organisations, and society in general, to willingly adopt equality policies and underlines the barrier of human nature and behaviour as discussed above. Equality legislation in the UK has expanded rapidly in recent years with duties brought in for disability, race and gender requiring employers, specifically those in the public sector, to work in a particular way and with further legislation introduced to encompass age, sexual orientation and religion and belief. Such a large body of legislation places demands on the equality specialist to interpret the law and to produce policies, action plans, impact assessments and audits as a response. It is this legislative-driven activity that has moved the equality agenda forward in many organisations. However some would say that it has added to the negative feelings of those employees who question the need for such policies, regarding them as unnecessary political correctness and a cause for increased workload, thus creating resistance and fuelling a lack of engagement. Other critics of the outcomes-based, legislative-driven approach have suggested that it encourages organisations to do the minimum possible to achieve required objectives without due regard for the processes by which outcomes may be achieved (Spracklen *et al.*, 2006, cited in Shaw, 2007).

One aspect of the implementation of equality policies has been the requirement to monitor the workforce in order to provide evidence that procedures/cultures are not inadvertently discriminating. Asking people within an organisation to complete questionnaires concerning their diversity status, even if they understand the reasons for the request, can often be seen as overly intrusive. Extending these questions into the more sensitive areas of religion and sexual orientation often leads to cries of invasion of privacy (Spittal, 2002, cited in Shaw, 2007), especially in recent times where the security of such personal data has been brought into question. The validity and accuracy of such data is also uncertain and these problems can lead to anger with the law for necessitating this line of questioning.

The problematic nature of the actions necessitated by the legislation leads one to ask whether it assists in changing the culture of an organisation. This requirement to monitor can become a barrier in itself as it frequently alienates people when they become aware that the reason for such monitoring links back to equality legislation. Does an analysis of the data or the implementation of procedures to increase the numbers of people of a certain group help bring about organisational culture change? Acker (1990) argues that increasing the numbers of people who represent diverse groups does nothing to ensure that equality is a central part of organisational processes if the organisation continues as it always has and does little to question its culture and structures (cited in Shaw, 2007). It is argued that all this achieves is an increasing number of marginalised groups within organisations that remain culturally and structurally unchanged. The results would be that minorities would be present in an organisation but they would have to adopt the behaviour and attitudes of the existing organisational culture (ibid.).

In an attempt to tackle more deeply ingrained organisational attitudes, legislation requires public sector employers to go further than just monitoring their workforces statistically. Under the Race Relations Amendment Act (2000) and the Equality Act (2006) which introduced both the Disability Equality Duty and the Gender Equality Duty amongst other legislation, all public authorities must ensure that they take action to assess the impact of all policies, procedures and practices on race, disability and gender equality and to report on the findings. Unfortunately in an attempt to comply with this legislative requirement, a whole new bureaucratic framework of forms and guidelines, entitled Equality Impact Assessment, has developed. Many equality specialists are now torn between attempting to respond to the legislation and the practicalities of implementing the process. The practice of asking mangers to review all polices, practices, provisions or functions to ensure that all are checked for any adverse impact on the different sections of society is a mammoth task for many public authorities operating in a procedure-led organisational culture. Used correctly, this process of assessing the impact of activities on all of society could be a useful way of identifying inbuilt inequality and promoting a deeper level of analysis of organisational operations.

Unfortunately, the legislative requirements are in danger of creating yet another process-driven procedure that is rarely understood and undertaken without any real commitment. The role of the equality specialist in attempting to embed this practice is particularly difficult, as it requires time and resources which are simply not available to many organisations. It remains to be seen if this process can be implemented in a way that achieves the aims of the encouraging equality and diversity issues to be considered at all levels, whilst avoiding the backlash against such policies accompanied by cries of political correctness gone mad.

The attempt to measure and assess the level of equality and acceptance of diversity within an organisation is a crude effort to deal with a subject as subtle as diversity. 'As many researchers within the non-profit sector have argued, conceptualising a social justice aim like equality, which is fluid and broadly defined, as achievable and thus measurable is deeply flawed and misleading' (Shaw and Allen, 2006, cited in Shaw, 2007). Interestingly research investigating the links between the perception of organisational performance and the perception of diversity (Allen, *et al.*, 2008) suggests that it is important for organisations to not only focus on achieving diversity in a statistically objective sense, but to aim to increase the perceptions of diversity within their workforce. They argue that it is the perceptions of diversity within an organisation which are important in 'influencing employee motivation and behaviour which in turn lead to higher levels of organizational performance'.

So, if legislation and monitoring are barriers to embedding equality and diversity why do these processes continue to be used to promote equality? The response is that if society is unable to readily embrace equality and diversity, but still has a desire to do so, then it has little option but to enforce diversity through legislation, however unsophisticated or crude this may feel. As the now decommissioned Commission for Racial Equality argued on the collection of data, 'To have an equality policy without ethnic monitoring is like aiming for good financial management without keeping financial records.' In addition to this, a legal framework can be 'seen as valuable in giving legitimacy to the area of equal opportunities' (Lawrence, 2000) and emphasising the legal responsibilities of an employer adds weight to the argument for equality and diversity.

Despite these defences, one can still justifiably question whether society is monitoring the right variables and whether the legislation is moving in the right direction. While having the backing of the law can be a useful tool in embedding diversity within an organisation, if this is to be the only approach used, then at best it may stop any real change in the culture of an organisation, and at worst it may damage the acceptance of equality or diversity theories. The reasons are simple. An organisation that thinks that to embrace diversity it has only to adhere to the legislation on equality and achieve a statistically representative workforce will not benefit from any of the advantages put forward in the business case. As a consequence, an organisation may well dispute the benefits of equality policies at all.

The impact of level-playing field theory

A common aim of early equality movements was that of working towards the creation of a level-playing field in which everyone is treated equally. In fact, to compete on merit in a society or organisation that is structured so as to favour a certain type of person – either male or non-disabled for example – will never create this level-playing field ideal. Despite this fact, equality specialists frequently encounter the 'we treat everyone the same now' attitude which can lead to resistance to attempts to diversity initiatives. For example, initiatives taken by equality specialists to encourage under-represented groups such as women-only training schemes, disabled staff groups and ethnic minority fast track schemes are frequently seen as favouritism – sometimes by members of the very groups that the schemes aim to help. As Burke (2005) argues, 'Members of disadvantaged groups see this process as raising questions about the qualifications or merit of the people hired or promoted.'

Other examples abound. In a recent article in *The Times* it was reported that 'The British cabinet fields just 6 women to 16 men and though public opinion might favour action to address the imbalance, the evidence suggests that it is women themselves who might oppose it.' Furthermore, Jacey Graham is quoted from her recent book on women in boardrooms in Britain as stating that, 'There is an appetite to facilitate talented women coming through, but they must be seen to compete on the same terms as their male colleagues' (*The Sunday Times*, 8 June 2008). The recent announcement of proposals in the new Equality Bill to allow an element of positive discrimination in recruitment has similarly created an outcry in the press.

How though are people expected to compete on merit if they are hampered by the values and standards in the workplace that have developed over the period when one section of society had a dominant role? If it is simply a case of providing opportunities for all people to develop the same skills and then those with the best skills being chosen for the job on *merit*, then people from a minority background would surely not be as underrepresented at senior levels in organisations as they are. As suggested in a recent report by the Equality and Human Rights Commission '... merit and talent are not the exclusive preserve of one section of the population or another. Instead we are failing to adapt the way we work to the realities of people's lives and ignoring the talent that exists within the population' (Equalities and Human Rights Commission, 2008). Certainly, the homogeneous nature of the people at the top of their disciplines leads one to ask whether there really can be a level-playing field. It also leads one to ask whether talk of 'judging people on the basis of merit' really makes sense. Are concepts of 'merit' universal or do they vary according to different groups? In other words, does it make sense to speak of a level-playing field and people wining on 'merit'?

Moss and Daunton (2006) provide an interesting insight into how traditional organisational values are still perpetuated, despite procedures being put in place by those with responsibility for equality and diversity to encourage the adoption of a different attitude to working (in this case to leadership). Moss and Daunton conducted an investigation into a recruitment process where the capability sets or competences identified for the role differed from those that were generally exhibited by those in leadership positions within the organisation. The competences identified in the job description were those which are largely accepted as those that will produce superior long-term results for organisations and which are more readily exhibited, but not exclusively, in an underrepresented group (in this case women). The selection panel consisted mainly of senior male leaders. It was apparent from discussions held with male interviewers that a large proportion of the respondents ignored the capability sets or competences laid down in the job specification, the majority of which were non-traditional in character, and judged candidates against competences of their own devising. The phenomenon of recruiting in one's own image is not unusual. However the indication of this research is that even if procedures are adopted to encourage a different range of competences, human nature is such that without first ensuring that those involved in the process really understand *and* embrace the concepts, such procedures will be ignored or 'worked around' and the original values will be perpetuated. The recognition of the value of different styles of leading or working in general will never be accepted, and in this case the glass ceiling will never be broken by women exhibiting mainly female strengths. It is easy from this example to see how the leadership style of senior managers can then influence and perpetuate the culture of the organisation as a whole (see Moss and Daunton, 2006, for further discussion).

There are further implications for the competitiveness of an organisation which fails to consider the business case for encouraging diversity within its workforce. A recent report from Microsoft Windows Mobile suggests that workers in the new economic model based around finance, media, publishing and business will need to be lateral, collaborative, flexible and creative thinkers. This will mean that the most sought after employees will be people who use the right side of the brain (*The People Bulletin*, October 2008). These skills will need to be developed by both males and females and this suggests that any mentoring, coaching schemes mentioned previously should concentrate on ensuring that all people are able to make the best of their abilities, not by learning how to conform and adapt their styles to those of current leaders and managers. It should also be remembered that it is just as important for current leaders and managers to be aware of the ways in which a different style of leadership could be equally as valid as their own. There is perhaps a greater need to focus on the individuals who are the majority type in organisations and display more traditional traits and methods of working – both existing managers and those seeking to be managers – than on the individuals from the minority groups in organisations who we are seeking to encourage and promote within organisations. This would suggest that the focus should be less on assertiveness courses for women and racial minorities than on Diversity awareness courses for senior managers in organisations.

Conclusion

The issues discussed above illustrate some of the complexities of the situation faced by equality specialists in an area that can, from a cursory glance, seem very straightforward. Instead of creating a framework by which equality can be embedded, over-zealous implementation of legislation and policies may serve only to alienate managers who see it as an increase in form-filling and data-gathering. By the same token, an appeal to people's social consciences may be equally unsuccessful and may, on its own, not bring about the sought-after change in people's attitudes and behaviour. In reality it is the combination of these methods which will assist an equality specialist to overcome barriers in embedding equality and diversity. There will never be a one-size-fits-all approach that will work in all organisations but we need to understand the strengths and weaknesses of each approach and the situations in which each can best be applied. Equality specialists are in essence change managers and perhaps we need to remember that in the field of organisational change, Beer and Nohria (2000) (cited in Burnes, 2004) claim that nearly two-thirds of change efforts fail. Equality specialists need to be resilient and persevere.

Bibliography

Allen, R. S., Dawson G., Wheatley K., and White C. S. (2008) Perceived diversity and organizational performance, *Employee Relations*, 30, 20–33.

Bagilhole, B. (2006) Family-friendly policies and equal opportunities: A contradiction in terms?, *British Journal of Guidance & Counselling*, 34(3), 327–43.

Barbosa, I. and Cabral-Cardosa, C. (2007) Managing diversity in academic organizations: A challenge to organizational culture, *Women in Management Review*, 22(4), 274–88.

Burke, Ronald J. (2005) Backlash in the workplace, *Women in Management Review*, 20(3), 165–76.

Burnes, B. (2004) *Managing Change*, 4th Edition. Pearson Education, UK.

Commission for Racial Equality archived website http://83.137.212.42/sitearchive/cre/gdpract/monitoring.html

Damasio, A. (2003) *Looking for Spinoza*, Harcourt Inc., USA.

Durbin, S., Lovell, L., and Winters, J. (2008) Diversities in an organizational context. *Equal Opportunities International*, 27(4), 396–400.

Equalities and Human Rights Commission (2008) Sex and Power.

Kochan, T. et al. (2002) The Effects of Diversity on Business Performance: Report of the Diversity Research Network. *Alfred P. Sloan Foundation and the Society for Human Resource Management*.

Lawrence, E. (2000) Equal opportunities officers and managing equality changes, *Personnel Review*, 29(3), 381–402.

Maxwell, G. A., Blair, S., and McDougall, M. (2001) Edging towards managing diversity in practice, *Employee Relations*, 23(5), 468–82.

Microsoft research sees women on top. *The People Bulletin*, 3 October 2008.

Moss, G. and Daunton, L. (2006) The discriminatory impact of non-adherence to leadership selection criteria. *Career Development International*, 11(6), 504–21.

Ryan, M. and Haslam, A. (2006) What lies beyond the glass ceiling? *Human Resource Management International Digest*, 14(3).

Scott-Thomas, S. (2008) Is the diversity brand-wagon moving on? *Equal Opportunities Review*, 176.

Shaw, S. (2007) Touching the intangible? An analysis of the equality standard: A framework for sport. *Equal Opportunities International*, 26(5); http://www.emeraldinsight.com/Insight/viewContentItem.do;jsessionid=BCE6558B222A-106321DC030564477C71?contentType=Article&contentId=1615759

Toomey, C. (2008) Quotas for Women on the board: Do they work? *The Sunday Times*, 8 June.

9
Design Diversity: The Organisational Obstacles

Gloria Moss

The congruity principle

We saw earlier how important it is for products to be configured around the 'unique and particular needs' of the customer (Hammer, 1995, 21). Organisations that can do this are more likely that products offer a vehicle for self-expression (Karande *et al.*, 1997) and organisations with products that consumers find beautiful are more likely to be able to charge a premium price (Bloch *et al.*, 2003; Hassenzahl, 2007).

We also saw how a study of earlier research on drawings and paintings as well as new research on design highlights the aesthetic range in people's design *productions* and *preferences* (Moss, 2009). Despite the range, we saw that there was a tendency for people of one demographic grouping (say men, or women) to have preferences that matched the productions that were typical of that group. For example, women would tend to produce female-typical design and they would also tend to prefer designs with these female tendencies. We found that the same was true of men (Moss, 1995, 1996b; Moss and Colman, 2001) although when it came to webdesign, men preferred male-typical webdesign overall but had no strong preferences as between male and female-typical shapes, and when it came to pictures, actually preferred those produced by women (Moss and Gunn, 2009).

This research provides an understanding of what one might term 'Design Diversity' and the detail that it provides offers pointers as to how to satisfy the congruity principle. In essence, it suggests that demographic groupings (e.g. men, or women) would be most likely to perceive beauty in design if they were offered designs that reflected the designs that are typically produced by that grouping. This notion is illustrated in Figure 9.1:

```
┌──────────────┐    ┌──────────────────┐    ┌──────────────┐
│  Production  │◄───│  Match between   │───►│  Preference  │
│  aesthetic   │    │  production and  │    │  aesthetic   │
└──────────────┘    │preference aesthetic│   └──────────────┘
                    └──────────────────┘
                             │
                             ▼
                    ┌──────────────────┐
                    │  Perception of   │
                    │     beauty       │
                    └──────────────────┘
                             │
                             ▼
                    ┌──────────────────┐
                    │  Preparedness to │
                    │  pay a premium   │
                    │     price        │
                    └──────────────────┘
```

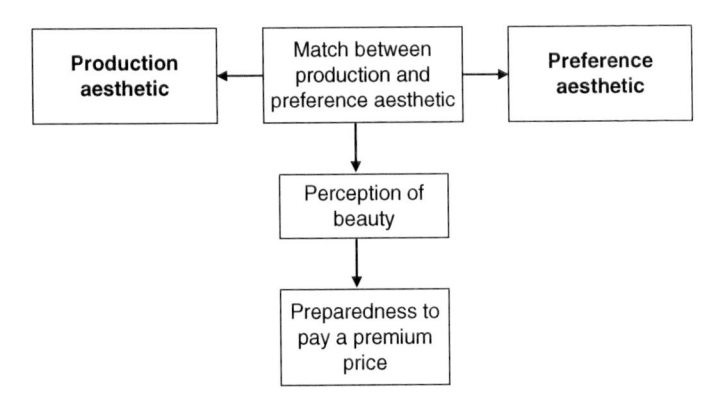

Figure 9.1 The gains to be derived from achieving a match between production and preference aesthetics

What the notion of Design Diversity does not do, however, is inform us as to the relative ease with which Design Diversity can be introduced into organisations. Only an understanding of the potential match that exists between organisational and consumer demographics can bring a realisation of the relative ease or difficulty in achieving congruity. In fact, as we shall see, there are a number of potential difficulties which are frequently overlooked in discussions of diversity, whether in specific relation to design or to diversity more generally. The practical issues and difficulties relating to the practical fulfilment of Design Diversity are the focus of this chapter.

Practicalities of achieving diversity

Inside-outside perspective

A starting point for considering the practicalities of introducing Design Diversity is the link between the outside processes of competition and the internal processes of creating and sustaining change, what Baden-Fuller (1995) has described as the 'inside-out' and 'outside-in' perspectives. It builds on the 'strategy innovation' approach of Van den Bosch (1993) and Van de Ven (1992) which assumes a link between a new organisational configuration (with new routines, new skills and new competences) and the construction of new competitive rules within the industry. The transfer of these ideas to Design Diversity invites a comparison of the perceptions of those *inside* and those *outside* the organisation. In practical terms, this means comparing the perceptions of the internal Design and Marketing team (insiders) and those of customers (outsiders).

Much has been written about customer demographics but a focus on gender reveals that the consumers in a large proportion of sectors are female (Johnson and Learned, 2004; Barletta, 2006; Moss, 2009). In this way, buying statistics from the US and the UK highlight the fact that women have equal or greater buying power than men in a large number of sectors. These sectors include groceries, furniture, books, education, housing, cars, small electrical goods and holidays. These customers constitute the 'outsiders'.

Where 'insiders' are concerned, these are likely to be the managers in the Marketing and Design departments, and the design staff employed. Date reveals that the majority of these tend to be men. Therefore we have a situation in which there is a potential mismatch between the perceptions and preferences of those *inside* and *outside* the organisation and one which may make it difficult to provide customers with products that fully match their preferences. The extent to which an inside-outside perspective can render Design Diversity problematic is shown in Figure 9.2:

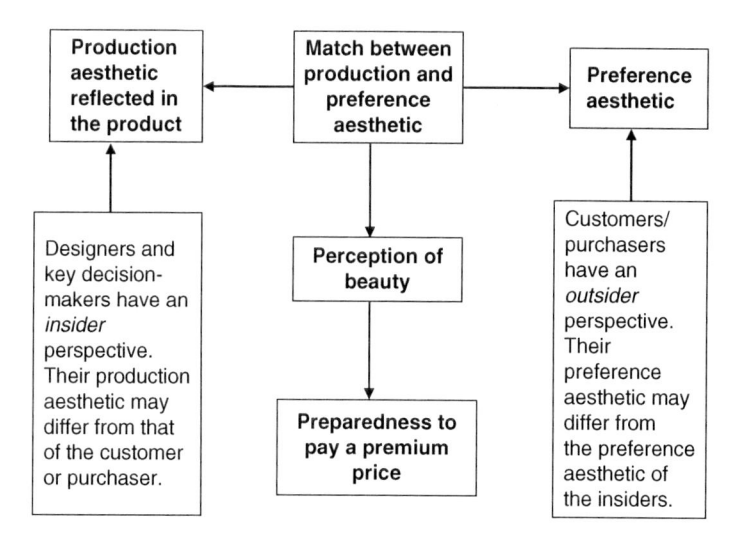

Figure 9.2 The gains to be derived from achieving a match between production and preference aesthetics

Moreover, the scope for conflict between the Design preferences of *insiders* and *outsiders* has been examined in the work of this author (Moss, 2007; Moss, 2009) but has otherwise been widely overlooked. In the sections that follow, we will look briefly at *inside* and *outsider* demographics and consider the extent to which these might, in practice, differ. Where they differ, we will explore some of the options for achieving a match so that customers are offered products that appeal to them and Karande's mirroring principle is satisfied.

Demographics

Customer demographics

The question of who has the major say in purchasing decisions is an important one and I have attempted to summarise what we know of this elsewhere (Moss, 1996a, 1999, 2009). What we find is that research has focused on the cross-industry spending habits of household members as well as on spending habits within particular sectors. Where the first is concerned, there is a wealth of interesting research conducted in the UK, the US and Belgium. If we start chronologically with the Belgian study (Davis and Rigaux, 1974), this showed that there was a tendency at that time for husbands and wives to make purchasing decisions jointly or in partnership, with very few decisions being the unique preserve of the husband. Studies conducted in the 1980s and 1990s showed a continuing trend away from husband-dominated decision-making. In the UK, for example, a study by Vogler and Pahl (1993), men were likely to have sole control of household income in just 12 per cent of decisions, having a shared role in decision-making with women in 60 per cent of cases. A second study (Buck *et al.*, 1994) showed that only 9 per cent of men were likely to have sole control over purchasing decisions compared with 24 per cent of women.

These studies of purchasing patterns show a large proportion of decisions involving men as well as women and these studies on their own would lead organisations to think of decision-making as an interactive process between couples, rather than a process dominated by male consumers.

Where information on sectors is concerned, studies in the UK have shown men than female purchasers of computers, fridges, washing machines, SLR cameras, alcohol, garden tools, petrol, recorded music, sports goods, video cameras and DIY items (Moss, 1996a, 1999). By contrast, women were found dominating purchasing decisions relating to clothing and major appliances (Mohan, 1995), as well as decisions relating to chocolate, china glass, cosmetics, books, electric kettles, furniture, kitchen equipment, jewellery, photographic equipment, small electrical goods, stationery, toys and homes (Moss, 1999).

The dominant position of women as purchasers is recognised by a former marketing director of Lever Brothers who expressed the view that 'the bulk of our brands are targeted at women who still do the bulk of the shopping' (Batstone, 1994). Similarly, Michael Silverstein, principal at Boston Consulting Group and author of *Trading Up: The New American Luxury* (Silverstein and Fiske, 2003), has said that 'Today's woman is the chief purchasing agent of the family and marketers have to recognize that.' In a similar vein, Fara Warner, author of *The Power of the Purse* (2006), describes women as the majority market (p. 5) and the world's most powerful consumers' (p. 6) while Marti Barletta, author of *Marketing to Women*, quotes women as responsible for 83 per cent of all consumer purchases.

Creative sectors

Design

In the UK, figures from *The Business of Design: Design Industry Research*, a UK Design Council Report in 2005, put the proportion of male designers at 61 per cent, and female at 39 per cent. A more detailed picture of the gender demographics of the industry emerges from membership statistics of the Chartered Society of Designers (CSD), the professional body as we have seen for designers in the UK. The proportion of male and female members for 2006, by design discipline, is shown in Table 9.1.

A quick look at the table shows that men outnumber women in all the design disciplines with the exception of fashion and textiles, with ever-decreasing proportions of female members as you advance up the profession. Overall, 9 per cent of Fellows are women, 18 per cent of Members and 40 per cent of Graduates. The absence of women is particularly acute in product design (a discipline classed as covering furniture, ceramics, jewellery, automotive, glass and industrial products) where women constitute a meagre 8 per cent of members at all levels.

The CSD does not keep data on the relationship of membership grade to job seniority but one might reasonably expect membership seniority to correlate with professional status. So, following this logic, one might assume from the CSD's figures that the vast majority of middle and senior ranks of design managers, design educators and product designers in the UK are male. It is only in the case of fashion and textile design

Table 9.1 The proportion of men and women members (and by grade of membership) according to membership statistics held by the Chartered Society of Designers

Discipline	Males (%)	Females (%)
Design management		
MCSD	86	14
FCSD	84	16
Design education		
MCSD	86	14
FCSD	70	30
Product design		
Graduate members		34
MCSD	92	8
FCSD	92	8
Graphic design		
Graduate members	44	56
MCSD	79	21
FSCD	88	12
Fashion and textiles		
Graduate members	25	75
MCSD	30	70
FCSD	53	47
Interiors		
Graduate members	30	70
MCSD	30	25
FCSD	75	12

(and then only at Member and Graduate level) that female members outnumber males. At the highest level of Fellow, even in this otherwise female-dominated field, men outnumber women. A tentative conclusion, therefore, might be that the design profession is one in which small proportions of women move up the ranks.

We should note that the declining position of female designers in institutional life contrasts with the position of boys and girls at school leaving stage. In 1996, an analysis of Art and Design examinations showed that the majority of candidates at both GCSE and particularly 'A' level were girls (Moss, 1996b), and also showed that the majority of those achieving 'A' grades were also girls. Ten years on, the situation at this stage remains largely unchanged since the 2006 report by the Women and Work Commission refers to 'A' level Art and Design as a subject favoured by female candidates. Not surprisingly, the majority of design students at tertiary level are then female (60 per cent) but the big question remains whether women will stay the course in design or fall away from the profession as the statistics suggest they do.

Another fact of note is the high proportion of people working on a self-employed basis in this industry. The Design Council Report *The Business of Design: Design Industry Research* (2005) shows that 40 per cent of designers are self-employed and since there is a view that the lack of full-time or part-time opportunities are the major prompts for women working on a freelance basis (Moss, 2009), one might expect the proportion of women in the self-employed category to be high.

Webdesign

The final area of design yet to be investigated is webdesign. Given the importance of webdesign, it may come as a surprise to learn that there is a relative dearth of information on the demographics of this new industry. Until recently, there were only two studies of relevance, one of which was concerned with small businesses (Thelwall, 2000) and the other with the extent to which webdesign was a male-dominated discipline (Simon and Peppas, 2005). This finding was confirmed in a survey conducted by E-consultancy on the UK affiliates (organisations creating websites for other companies – see E-Consultancy, 2007) showing that 83 per cent of the staff employed by affiliates were male. Corroboration of the low involvement of women in web development emerges from a report highlighting the consistently low proportion of women speakers at web conferences (Kottke, 2007).

With the exception of these studies, there was no published data on the demographics and *modus operandi* of this relatively young industry so new research was called for. This research was conducted through telephone interviews and in the first phase, webdesign managers in three sectors were questioned about the gender distribution of webdesigners and in the second, Project and Human Resource managers were questioned about the skills-base of webdesigners.

The results of these phases are reported in detail elsewhere (Moss *et al.*, 2008; Moss, 2009) and show the existence of a male-dominated industry. In phase one, the three sectors examined were markets dominated respectively by (i) men, (ii) women and (iii) equal proportions of men and women, and in no more than 18 per cent of cases did respondents use the services of female webdesigners. In the second phase, interviewees gave the background of webdesigners as being either graphic design or Information Technology (IT). Currently, as we have seen, Graphic Design is dominated at the highest levels of CSD membership by men and IT is also male-dominated. During the 1990s, average participation rates for women fluctuated between 19 per cent and 22 per cent (Robertson *et al.*, 2001) with a dominance of men at all levels and across the three fields of information systems, information technology and computer science (ibid.). The situation varies only in different parts of the world and different IT specialisms. In the UK in 1994, women made up 30 per cent of computer scientists, 32 per cent of systems analysts, 35 per cent of computer programmers, 10 per cent of IS directors, 18 per cent of project leaders and 14 per cent of applications development managers (Baroudi and Igbaria 1994/5). In terms of trends, the proportion of women in IT is on the decline. So, while the 1980s saw an influx of women into IT, with a fourfold increase between 1980 and 1986 in the number of women awarded bachelor's degrees in computer science and a threefold increase in the number of women with master's degrees (Igbaria and Parasuraman, 1997), recent years have seen a sharp decline in the number of women pursuing undergraduate and postgraduate degrees in computer-related fields (ibid.). Relatedly, in the US, the proportion of women among computer professionals fell in the 1990s from 35.4 per cent to 29.1 per cent.

This skewed gender distribution in IT has purportedly produced a 'masculine computer culture' with a 'masculine discourse' and a prioritisation of technical issues (Robertson *et al.*, 2001), all of which are thought to deter women from entering or remaining in the field (ibid.). The authors suggest that it is only by including a 'broader set of skills and discursive practices' that a more diverse group of people can be attracted into the profession, and that the masculine nature of the culture can be altered.

What we have seen of the demographics of the design and webdesign industries suggest industries that are heavily male-dominated. The next section will explore the related area of advertising.

Advertising

The worldwide market for the conception and development of advertising campaigns is in the area of $45 billion with three main advertising centres in the world, namely New York, Tokyo and London. The US market dominates and the UK is the fourth largest advertising market in the world in terms of revenues after the US, Japan and Germany. The UK advertising industry employs around 92,000 people (Andriopoulos and Dawson, 2009).

Where gender demographics are concerned, a survey by the Institute of Practitioners in Advertising into the media buying, advertising and marketing communications sectors (Brooke, 2006) showed that women make up approximately half of the workforce but only 15.1 per cent of managing directors or chief executives. According to this survey, the percentage of women at the top of the advertising industry has more than doubled from a low of 7 per cent in 1998, but increased by only one percentage point since 2004. Meanwhile, at lower management levels, the survey shows female representation in the industry to be under 30 per cent (ibid.).

The results of this survey do not come as a surprise since earlier research highlighted low female numbers both in senior positions and creative functions. In 2000, for example, research by the UK's Institute of Practitioners in Advertising showed that while women's presence as account handlers had increased from 27 per cent in 1986 to 54 per cent in 1999 (with women accounting for half of those in planning and research), just 14 per cent of art directors and 17 per cent of copywriters were women (*The Independent*, 2001). A more recent article shows the figures largely unchanged with figures quoted of 83 per cent of 'creatives' being men, a figure said to be worse than 30 years ago (Cadwalladr, 2005). It is not surprising, given the male domination of the creative side of advertising, that women's representation in creative roles should be referred to as 'a closed shop when it comes to bridging the gender divide' (Doward, 2000). It is not surprising, either, that the creative arm of the advertising industry should be described as one that 'does not seem to be too keen on thinking out of the box on gender issues' (ibid.). A contributory factor may, according to a report on women in the advertisement industry by Debbie Klein, Chief Executive of WCRS, be the 'stereotypical laddish atmosphere' which is said to be still very much in existence (ibid.).

So much for the UK. In the US, as we have seen, a 2002 survey of advertising staff by AdAge found that on average 35 per cent of creative staff were female. This is a low figure, but almost twice that of the proportion of women in creative roles in the UK (Barletta, 2006). So, the staunchly masculine aspect of the creative arm of advertising seems to be particularly pronounced in the UK (Moss, 2009).

Achieving congruity: Insider versus outsider perspectives

Now that we have explored the demographics of those *outside* and *inside* the design and advertising industries, we can consider the likelihood of congruity between these two groups. To what extent are consumers like to share the perceptions of those creating designs and advertising for organisations?

As we have seen, many markets are strongly segmented by gender, with women the dominant consumer in many markets, and yet the design and advertising professions still appear to be male-dominated organisations. Since we saw earlier how men tend to prefer designs displaying the male production aesthetic, and women designs displaying the female production aesthetic, one could well question the ability of design and advertising agencies to deliver the male *and* female production aesthetic. In the face of a customer base that consists of male and female purchasers, Rita Clifton, chairwoman of Interbrand, describes the shortage of female creatives in the advertising industry as 'absolutely bizarre and extraordinary' (Cadwalladr, 2005). A similar sentiment comes from Debbie Klein, Chief Executive of WCRS and author of the Institute of Practitioners in Advertising report on women in advertising (2000), who writes that 'the balance between people who write the ads and those whom they should be aimed at is completely out of whack' since 'more than 70 per cent of expenditure is made by women' (Doward, 2000).

So, given the skewed nature of the demographics in the design and advertising industries, what steps can be taken to deliver product congruity to customers? One might also ask what obstacles exist to the achievement of congruity.

Achieving congruence within existing structures

The underlying assumptions in this chapter are that people can most easily reflect the perceptions/preferences of the external market where they share the demographic characteristics of that market. In this chapter, the spotlight has been on gender and it needs to be said that not all men, or women, share the same design production and preference aesthetics. However, in the research I have conducted, the majority of people of one gender (say 75–80 per cent) produce work that conforms to the norms discussed in the earlier chapter on design (see Part I). As we have seen, the strength of preference tests suggests that, in a similar way, high proportions conform to gender-specific preference norms. This leaves an important question as to how organisations can configure themselves to deliver the design diversity implied by this research. This is a vital question since the marketing literature emphasises the benefits of mirroring customer preferences in the products offered (Brock, 1965; Crozier and Greenhalgh, 1992; Groppel, 1993; Yahomoto and Lambert, 1994; Donovan *et al.*, 1994; Hammer, 1995; Karande *et al.*,

1997; De Chernatoney *et al.*, 2004) This is not necessarily an easy question to answer since the research on design diversity emphasises the extent to which productions and preference aesthetics can be segmented by gender.

Some of the issues involved in configuring organisations to deliver design diversity have been considered elsewhere (Moss, 2007, 2009) and are summarised in the sections that follow. In essence, the problems turn on the ability of the *internal* market to make the changes necessary to produce design solutions that are appropriate to the *external* market. These solutions may involve the use of *production* and *preference* aesthetics that are at odds with the natural preferences of those in the *internal* market. The groups within an organisation that are key in this are those responsible for decisions concerning design and advertising staff, as well as those creating and executing design briefs. These groups are likely to be managers on the one hand and designers and creatives on the other. We will look in more detail at the issues relating to culture and the potential for change in these areas.

Internal labour markets

The internal labour market has been described as difficult to change (Boxall and Purcell, 2003) and frequently conservative, sticky systems, often demarcated internally on hierarchical and gender lines (Lepak and Snell, 1999). The latter point is reinforced by Wajcman (2000; quoted in Boxall and Purcell, 2003, p. 119) who describes organisations as 'profoundly gendered'. The dominant male model prevalent in organisations makes it difficult to hire staff whose perceptions and preferences are at odds with those of the male model.

In terms of the gender balance in organisations, statistics relating to managers show a dramatic increase in the number of women pursuing managerial and professional careers. However, they still appear to be experiencing vertical segregation and encountering a 'glass ceiling' in private and public sector organisations in all developed countries (Burke, 2002; Burke and Nelson, 2002). According to Vinnicombe and Singh of Cranfield University (2002), women hold only 32 per cent of managerial positions and 6 per cent of top directorships in the UK.

As far as the gender balance in design is concerned, we have already seen how male-dominated various branches of the design profession are. We are not alone in this conclusion. According to Peter Souter, executive creative director of AMV and a former president of the British

Design and Art Direction Association (D & AD), the demographics of the marketing world are predominantly male (Moss, 2007). Importantly, his explanation for the male domination of these industries is that 'people are slightly guilty of hiring themselves' (Moss, 2007) and this is tantamount to acknowledging the all pervasive impact of the homogeneity principle in the marketing sector, with men appointing other men into management positions.

The problems identified by Peter Souter get to the heart of what we have been discussing in this chapter, and show how the internal labour market and forces of congruity *within* an organisation may impede the achievement of congruity with customers *outside* it. Clearly, the process by which managers are selected is of enormous importance and a realisation is needed of the cascade effect of appointing managers of a particular kind at the top. Given the tendency of people to appoint others like themselves – known as the homogeneity effect – the characteristics of the top person could well pervade the appointment of managers and staff all the way through the organisation. This could be general managers, or specialist staff in the areas we are focusing on here, namely design, brand and marketing managers. Since research has shown that brand managers permeate the brand with their own values (Schneider, 2001) and that senior managers often spearhead new brand values (Driscoll and Hoffman, 2000; Moss and Gunn 2009), the appointment of these managers will influence design and branding in the rest of the organisation. For example, if an organisation has a senior management that consists predominantly of men, they will tend to appoint other men and these men, if they are designers or brand managers, will tend to produce designs and brands that are at the masculine end of the production aesthetic continuum. In this situation, achieving congruity with a largely female customer base may be difficult and this would deprive organisations of the many assumed benefits of congruity.

The nature of the internal labour market is therefore an important one. According to the authors of a book on Human Resources strategy, the negative effect of poor recruitment has been linked with organisational 'failure or, at the very least... stunted growth' (Boxall and Purcell, 2003, p. 140). This suggests that a way of overcoming the practical effects of the homogeneity principle *inside* and *outside* the organisation needs to be found. Before looking at ways of overcoming the effects of the homogeneity principle, we will explore what we know of the homogeneity principle.

The homogeneity principle

Studies have highlighted the tendency for the homogeneity principle or 'similarity-attraction paradigm' (Byrne, 1971) to influence recruitment, appraisal and promotion (Schneider, 1987; Dipboye and Macan, 1988; Byrne and Neuman, 1992). As Stockdale and Crosby (2004, p. 105) write, 'Most organizational leaders continue to be white males [and] there is a natural bias for such leaders to attract and select other white males.' Schneider's model shows organisations becoming increasingly homogeneous, not only because individuals are attracted to organisations where they believe they will 'fit in' but because organisational members are likely to feel comfortable with applicants who are similar and thus are likely to hire new employees who hold similar characteristics (Stockdale and Crosby, 2004). Perceived similarity will also impact retention since employees are more likely to be satisfied and remain with an organisation where they feel that they 'fit in'.

Overcoming the homogeneity principle

What steps can organisations take to overcome the impact of the 'similarity-attraction paradigm'? (Byrne, 1971). According to Stockdale and Crosby (2004), an earlier study in 1993 by Powell describes organisations as proactive, reactive or benignly neglectful with the proactive amongst them taking action without external prompting. Cox's categorisation (1991) of organisations as monolithic, pluralistic or multicultural helps anticipate the reaction that might be found in an organisation since a pluralistic organisation is likely to pay lip service to the value of diversity but only fully embeds it when it reaches the multicultural state. At that point, according to Stockdale and Crosby (2004), the organisation is likely to have modified its structure in order to take full advantage of its diverse workforce (ibid., p. 59) and is likely to have 'developed policies, practice and culture to support diversity' (ibid., p. 67). In order to arrive at this point, however, the organisation will need to have changed its core culture to sustain the coordinated efforts of a diverse workforce (Thomas, 1996). In fact, Thomas recommends diagnosing the current organisational climate before undertaking an initiative and also suggests that organisations with a tendency to learning effectiveness are most likely to have the orientation needed to implement diversity (ibid.). In a similar way, Allen and Montgomery (2001) suggest that managing diversity is first about managing the change process.

What are the change options? Less radical approaches to change have been said to be based on 'realignment' while more radical approaches are said to rely on 'transformation' with the option of faster change ('revolution') and slower change ('evolution') (Balogan and Hope-Hailey, 2008). One of the transformational routes to revolutionary change would be the option of 'buying in' appropriate skills to the organisation, while a more evolutionary approach might consider the use of education to change the attitudes of those within the internal system. These solutions would rely, to a greater or lesser extent, on the *internal* or *external* labour market with the option of buying-in skills placing reliance on the *external* market (with staff bought in either on a permanent or contract basis) and the option of education relying instead on the *internal* labour market.

Windolf's recommended move from *status quo* to *innovative* recruitment (1986) can help creative firms mitigate the problems posed by the homogeneity principle. Boxall and Purcell (2003, p. 141) describe *status quo* recruitment as recruitment that is 'conservative, often recruiting from the same social strata and age groups' while innovative recruitment has very different characteristics:

> innovative firms attempt to recruit talented people who can help them develop a stream of new products and processes. They therefore use all possible channels to generate a heterogenous group of applicants.

Design and ICT specialists are the kind of staff that could be brought into an organisation (Lepak and Snell, 1999) but how realistic is this option of recruitment as against that of education?

Recruitment versus education

In the course of this book, we have recommended two strategies for achieving congruence with external customers the first of which is to select personnel with similar demographics to those of the target market. The second is to educate those who may not reflect the demographics of the target market in the ways of seeing characteristic of that group. Just how feasible are these strategies? The first option appears, on the face of it, to be an attractive one. In 1995, with the growing awareness that 80 per cent of television advertisements are targeted at women, the group managing director of brand consultancy at Leo Burnett (a leading London advertising agency) commented that 'agencies began to realise that it was a great advantage to appoint people to the team who intimately understood their target audience' (Horsman, 1995). More recently, Debbie Klein, Chief Executive of WCRS and author of the 2000 Institute of Practitioners in Advertising report on women in advertising, supported the notion of employing more women in the creative industries on the basis that 'it would bring different ways of looking at things' (Doward, 2000).

However, while there are attractions to involving people in organisations who offer a different perspective, academics have long been aware, at a theoretical level, of the extent to which design paradigms are concentrated around the male production and preference aesthetic, and the way this can create barriers for those whose thinking may be different. Buckley (1987), for example, speaks of the fact that male designers promote a particular approach to design and also mentions the fact that the dominance of the profession by men makes it difficult for a female approach to gain acceptance. The male influence on design can be seen in the fact that design is defined in terms of mass production design, the design favoured by the male sex, while craft design, the design traditionally favoured by women, is accorded secondary status. In this way, the interests of the dominant group are presented as 'universal' rather than just a reflection of the interests of the dominant group and this leads Attfield and Kirkham (1989) to describe a hierarchy of design values in which industrial design and the 'machine aesthetic', areas which she describes as 'more obviously masculine', are accorded pride of place.

Meanwhile, areas which are more obviously 'feminine' are ascribed lesser importance. This notion that there is a specifically male set of values has been further developed by Professor Penny Sparke, Pro Vice-Chancellor for the Arts at Kingston University and a prolific writer on design. As we saw earlier, she writes in *As Long As It's Pink* (1995), her book on gender and design, that 'women's tastes stand outside the "true" canon of aesthetic values of the dominant culture', noting that

> architectural and design modernism imposed on goods and their design a stereotypically masculine aesthetic, not only because it was undertaken by men but because it was now embedded within masculine culture. (Ibid., p. 10)

So, while injecting staff with a new way of thinking into an organisation may appear on the face of it to be a useful strategy, in practice it can be problematic. Aside from the demographic difficulties in finding the necessary staff (we have already discussed the male domination of many areas of design and the shortage of female graphic, product and webdesigners), succeeding in hiring a new style of recruit whose demographics and values may differ from that of the majority in the organisation may be difficult. There are two main factors that serve as obstacles. The first of these is that people are unwittingly subject to the congruity principle and, unless a concerted attempt is made to counter this such as was the case with the organisation that initiated a new leadership framework (Moss *et al.*, 2006), the congruity principle will lead people to favour people like themselves (Klohnen and Shanhong, 2003). As Stockdale and Crosby write (2004), 'organizational leaders will feel more comfortable with individuals who are similar in demographic characteristics, and thus be far more likely to select those individuals for the work team' (ibid., p. 105).

The second factor relates to the problems that surface when people are recruited with norms at odds with those of the majority. As Amanda Walsh, founder of the agency Walsh Trott Chick Smith, has said, 'You do feel slightly lonely and there are situations when you feel alien and wish you weren't in the room' (*The Independent*, 2001). In a similar vein, the chairman of the PHD media agency, Tess Alps, says that men 'just don't value the kinds of ads that women write and that women like' (Cadwalladr, 2005). This can lead men in the agencies to freely offer negative feedback to the female employees as Christine Walker, founder of Walker Media, writes, 'If they [the men] don't like it', the women are 'often told they've got no sense of humour. If I've heard that once, I've heard it 50 times. It can be hurtful, but what's more worrying is the guys don't know that they're doing it' (*The Independent*, 2001). The problem of different values has led Rita Clifton, chairman of Interbrand, to suggest that a strategy of employing people who match the values of the customer base but not those of the organisation (e.g., employing a female creative team in a male-dominated environment) is not necessarily the solution. As she says, she has found that 'female creatives are working within this culture, and they are being judged by these standards so they're creating stuff that's framed by that'.

Working cultures

The problems can extend to working cultures too. Christine Walker, founder of Walker Media, writes of the laddish culture in place in advertising agencies: 'I can see why women may not want to work in media agencies', says Walker. 'Media owners are dominated by men. There is a very laddish culture where people are expected to work hard and play hard. In order to be successful you have to network. You have to be out every night and for most women, the priorities lie elsewhere' (*The Independent*, 2001). Changing these cultures can be difficult as Kathy Gornik, former chairwoman of the American Consumer Electronics Association, has said: 'There's a lot of inertia when things are done in a particular way. You are talking about having to change the entire orientation and culture of a company' (Palmer, 2003).

Clearly, for as long as organisations are unbalanced demographically (e.g., employing a higher proportion of men than women) it will be difficult for new people with a different way of seeing not to feel tempted to model their performance on that of the majority. The impulse to do this has been demonstrated in the case of leadership (Gardiner and Tiggerman, 1999) and the same may apply where aesthetic responses are concerned. It may only be possible to subvert this natural tendency to conformity through a radical and innovative recruitment strategy that seeks a match between *performance* and *preference* elements and that offers continued support to demographic minorities in the organisation. This focus may be on the key stages of recruitment, appraisal and promotion until the demographic has become more balanced at which point the minority will be mainstream and better able to maintain its separate identity.

Education and evolutionary change

Until that point, it may be helpful to educate the mainstream in the values of the customer, an 'evolutionary' option which is longer term in its time span and focus than 'revolutionary' change. Research by Hanover and Cellar (1998) showed that diversity education could indeed be effective at changing the attitudes of middle managers of a Fortune 500 company and other commentators have likewise recorded a positive impact on attitudes (Roberson *et al.*, 2001; Stockdale and Crosby, 2004). However, the successful introduction of diversity is facilitated, according to Agars and Kottke (2002), by a three-stage process. The steps in this are: (i) issue identification during which organisations make diversity management a priority; (ii) implementation during which new policies are implemented that support a diverse workforce; (iii) maintenance of the diversity initiative. According to Stockdale and Crosby (2004) there are a number of obstacles to the successful passage through these stages and these can include social stereotypes, perceptions of threats, perceptions of injustice in the introduction of diversity and little understanding of the financial benefits of diversity.

So, although evolutionary change is often presented as easier to achieve than transformational change, it may still be challenging. In this respect, Rita Clifton, chairwoman of Interbrand, wrote that 'while a good creative should be able to think themselves into any role or profile, and men can do this as well as women, the difference is they don't feel it'. She spells out what she sees as the consequence when she says that 'this comes across in the ads. In lingerie ads the women are very observed figures. These are women who are set up to be watched. The same with some of the supermarket ads' (Cadwalladr, 2005).

This recognition of people's limited ability to think beyond their own way of seeing into that of others suggests that effecting evolutionary change in the context of existing organisational and skills demographics, although perhaps easier and more long-lasting than revolutionary change, is still challenging. It may yet be possible to train a man to think more like a woman, and vice versa, but targeted and repeated training is likely to be necessary. I can recall the time, for example, when I trained a company in how to optimise its website for its female market and how quick the male webdesigners were to introduce the recommended female features. However, within a short time, the website had reverted to type and was displaying the same masculine aesthetic it displayed before the training. This suggests that the effectiveness of any interventions relies on regular inputs over time, and not just one-off inputs. Moreover, the message conveyed in the first session may meet with resistance, and so repeated sessions will be necessary to get past this stage.

Conclusions and practical lessons

Ensuring that congruence is achieved between product and customer preferences may not be a simple process. It faces a number of obstacles, not least of which is the presence of values in the workforce (design values and management or teamwork values) that fail to achieve congruence with those of the target market. Careful discussion of these issues and well-organised training may assist in achieving the congruence between staff and customer segmentation variables needed to achieve product/customer congruence but any such initiatives will need to be prepared with great care and accompanied by regular interventions and evaluation. The male domination of the design profession raises the issue of whether the male and female aesthetic can be equally well produced by IT professionals of either gender. This is a question for future research. We have seen the extent to which webdesign, in line with other forms of design, can reflect aspects of its creator. In this case, we have seen the extent to which the design can leave fingerprints of its creator's gender.

References

Agars, M. and Kottke, J. (2002), An integrative model of diversity. Paper presented as part of M. D. Agars and J. Kottke (Chairs), *Integrating Theory and Practice in Gender Diversity Initiatives*. Symposium presented at the 17th Annual Conference of the Society for Industrial and Organizational Psychology, April. Toronto, Canada.

Allen, R. and Montgomery, K. (2001), Applying an organizational development approach to creating diversity, *Organisational Dynamics* 30, 149–61.

Andriopoulos, C. and Dawson, P. (2009), *Managing Change, Creativity and Innovation*, Los Angeles: Sage.

Attfield, J. and Kirkham, P. (1989), *A View from the Interior: Feminism, Women and Design*, London: Woman's Press.

Baden-Fuller, C. (1995), Strategic innovation, corporate entrepreneurship and matching outside-in to inside-out approaches to strategy research, *British Journal of Management* 6, Special issue, 3–16.

Balogan, J. and Hope-Hailey, V. (2008), *Exploring Strategic Change*, London: Prentice Hall.

Barletta, M. (2006), *Marketing to Women*, New York: Kaplan.

Baroudi, J. J. and Igbaria, M. (1994/05), An examination of gender effects on career success of information system employees, *Journal of Management Information Systems* 11, 3, 181–201.

Batstone, M. (1994), Men on the supermarket shelf, *The Financial Times* 27 October, 15.

Bloch, P. H., Brunel, F. F. and Arnold, T.J. (2003), Individual differences in the centrality of visual product aesthetics, *Journal of Consumer Research* 29, 551–65.

Boxall, P. and Purcell, J. (2003), *Strategy and Human Resource Management*, Basingstoke: Palgrave Macmillan.

Brock, T. C. (1965), Communicator-recipient similarity and decision change, *Journal of Personality and Social Psychology* 1, 650–4.

Brooke, S. (2006), Women miss out on top advertising jobs, *The Guardian* 25 January. http://www.guardian.co.uk/media/2006/jan/25/marketingandpr.advertising

Buck, N., Gershuny, J., Rose, D. and Scott, J. (eds) (1994), *Changing Households: The BHPS 1950 to 1992*, Essex: ESRC Research Centre on Micro-Social Change.

Buckley, C. (1987), Made in patriarchy: Towards a feminist analysis of women and design, *Design Issues* 3, 2, 3–14.

Burke, R. (2002), Career development of managerial women, in Burke, R. and Nelson, D. (eds), *Advancing Women's Careers*, Oxford: Blackwell.

Burke, R. and Nelson, D. (2002), Advancing women in management: Progress and prospects, in Burke, R. and Nelson, D. (eds), *Advancing Women's Careers*, Oxford: Blackwell.

Byrne, D. (1971), *The Attraction Paradigm*, New York: Academic Press.

Byrne, D. and Neuman, J. (1992), The implications of attraction research for organizational issues, in Kelley, K. (ed.), *Issues, Theory and Research in Industrial and*

Organizational Psychology, New York: Elsevier.

Cadwalladr, C. (2005), This advertising boss thinks women make 'crap' executives. It seems he's not alone, *The Observer* 23 October. http://observer.guardian.co.uk/focus/story/0,6903,1598649,00.html

Cox, T. (1991), The multicultural organization, *Academy of Management Executive* 5, 34–47.

Crozier, W. and Greenhalgh, P. (1992), The empathy principle: Towards a model for the psychology of art, *Journal for the Theory of Social Behaviour* 22 1, 63–79.

Davis, Harry L. and Rigaux, Benny P. (1974), Perception of marital roles in decision processes, *Journal of Consumer Research* 1 June, 51–62.

De Chernatony, L., Drury, S. and Segal-Horn, S. (2004), Identifying and sustaining services brands' values, *Journal of Marketing Communications* 10 2, 73–94.

The Design Council (2005), *The Business of Design: Design Industry Research*, London: Design Council.

Dipboye, R. and Macan, T. (1988), A process view of the selection/recruitment interview, in Schuler, R. *et al.* (eds), *Readings in Personnel and Human Resource Management*, St Paul, MN: West.

Donovan, R. J. *et al.* (1994), Store atmosphere and purchasing behaviour, *Journal of Retailing* 70, 3, 283–94.

Doward, J. (2000), Why adland is still lad land, *The Observer*, 19 November http://www.guardian.co.uk/business/2000/nov/19/pressandpublishing. media1 or http://www.guardian.co.uk/Archive/Article/0,4273,4093039,00.html

Driscoll, Dawn-Marie and Hoffman, W. Michael (2000), *Ethics Matters: How to Implement Values-Driven Management*, Waltham, MA: Bently College Center for Business Ethics.

E-Consultancy (2007), *UK Affiliate Census Report*. http://www.e-consultancy.com/publications/affiliate-census/

Gardiner, M. and Tiggerman, M. (1999), Gender differences in leadership styles, job stress, and mental health in male- and female-dominated industries, *Journal of Occupational and Organizational Psychology* 72, 301–15.

Groppel, A. (1993), Store design and experience orientated consumers in retailing: comparison between the United States and Germany, in Van Raaij, W. F. and Bassomy, G. J. (eds), *European Advances in Consumer Research*, Amsterdam: Association for Consumer Research.

Hammer, M. (1995), *Reengineering the Corporation*, London: Nicholas Brealey.

Hanover, J. and Cellar, D. (1998), Environmental factors and the effectiveness of workforce diversity training, *Human Resource Development Quarterly* 9, 105–24.

Hassenzahl, M. (2007), Aesthetics in interactive products: Correlates and consequences of beauty, in Schifferstein, H. N. J. and Hekkert, P. (eds), *Product Experience*, Amsterdam: Elsevier.

Horsman, M. (1995), What a week it was for...ad women, *The Independent* 17 March. The Independent, http://www.independent.co.uk/news/media/how-to-get-ahead-in-advertising-692900.html, 2 January 2001.

Igbaria, M. and Parasuraman, S. (1997), Status report on women and men in the IT workplace, *Information Systems Management* 14 3, 44–54.

Johnson, L. and Learned, A. (2004), *Don't Think Pink*, New York: American Management Association.

Karande, K., Zinkhan, G. M. and Lum, A. B. (1997), Brand personality and self concept: A replication and extension, *American Marketing Association*, Summer Conference, 165–71.

Klohnen, E. C., Luo, S. (2003), Interpersonal attraction and personality: What is attractive-self similarity, ideal similarity, complementarity or attachment security? *Journal of Personality and Social Psychology* 85, 4, 709–722.

Kottke, Jason (2007), Gender diversity at web conferences, http://www.kottke.org/07/02/gender-diversity-at-web-conferences.

Lepak, D. and Snell, S. (1999), The strategic management of human capital: Determinants and implications of different relationships, *Academy of Management Review* 24, 1, 1–18.

Mohan, M. (1995), The influence of marital roles in consumer decision-making, *Irish Marketing Review* 8, 97–107.

Moss, G. (1995), Differences in the design aesthetic of men and women: Implications for product branding, *Journal of Brand Management* 3, 3, 51–61.

Moss, G. (1996a), Sex: The misunderstood variable, *Journal of Brand Management* 3, 5, 296–305.

Moss, G. (1996b), Assessment: Do males and females make judgements in a self-selecting fashion?, *Journal of Art and Design* 15, 2, 161–9.

Moss, G. (1999), Gender and consumer behaviour: Further explorations, *Journal of Brand Management* 7, 2, 88–100.

Moss, G. (2009), *Gender, Design and Marketing*, Gower: Surrey.

Moss, G. and Colman, A. (2001), *Journal of Brand Management* 9, 2, 89–99.

Moss, G. and Gunn, R. (2009), *Behaviour and Information Technology*, DOI: 10.1080/0144929080

Moss, G. and Gunn, R. (2009), Gender differences in website production and preference aesthetics: Preliminary implications for ICT in education and beyond, *Behaviour and Information Technology*, 28, 5, 1362–3001, First published 2009, Pages 447–460.

Moss, G., Daunton, L. and Gasper, R. (2006), The positive impact of selection criteria on leadership diversity: a comparison of two organizations, *European Academy of Management* 16-19 May, Oslo.

Moss, G. (2007), Psychology of performance and preference: Advantages, disadvantages, drivers and obstacles to the achievement of congruence, *Journal of Brand Management* 14, 4, 343–358.

Moss, G., Gunn, R. and Kubacki, K. (2008), Gender and web design: The implications of the mirroring principle for the services branding model, *Journal of Marketing Communications* 14, 1, 37–57.

Palmer, K. (2003), Tech companies try wooing women with girlie marketing, *The Wall Street Journal August*, 26.

Roberson, L., Kulik, C. and Pepper, M. (2001), Designing effective diversity training: Influence of group composition and trainee experience, *Journal of Organizational Behavior* 22, 871–85.

Robertson, M., Newell, S., Swan, J., Mathiassen, L. and Bjerknes, G. (2001), The issue of gender within computing: Reflections from the UK and Scandinavia, *Information Systems Journal* 11, 111–26.

Schneider, B. (1987), The people make the place, *Personnel Psychology* 40, 437–53.

Schneider, R. (2001), Variety performance, *People Management* 7, 9, 27–31.

Silverstein, M. and Fiske, N. (2003), *Trading Up: The New American Luxury*, New York: Portfolio Press.
Simon, J. and Peppas, S. (2005), Attitudes towards product website design: A study of the effects of gender, *Journal of Marketing Communications* 11, 2, 129–44.
Sparke, P. (1995), *As Long As It's Pink*, London: Pandora Press.
Stockdale, M. and Crosby, F. (2004), *The Psychology and Management of Workplace Diversity*, MA and Oxford: Blackwell Publishing.
Thelwall, M. (2000), Effective websites for small and medium-sized enterprises, *Journal of Small Business and Enterprise Development* 7, 150–9.
Thomas, R. (1996), *Redefining Diversity*, New York: AMACOM.
Van den Bosch, F. A. J. and de Man, A.-P. (1993), 'Towards a Conceptual Definition of Organizational Innovation: The Case of Strategic Alliances', *Management Report Series No 159*, Rotterdam School of Management, Erasmus University.
Van de Ven, A. H. (1992), Suggestions for studying strategy process: A research note, *Strategic Management Journal* 13, Special Summer issue, 169–88.
Vinnicombe, S. and Singh, V. (2002), Developing tomorrow's women business leaders, in Burke, R. and Nelson, D. (eds), *Advancing Women's Careers*, Oxford: Blackwell.
Vogler, C. and Pahl, J. (1993), Social and economic change and the organisation of money within marriage, *Work, Employment and Society* 7, 1, 71–95.
Wajcman, J. (2000), Feminism freeing industrial relations in Britain, *British Journal of Industrial Relations* 38, 2, 183–202.
Warner, F. (2006), *The Power of the Purse*, Pearson: Prentice Hall.
Windolf, P. (1986), Recruitment, selection and internal labour markets in Britain and Germany, *Organisational Studies* 7, 3, 235–54.
Yahomoto, M. and Lambert, D. R. (1994), The impact of product aesthetics on the evaluation of industrial products, *Journal of Product Innovation Management* 11, 309–24.

10
Obstacles to Greater Design Diversity: Gender and Webdesign Software

Gabor Horvath, Gloria Moss, Rod Gunn and Eszter Vass

Introduction

The last chapter explored some of the practical issues that stand in the way of achieving greater design diversity. This chapter will take this further by looking at the practical case of grocery websites, noticing how they fail to reflect the aesthetic diversity that would allow them to maximise their impact. In the second half, we will see how the majority of free webdesign software is similarly failing to deliver on diversity, and we suggest that at root is a male-dominated webdesign and Information Technology (IT) culture. We show here how this culture produces free webdesign software that is overwhelmingly masculine in its orientation.

Importance of the web

The basics of the Internet communication, web surfing and online shopping are the websites. The websites can serve a variety of functions, ranging from informing, persuading and reminding users (Anderson and Rubin, 1986) as well as sustaining traffic, that is, attracting the casual surfer to linger (Schenkman and Jonsson, 2000) and revisit the site (Joergensen and Blythe, 2003). Because there is huge and increasing number of websites on the Internet the competition for the user's attention as well as the shift to consumer-controlled interaction (Wedande *et al.*, 2001) created a need for websites to look for new ways to stay competitive, to draw users and increase revenue (Hoffmann and Krauss, 2004).

The search for the factors that may influence the usefulness, enjoyment and ease-of-use of the websites (Van der Heijden, 2003) and customer satisfaction (Van Iwaarden *et al.*, 2004) has led Human Computer Interaction (HCI) researchers to attempt to understand the elements (technical, visual and content) in webdesign that are valued (Schenkman and Jonsson, 2000) and those that currently produce a deficit between expectations and experience. Although there are many definitions of HCI (Shneiderman, 2003; Dix *et al.*, 2004), the one fairly extensively used is of a discipline concerned with the design, evaluation and implementation of interactive computing systems for human use and the study of major phenomena surrounding them (Hewett *et al.*, 2006).

Searching and identifying these factors could be a key element for the success of online businesses. Retailing research is driven by the notion that the physical form of a product is an important element in its design (Bloch, 1995) and that it creates certain effects in buyers (Kotler, 1973/74). As Yahomoto and Lambert (1994) found products which perceived as pleasurable are preferred and used more frequently than those not perceived as pleasurable (Jordan, 1998), leading to enhanced purchasing (Groppel, 1993; Donovan *et al.*, 1994) and readiness to pay premium prices (Hassenzahl, 2007).

It is important to understand the factors which determine whether webusers (potential buyers) remain on a website or not (Moss, *et al.*, 2006b). One of these factors is the aesthetics of the website (Schenkman and Jonsson, 2000). The aim of visual aesthetics is to forward the message to the user (Krauss, 2004). According to Zettl (1999) visual aesthetics, and the process of applying it, involves selecting elements and techniques that are most appropriate for shaping a message or content to make it as effective as possible, and that this message is influenced by its context therefore the context can change the way the message is received or interpreted. Therefore as Zettl (1999) stated the aim of visual aesthetics should be to support the message, but if the aesthetics used in the website design does not support the message the site may look beautiful but will loose the original function and will not be effective in the communication. In this situation the incorrect website design or misused aesthetics elements can be a disadvantageous (Krauss, 2004). Hoffmann and Krauss (2004) highlighted another important function of the visual aesthetics for the web. They stated that it can influence the decision-making process when the costumer wants to buy a product online. Zettl (1999) agrees with this opinion saying that visual aesthetics can influence the viewer's decision-making process. Heimlich and Wang (1999) went further claiming that aesthetics can be used to keep users on a website.

As Hassenzahl *et al.* (2008) highlighted 'industrial designers have long been concerned with the aesthetic qualities of their products, but appearance and the responses to appearance of software as an integral part of the user experience has only captured the imagination of human-computer interaction (HCI) researchers in the past few years' (p. 1). They have also argued that as the number of researchers who contribute to this research topic is increasing, it becomes clear that aesthetics does make a difference in HCI and that more research is needed on many fronts of this area.

Having a complete grasp of research relating to online visual aesthetics is difficult since, as Hoffmann and Krauss (2004) argue, there is a paucity of information on this topic. There has been a strong focus on usability issues (Tractinsky, 1997; Heimlich and Wang, 1999; Van der Heijden, 2003) with a relatively small number of authors (Haig and Whitfield, 2001) focusing on visual aesthetics (Miller and Arnold, 2000; Flanagin and Metzger, 2003; Moss *et al.*, 2006a; Moss and Gunn, 2009) focusing on visual aesthetics. The studies of usability tend to follow the universalist approach, seeking universal rather than segmented values, and as a consequence they have no information on website type or designer or the age, gender and so on of respondents. The studies of visual aesthetics, on the other hand, are interactionist in approach and seek to establish whether there is a connection or interaction between the website and the user. Many of the earlier interactionist studies of visual aesthetics have serious methodological flaws while the more recent studies (Moss *et al.*, 2006a, 2006b, 2006c; Horvath *et al.*, 2007) appear to avoid these methodological shortfalls.

Internet use and genders

As Sheehan and Bartel (1999) stated, the two genders use the web differently and Schlosser *et al.* (2006) noted that differences could be seen in the way male and female users perceived web advertising. The differences are such that Wolin and Korgaonkar (2005) said that further research on the reactions of men and women to web advertising was warranted.

The need for research on gender differences is particularly highlighted by the fact that young women (18–34 year old) is the most dominant constituency online in the UK (NetRatings, 2007), making up 18 per cent of the total Internet audience and using 21 per cent of all computer time. This strong presence of female computer users is particularly true in the household sector and an analysis of six studies

(Berning *et al.*, 2004) concluded that that the typical e-grocery consumer is female, 25 to 44 years old, has at least a college degree, household income between $50,000 and $100,000, and is likely to have children. The authors also argued that these consumers are also less price sensitive than in-store shoppers because they have high opportunity costs of their time and are more interested in convenience than price. A more recent survey confirms the dominance of female consumers online (STORES, 2007), finding that most of the top 10 online retailers in the US have majority-female customer bases. The case is similar in the UK with two-thirds of online grocery shoppers being female (Mediaweek survey, 2004).

Web aesthetics and gender differences

A recent study (Moss *et al.*, 2006a) reported on an interactionist approach to web aesthetics involving an analysis of 60 male and female-produced websites and found statistically significant differences between the male and female-produced websites on 13 out of the 23 factors analysed. These factors included the number of separate subject areas covered, the character of the language (men favouring formal and expert language, infrequent use of abbreviations), visual elements (men favouring the use of straight as opposed to rounded lines, and a conventional horizontal layout) and the character of the typography (men favour formal typography and a smaller number of typeface colours). The results of this study were sufficiently numerous and significant to be suggestive of a masculine/feminine design production aesthetic continuum. Recent studies (Moss and Gunn, 2007, 2009) added that women's preferences for websites produced using the female aesthetic is stronger than male preferences for websites produced using the male aesthetic. Extrapolating these results to male- and female-dominated markets, and building on the mirroring principle in marketing (Hammer, 1995; Karande *et al.*, 1997; De Chernatony *et al.*, 2004) suggest the need to create webdesigns modelled on the aesthetics of the target market. In this way, an industry operating in a male-dominated market would produce websites displaying the masculine aesthetic while a female-dominated market (for example the household sector) would produce websites displaying the feminine aesthetic.

Currently, there are only a limited number of studies examining the extent to which commercial websites reflect these expectations. The aim of the study reported here was to establish whether the websites of the largest UK food retailers contain an aesthetic that is tailored to the preferences of the target market, in other words largely women. This was the starting point for the study reported in the first part of this chapter. In the second part of the chapter, we analyse the visual aesthetic of free webdesign software.

Scoring criteria

In this study the authors followed the criteria worked out by Moss *et al.* (2006a). The characteristics investigated were (in brackets are the possible maximum scores):

Language

Expert language: Whether expert/technical language is used (2)
Abbreviations: Whether the language includes abbreviations (3)
Formal language: Whether the language used is formal or informal (2)

Visuals

Straight lines: Predominance of straight or rounded lines or a mixture of both (3)
Horizontal line: Appearance, or not, of a horizontal line in the layout (2)
Layout: Whether conventional or unconventional layout is used (2)
Typeface colour: Number of typeface colours used (4)
Text colour: Type of colours used in the typeface (3)
Typography: Whether typography is regular or irregular (3)
Font: Whether the fonts used are basic formal letter types or more informal ones (3)

When analysing the grocery website, the sites were rated against the above-mentioned criteria. Then, based on the scores given, individual index numbers were created for each criterion with 0 as the minimum score, 1 for the maximum score and intermediate values expressed as fractional values. Therefore in a case when the minimum score was 1 and the maximum was 4 a score of 1 received an index value of 0. A score of 2 received 0.33, a score of 3 received 0.66 and 4 received an index value of 1. This index marks a relative position on the masculine–feminine aesthetic scale, where 0 is the masculine end and 1 is the feminine end. It means that – for example – an index value of 1 shows that a given website has strongly feminine characteristics for the criteria examined.

The researchers also created an overall Gender Index which is based on the summarised scores for the previous elements. The index was calculated by adding the scores for the ten criteria group together and then deducting 10 from this sum. The authors decided not to weigh the scores despite having elements with different possible highest values (for example: abbreviations – highest score 2, type of colour – highest score 3, number of colours – highest score 4), because the high scoring components denoted even higher level of femininity. Since the aim of using this index was to highlight these differences, it seemed justified to use the values as they are.

Therefore a site which has the minimum scores (1 for all the criteria) for every element (showing high level of masculinity) received an index score of 0 (zero). If there was a home page with a complete set of feminine characteristics, it would receive a score '17'. The two ends of the 'Gender index' scale represent the two ends of the masculine–feminine aesthetic continuum (Moss *et al.*, 2006a) with the lowest score marking the masculine end and the highest score marking the feminine end of the continuum.

Results of the grocery websites analysis

It was found that most of the commercial websites analysed used mainly straight lines which typify masculine-type websites. Only three of the websites contained a mixture of straight and non straight lines (index score 0.5) and none of the websites analyzed were designed with a predominance of rounded lines, a feature typical of the female webdesign aesthetic (Figure 10.1).

As can be seen, the use of horizontal lines is a favourite among the supermarket websites, with only two of the websites missing this feature. Where the layout of the home pages is concerned, it can be seen that the bias towards the masculine characteristic is even higher there. There are no websites showing – even slightly – an unconventional layout.

The colour of typefaces (both the number of different colours and the colours used) is also a very important characteristic when analyzing and describing the gender of a website. The results of this study show that the generality (eight out of nine) of the grocery home pages are using a two-three colour scheme (index score 0.33) which is a typical masculine feature. There are no websites using only one colour. The reason for this is that the hyperlinks have traditionally different colours (mainly blue) from the normal text and all the websites start with at least two colours. However, most of them do not add more colours and only the

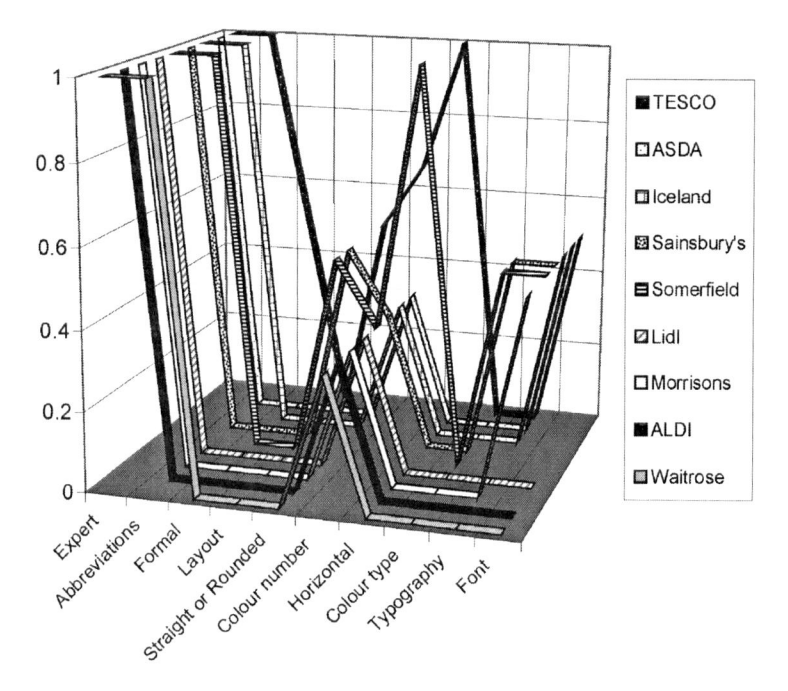

Figure 10.1 Gender characteristics of grocery websites

Tesco website uses more than four colours. Regarding the colours used in home pages, it would appear at first glance that none of them employ feminine colour schemes (all of them have a 0 index score). This means that the use of black or blue text is typical and none of the websites have pink or mauve typography. However, it is worth mentioning that for most of the websites, the use of a colour different from black or blue is restricted to white. Therefore, it is not necessarily the case that all of the websites featuring colours other than black and blue have feminine characteristic.

As regards typography, the study revealed also the overwhelming dominance of masculine design. Only two of the home pages feature informal/irregular typography. Most of the websites, however, feature informal font types together with formal ones.

Figure 10.2 shows that most of the grocery home pages are situated close to the masculine end of the masculine–feminine aesthetic continuum. Even the highest scoring sites – Somerfield and Tesco – are only halfway along on the scale. This shows that these websites do not mirror the preferences of the majority of their target market which, as we know from recent studies, consists largely of female customers. We know

178 Obstacles to Diversity Initiatives

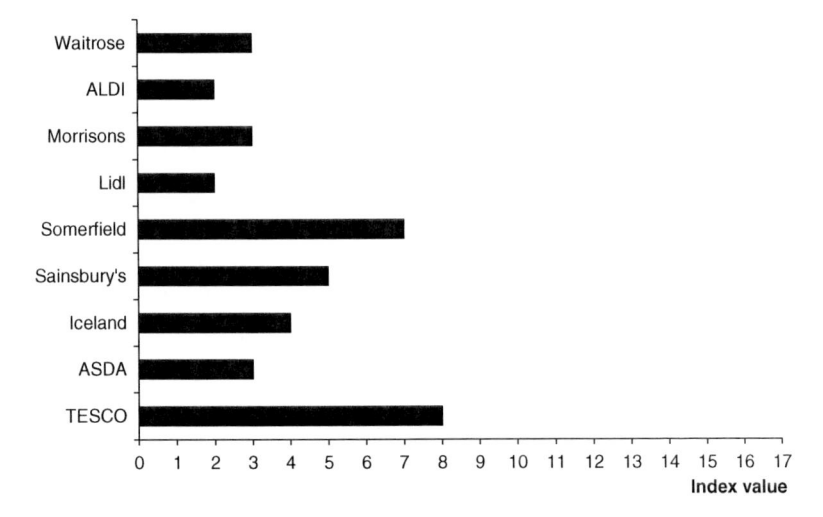

Figure 10.2 The Gender Index of grocery homepages

that the Information Technology and Webdesign industries are staffed predominantly by men (Moss *et al.*, 2008) and presumably the male majority in these industries have a preference for the masculine end of the aesthetic continuum. The aesthetic reflected in the grocery websites could therefore reflect the preferences of the webdesigners rather than those of online customers.

The results, taken with earlier studies showing the extent to which women prefer websites using the female production aesthetic over the male production aesthetic (Moss and Gunn, 2007, 2009), show that there is a room for improvement. Women's strong preference for websites produced using the female production aesthetic show that if any of these websites were redesigned to suit the preferences and expectations of female buyers, it would lead to higher customer satisfaction and therefore higher customer retention. Given the high level of competition in the grocery sector it could give them a certain advantage over their competitors.

This first study investigated the gender characteristics of websites of big commercial companies. They usually employ webdesigners who use sophisticated software to create the sites. If these large organisations cannot create websites mirroring the preferences of their target market, then what are the options for smaller companies? Could they create the optimal website with their limited skills? What is the reason for the low number of feminine websites? The second part of this chapter attempts to identify some answers.

Webdesign and gender

A recent study of Lavie and Tractinsky (2004) refers to the relative 'paucity of research' (p. 269) when summarising the work on webdesign aesthetics. Joergensen and Blythe (2003) adds that 'no principles of good www design...set in stone' (p. 48). The fact that some webdesign is perceived as less than optimum is demonstrated by the fact that the ten factors with the greatest deficit amongst Internet users in the US and Netherlands included a factor relating to graphics (Van Iwaarden *et al.*, 2004).

The design of websites of course can most easily be affected by Information Technology (IT) professionals and IT is a profession in which participation rates for women across the board have fluctuated during the 1990s somewhere between 19 per cent and 22 per cent (Robertson *et al.*, 2001). The position varies slightly in different parts of the world and in different IT sectors. Thus, in the US, the proportion of women among US computer professionals fell in the 1990s from 35.4 per cent to 29.1 per cent. In the UK in 1994, women made up 30 per cent of computer scientists, 32per cent of systems analysts, 35 per cent of computer programmers, 10 per cent of information system security directors, 18 per cent of project leaders and 14 per cent of applications development managers (Baroudi and Igbaria, 1994/95). The trend is downward. The 1980s saw an influx of women into IT, with a fourfold increase between 1980 and 1986 in the number of women awarded bachelor's degrees in computer science and a threefold increase in the number of women awarded master's degrees (Igbaria and Parasuraman, 1997). Since then, there has been a sharp decline in the number of women pursuing degrees in computer-related fields, together with a reduction in the numbers of women taking advanced-degree programmes (Igbaria and Parasuraman, 1997). The result is a male dominated profession, a point highlighted by figures from the Equal Opportunities Commission showing the horizontal and vertical segregation (Robertson *et al.*, 2001) present in the IT profession in the UK.

In terms of webdesign, there is a study examining the use of websites in small businesses (Thelwall, 2000) and also one examining the gender demographics of the industry (Moss and Gunn, 2005). This examination appears in the context of a study focused on Higher Education websites, revealing that the majority of websites in the sample of 32 websites under consideration were produced by a man or predominantly male team, with just 7 per cent produced by a female or predominantly female team, and just 19 per cent produced by an equal mixture of men and women (Moss and Gunn, 2005). This information, if representative of the website sector as a whole reveals a sector which, in parallel with the related IT sector (WWW-ICT, 2002), is male-dominated.

According to the research of Robertson *et al.* (2001) one of the effects of the male domination, vertically and horizontally, of the IT profession is the creation of a 'masculine computer culture' (p. 116) that produces a 'masculine discourse' (p. 116) and a prioritisation of technical issues, both of which serve to deter women from entering the field. The authors suggest that it is only by including a 'broader set of skills and discursive practices' (p. 124) that a more diverse group of people will be attracted into IT (including a critical mass of women) and that the masculine culture can be altered.

There are some studies dealing with the differences between sites originated by men and women (Moss and Gunn, 2005; Moss *et al.*, 2006a; Horvath *et al.*, 2007). However, these references are mainly related to the 'output', in other words analysing the final website. In the second part of this chapter the authors examine the input side of webdesigning, analysing nine different webdesigner softwares.

How to design a good website?

There are several webdesigner companies offering their services to the public. They can prepare and maintain professional websites but their services are relatively expensive, especially if one only needs a low cost/personal website. What can lower budget organisations do if they have just entered the world of WWW (without or with only a limited programming knowledge) and want to launch their own website? One possibility is for these organisations to create a website with the help of one of the web builder softwares and using their pre-programmed templates.

The authors analysed and rated a large number of randomly selected webdesigner softwares to ascertain whether, and to what extent, the templates they offer are positioned across the full spectrum of the web aesthetic design continuum. This continuum could be thought to contain at either extreme features that typify the masculine or feminine webdesign aesthetic and the aim of this study was to identify where on this continuum the templates associated with the softwares were positioned.

The hypothesis was that the aesthetic character of the majority of templates would be located at the masculine end of the continuum rather than across the range of the spectrum, a hypothesis based on the observation that a large proportion of commercial websites are anchored at the male end of the webdesign continuum (Moss and Gunn, 2005, 2009; Moss et al., 2006b). If this hypothesis is supported by the findings of this study, then one consequence might be difficulties in constructing a website with features more typical of the feminine end of the webdesign continuum. Given evidence of women's positive response to design anchored at the feminine end of the webdesign continuum, this could have negative consequences on companies' ability (especially of those on a limited budget) to mirror the aesthetic preferences of women. This would have a knock-on impact on the ability of these organisations to retain these women as customers.

Webdesign software

There are several examples of easy-to-use website builder software available through the Internet. The researchers selected the test softwares randomly from the www.tucows.com website, which is a good collection of such programmes and widely accessible. Although most of the software on this site was available only as trial versions with limited functions, a number of templates could be viewed. The authors also included Microsoft FrontPage in the study, because this is the software most Windows user has access to. The following is a list of the software tested:

1 Website Mentor Professional R1
(WRAPTECH LIMITED · DARK-STREET.CJB.NET)
This software allows the user to create a personal or business website. It includes 25 templates and is cross-browser compatible. It is also possible to add JavaScript and PHP functions to the web pages.

2 WYSIWYG Web Builder 2.7.2
(PABLO SOFTWARE SOLUTIONS · WWW.PABLOSOFTWARESOLUTIONS.COM)
The Web Builder 2.7.2 is a WYSIWYG (What-You-See-Is-What-You-Get) programme which means that the finished page will display exactly the way it was designed. The programme helps users to create a web page without their needing to learn HTML. Users can position objects anywhere they want and Web Builder gives them full control over the content and layout of their web page. The supporting website contains free downloadable templates for WYSIWYG Web Builder with which websites can be started.

3 TrendyFlash Website Builder 1.0
(TRENDYFLASH.COM · WWW.TRENDYFLASH.COM)

This programme allows users the means to create professional quality Flash Websites without Flash designing or programming knowledge. Users can add their own logo, JPG images and MP3 music; edit image size, image position and transparency; and modify text size and positioning. The trial version includes 29 themes covering different categories and 20 animated designs making 580 distinct Flash Website lay-outs possible.

4 IntroWizard Flash Website Builder 1.0
(INTRO WIZARD TECHNOLOGIES · WWW.INTROWIZARD.COM)

With this programme, users can make their own Flash Website by selecting a design, typing in their content and clicking 'Create'. They can select from 23 Flash Website template designs. They can add up to 13 sections or buttons with four images in each section. They can have 52 images in total and each section can have its own text colour. Users can also add a link to a Flash poll, chat box or guestbook.

5 Easy Website Pro 2.02
(PHOTONFX · WWW.PHOTONFX.NET)

This program helps to build home pages and publish them to the Internet. This version includes WYSIWYG (What-You-See-Is-What-You-Get) editor with MP3, MPEG and Flash support. It is possible to import pictures and create thumbnails in one click. It allows applying own logos, buttons, MP3s, videos, guest book and counter. There are 12 built-in templates to choose from.

6 A4Desk Flash Website and Menu Builder 5.45
(FAICO INFORMATION SOLUTIONS · WWW.A4DESK.COM)

This is template-based, WYSIWYG Flash site builder software. There are 169 templates to choose from, grouped in categories, such as Corporate and commerce, Family and so on. Users can create Flash menu headers and Flash Websites without Flash programming experience.

7 EZGenerator Website Builder 2.5.0.14
(IMAGE-LINE SOFTWARE · WWW.EZGENERATOR.COM)

This is a powerful programme which helps to create an entire website, including all navigation, artwork, buttons and sitemap. The users can include a blog, digital images and an online calendar and, using the

Newsletter Management system, create questionnaires. They can generate reports with the Flash Poll tool and can power their own website with an E-Commerce Web shop. The programme offers more than 2500 free web templates.

8 Namu6 – Website Editor 2

(NAMU6 LTD. · NAMU6.COM)

This very simplified programme allows you to create, maintain and publish a website.

9 Microsoft FrontPage 2002

(MICROSOFT – www.microsoft.com/office)

FrontPage is an award-winning web authoring tool programme that a number of people tend to regularly use to update their homepages, or sometimes to design full-blown sites.

The research method consisted of rating the templates (altogether 3682 templates were examined) from these website builder programmes against a number of different criteria based upon the earlier mentioned research of Moss *et al.* (2006c). Among their criteria were several which could be used only for the analysis of completed (with real content) websites; where templates were concerned, the criteria related to Navigation issues (e.g. How varied is the subject matter?) and Language (e.g. Denigration, Use of expert/technical language, Abbreviations, Seriousness/humour) could not be used.

The following five criteria, all related to visual elements, were applied to website templates:

Quality of shapes

Are straight lines dominant or there are rounded shapes as well?

Layout

Does it follow convention in having lines organised horizontally and vertically and text arranged within this?

Colour of typefaces

How many different coloured typefaces used throughout the site?

Text colours

What are the colours used?

Regularity of the typography
Is the typography formal or informal?
The scoring system (Table 10.1) used was as follows (high scoring components denote higher level of femininity):

Table 10.1 The scoring system

Criteria	Description	Score
Quality of shapes	Mainly straight	1
	Mixture	2
	Mainly rounded	3
Layout	Conventional layout	1
	Unconventional layout	2
Typeface colour	One colour	1
	2–3 colours	2
	4–6 colours	3
	7 + colours	4
Text colours	Mainly black or blue typography	1
	Some white, yellow, pink or mauve typography	2
	Mainly white, yellow, pink or mauve typography	3
Typography	Formal/regular typography	1
	Both	2
	Informal/irregular typography	3

Results: The analysis of the templates

The basic elements (quality of shapes, layout and typography) of the templates cannot (in most cases) be changed by the users and therefore they determine the final characteristics of the website that use them. In reporting on the results, they will be presented according to the features analysed.

Straight/rounded lines

The research found that most of the templates (84 per cent of total) used mainly straight lines, which typify the male production aesthetic with just 15 per cent of the templates using a mixture of straight and non straight lines (an example of a website with such a mixture is at www.bounty.com). Only 1 per cent of the templates analyzed were designed with a predominance of rounded lines, a feature linked to the

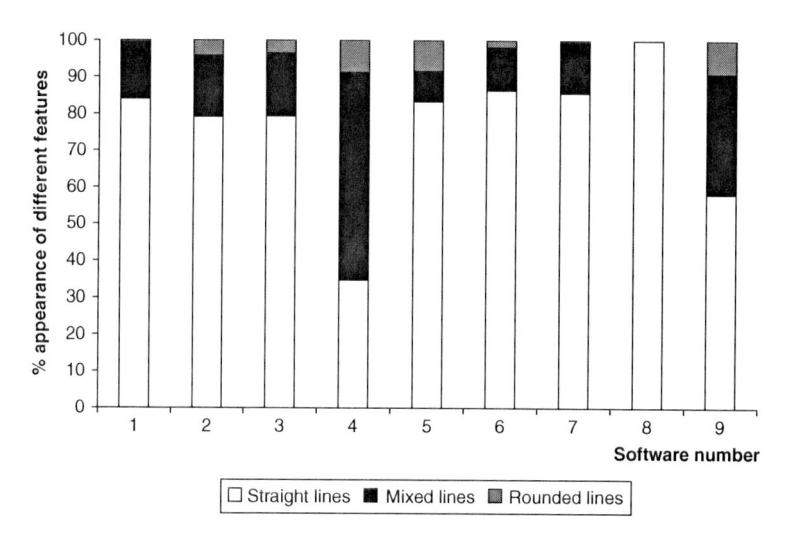

Figure 10.3 Shapes on the templates

female design production aesthetic. These results are shown in graphical form in Figure 10.3.

Layout of the templates

Looking at the figures relating to the layout of the templates, it can be seen that the bias towards the masculine characteristic is even higher there (Figure 10.4). There are only a very small proportion of templates (0.2 per cent of total) and only three out of eight programs which offer the possibility of creating websites with even a slightly unconventional layout.

The typeface colours

The colour of typefaces (both the number of different colours and the colours used) is a very important characteristic when analyzing and describing the gender of a website. However, the text colours used in templates are less important because they can be changed by the users in most cases. The reason why they are still included in this study is that the authors believe that the majority of users are likely to have limited programming skills and are therefore unlikely to change the colours of the templates.

The result of the study shows that the majority (99.6 per cent) of the templates are using two-three colours which is a typically masculine

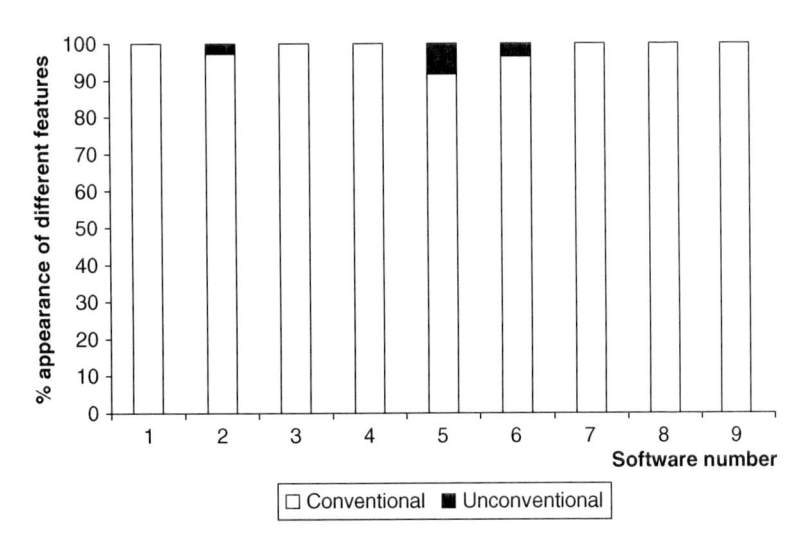

Figure 10.4 Layout of the templates

feature. One factor explaining why a lesser number of colours are not used is that the hyperlinks have traditionally different colours (mainly blue) from the normal text and this helps explain why all of the templates start with at least two colours. However, most of them do not add more colours and only 0.4 per cent of them offer more than four colours. These results are shown in Figure 10.5.

Regarding the colours used in templates, it would appear at first glance as though a number of templates employ feminine colour schemes (Figure 10.6). Although the use of mainly black and blue text is still typical (49 per cent), 45 per cent of the templates have some and 6 per cent of them have mainly white, yellow, pink or mauve typography.

However, it is worth mentioning that in the majority of templates, the use of colours other than black or blue is restricted to white so it is not necessarily the case that all of the templates featuring colours other than black and blue have feminine characteristic.

Style of typography

As for the typography there is an overwhelming dominance of masculine design. Only 0.2 per cent of the templates have informal/irregular typography and only three out of the programs offered such a template (see Figure 10.7).

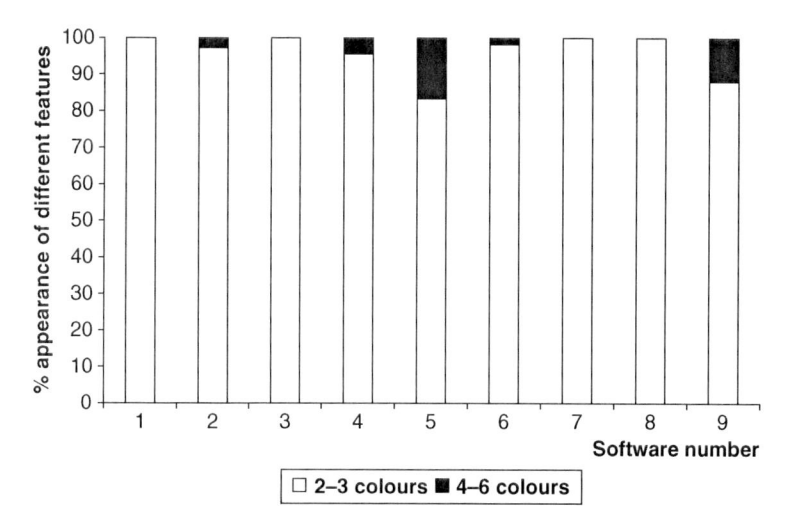

Figure 10.5 Number of different text colours used

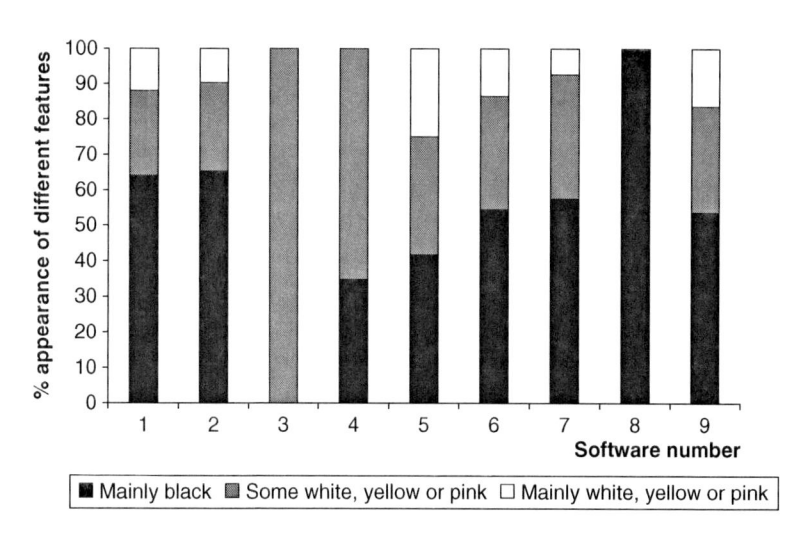

Figure 10.6 Types of different text colours used

In order to obtain a gender aesthetic index for any particular piece of software, a special index was created based on the ratio of templates bearing feminine or masculine characteristics within the software. This index was calculated by multiplying the relative frequency of each criterion by the weighting score given above. Then the values associated with

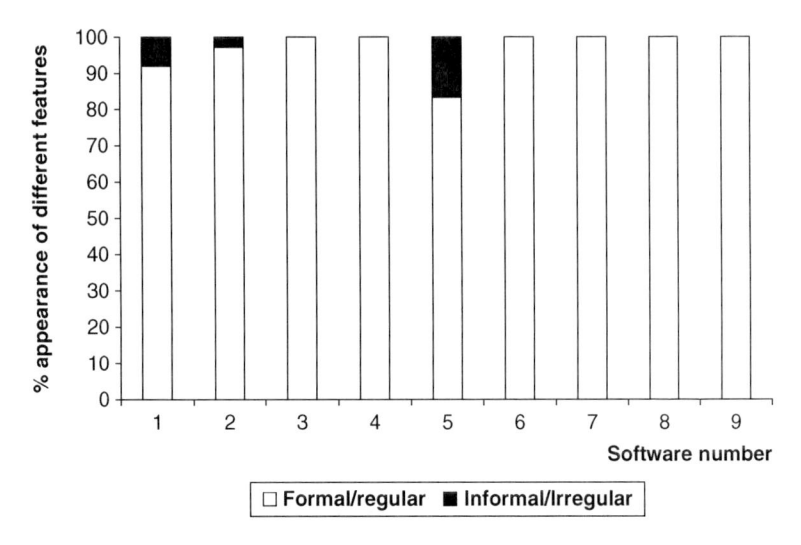

Figure 10.7 Typography of the templates

a particular criterion group (for example Quality of shapes, Layout and so on) were added together, producing a gender index for the templates sorted by visual features. Where this index approaches 1, the majority of the templates in the software examined are masculine in relation to the given criteria. Where the index approaches 2 (the maximum value), the majority of templates in a piece of software are feminine in character. However, as it can be seen there is no software programme that even approaches this value (Figure 10.8).

Figure 10.9 shows the summary of the indexes above. In this case, the value of the summarised indexes could be in the range of 5 to 10, with a score of 10 indicating software with exclusively feminine templates. We can see that software N.8 is a fully masculine programme showing no feminine features at all. This attracts the minimum score, namely 5.

Discussion

As mentioned earlier, there are a limited number of studies dealing with differences between sites originated by men and women. The focus here is on the 'output' aspects, namely the final website, with, some discussion of the input side in relation to the demographics of the webdesign and IT industries. There is no discussion in this earlier research on the

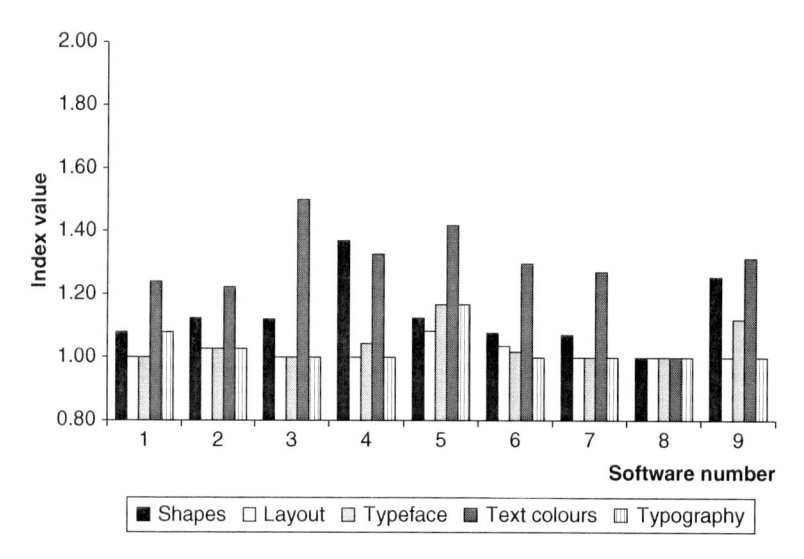

Figure 10.8 Visual gender index

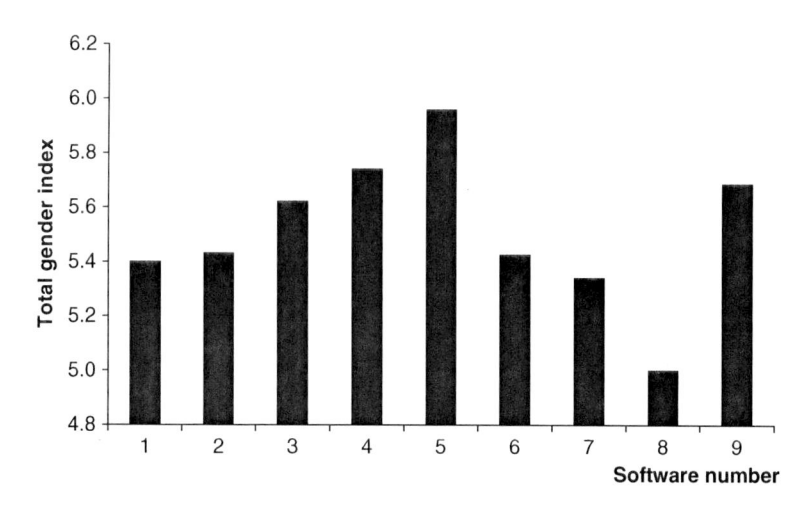

Figure 10.9 Index of gender – summary

webdesign software and the influence that this may have in relation to input. The data presented in this chapter helps fill this gap.

As we have seen, the authors conducted a thorough analysis of nine randomly selected examples of webdesigner softwares in order to establish whether, and to what extent, the templates they offer determine the final look of websites. The research revealed that most of the software offers templates that are typically masculine in their appearance. The use of these templates would make it very difficult to construct a feminine-looking website.

The results confirmed the initial hypothesis that there is a masculine hegemony within the webdesigner software, a not surprising result given the male dominance of the IT and webdesign industries (Moss et al., 2008; Moss and Gunn, 2009). Given that we know the efficacy of tools or messages can be maximised by ensuring that they contain features that mirror the preferences of the target market (the 'mirroring principle'), the fact that webdesign software is anchored largely in the male visual aesthetic is a limiting factor and one that will impede the production of websites anchored in the female visual aesthetic. To satisfy the mirroring principle would demand the availability of webdesign software anchored in both the male and female aesthetic paradigms. At the moment, this type of software is not freely available and this is an impediment, for many individuals and organisations, to the achievement of the mirroring principle. Whether it is this, or the male-dominated nature of the IT and webdesign industries that contributes to the masculine appearance of retailing websites, when research reveals that their target market would prefer more feminine websites, remains to be seen.

Meanwhile, the findings reported here document some of the obstacles to achieving greater diversity in diversity. The options for moving forward would include awareness training and from that, further training or recruitment of webdesigns who can mirror the visual preferences of the end-user. While these are not easy options, and may well encounter many organisational obstacles (see Chapter 10), they need to be tackled if the benefits of mirroring diverse aesthetic tastes is to be achieved.

References

Anderson, P. M. and Rubin, L. G. (1986) *Marketing Communications* (Englewood Cliffs, NJ: Prentice-Hall, Inc).

Baroudi, J. J. and Igbaria, M. (1994/95) 'An examination of gender effects on career success of information system employees', *Journal of Management Information Systems* 11, 3, 18–32.

Berning, C., Ernst, S. and Hooker, N. H. (2004) *E-Grocery: Who Is the Ideal Consumer?* (AED Economics, Ohio State University, AEDE-RP-0043-04).

Bloch, P. H. (1995) 'Seeking the ideal form: Product design and consumer response', *Journal of Marketing* 59, 16–29.

De Chernatony, L., Drury, S. and Segal-Horn, S. (2004) 'Identifying and sustaining services brands values', *Journal of Marketing Communications* 10, 73–94.

Dix, A., Finlay, J., Abowd, G. and Beale, R. (2004) *Human Computer Interaction* (Eaglewood Cliffs, NJ: Prentice Hall).

Donovan, R. J., Rossiter, J. R., Marcoolyn, G. and Nesdale, A. (1994) 'Store atmosphere and purchasing behaviour', *Journal of Retailing* 70, 3, 283–94.

Flanagin, A. and Metzger, M. (2003) 'The perceived credibility of personal web page information as influenced by the sex of the source', *Computers in Human Behaviour* 19, 6, 683–701.

Groppel, A. (1993) 'Store design and experience orientated consumers in retailing: Comparison between the United States and Germany', in Raaij, W. F. van and Bamossy, G. J. (eds), *European Advances in Consumer Research* 1, 99–109.

Haig, A. and Whitfield, T. W. A. (2001) *Predicting the Aesthetic Performance of Web Sites: What Attracts People?* (Australia: National School of Design, Swinburne University of Technology).

Hammer, M. (1995) *Reengineering the Corporation* (London: Nicholas Brealey Corporation).

Hassenzahl, M. (2007) 'Aesthetics in interactive products: Correlates and consequences of beauty', in Schifferstein, H. N. J. and Hekkert, P. (eds), *Product Experience* (Amsterdam: Elsevier).

Hassenzahl, M., Lindgaard, G. and Tractinsky, N. (2008) *The Study of Visual Aesthetics in Human-Computer Interaction* 13.07.08 – 16.07.08, Dagstuhl Seminar 08292, http://www.dagstuhl.de/en/program/calendar/semhp/?semnr=2008292.

Heimlich, J. E. and Wang, K. (1999) *Evaluating the Structure of Web Sites* (Environmental Education and Training Partnership, EETAP Resource Library, Ohio State University Extension).

Hewett, T. T., Baecker, R., Card, S., Carey, T., Gasen, J., Mantei, J., Perlman, G., Strong, G. and Verplank, W. (1996) *ACM SIGCHI Curricula for Human–Computer Interaction* [WWW document] 1996,. URL http://sigchi.org/cdg/cdg2.html#2_1 (accessed on 17 June 2006).

Hoffmann, R. and Krauss, K. (2004) 'A critical evaluation of literature on visual aesthetics for the web', *Proceedings of SAICSIT 2004*, 205–09.

Horvath, G., Gunn, R., Vass, E. and Moss, G. (2007) 'Gender and web design software', *Proceedings of the 4th International Conference on Cybernetics and Information Technologies, Systems and Applications: CITSA 2007* July 12–15, Orlando, Florida, USA. 48–53.

Igbaria, M. and Parasuraman, S. (1997) 'Status report on women and men in the IT workplace', *Information Systems Management* 14, 3, 44–54.

Joergensen, J. and Blythe, J. (2003) 'A guide to a more effective World Wide Web', *Journal of Marketing Communications* 9, 45–58.

Jordan, P. W. (1998) 'Human factors for pleasure in product use', *Applied Ergonomics* 29, 25–33.

Karande, K., Zinkhan, G. M. and Lum, A. B. (1997) 'Brand personality and self concept: A replication and extension', *American Marketing Association, Summer Conference*, 165–71.

Kotler, P. (1973/74) 'Atmospherics as a marketing tool', *Journal of Retailing* 49, Winter, 48–63.
Krauss, K. (2004) 'Visual aesthetics and its effect on communication intent: A theoretical study and website evaluation', *Proceedings of the Southern African Computer Lecturers Association* (SACLA).
Lavie, T. and Tractinsky, N. (2004) 'Assessing dimensions of perceived visual aesthetics of Web Sites', *Journal of Human-Computer Studies* 60, 269–98.
MediaWeek (2004) 'The guide to online grocery shoppers', *MediaWeek* December 8.
Miller, H. and Arnold, J. (2000) 'Gender and home pages', *Computers and Education* 34, 3–4, 335–9.
Moss, G. and Gunn, R. (2005) 'Websites and services branding: Implications of Universities websites for internal and external communications', *Critical Management Studies, 4th Critical Management Studies Conference* July, Cambridge.
Moss, G. and Gunn, R. (2007) 'Gender differences in website design: Implications for education' *Proceedings of the 4th International Conference on Cybernetics and Information Technologies, Systems and Applications: CITSA 2007* July 12–15, Orlando, Florida, USA, 35–40.
Moss, G. and Gunn, R. (2009) 'Gender differences in website production and preference aesthetics: Preliminary implications for ICT in education and beyond', *Behaviour and Information Technology*, DOI: 10.1080/0144929080.
Moss, G., Gunn, R. and Heller, J. (2006a) 'Some men like it black, some women like it pink: Consumer implications of differences in male and female website design', *Journal of Consumer Behaviour* 5, 328–41.
Moss, G., Gunn, R. and Kubacki, K. (2006b) 'Angling for Beauty: Commercial implications of an interactive aesthetic for web design', *International Journal of Consumer Studies* 30, 1–14.
Moss, G., Gunn, R. and Kubacki, K. (2006c) 'Optimising web site design in Europe: Gender implications from an interactionist perspective' *International Journal of Applied Marketing* 2, 1.
Moss, G., Gunn, R. and Kubacki, K. (2008) 'Gender and web design: The implications of the mirroring principle for the services branding model', *Journal of Marketing Communications* 14, 1, 37–57.
NetRatings (2007) 'Young women now the most dominant group online' *Nielsen//NetRatings*, NetView, UK, May 16.
Robertson, M., Newell, S., Swan, J., Mathiassen, L. and Bjerknes, G. (2001) 'The issue of gender within computing: Reflections from the UK and Scandinavia', *Information Systems Journal* 11, 111–26.
Schenkman, N. and Jonsson, F. (2000) 'Aesthetics and preferences of web pages', *Behaviour and Information Technology* 19, 5, 367–77.
Schlosser, A. E.,White, T. B. and Lloyd, S. M. (2006) 'Converting web site visitors into buyers: How web site investment increases consumer trusting beliefs and online purchase intentions', *Journal of Marketing* April, 70, 2, 133–48.
Sheehan, M. and Bartel, K. (1999) 'An investigation of gender differences in on-line privacy concerns and resultant behaviours', *Journal of Interactive Marketing* 13, 4, 24–38.
Shneiderman, B. (2003) *Leonardos Laptop: Human Needs and the New Computing Technologies* (Cambridge, MA: The MIT Press).

STORES (2007) 'Who's shopping where' *STORES Magazine* October 2007 http://www.stores.org/Current_Issue/2007/10/EditSidebar2.asp.
Thelwall, M. (2000) 'Effective websites for small and medium-sized enterprises' *Journal of Small Business and Enterprise Development* 7, 150–59.
Tractinsky, N. (1997) 'Aesthetics and apparent usability: Empirically assessing cultural and methodological issues' *In Proceedings of the SIGCHI conference on Human factors in computing systems*, Atlanta, Georgia, United States.
Van der Heijden, H. (2003) 'Factors influencing the usage of websites: The case of a generic portal in the Netherlands' *Information and Management* 40, 6, 541–49.
Van Iwaarden, J., van der Wiele, T., Ball, L. and Millen, R. (2004) 'Perceptions about the quality of web sites: A survey amongst students at Northeastern University and Erasmus University' *Information and Management* 41, 8, 947–59.
Wedande, G., Ralston, L. and t'Hul, S. van (2001) 'Consumer interaction in the virtual era: Some solutions from qualitative research' *Qualitative Market Research: An International Journal* 4, 3, 150–59.
Wolin, L. and Korgaonkar, P. (2005) 'Web advertising: Gender differences in beliefs, attitudes, and behavior' *Journal of Interactive Advertising* 6, 1, 125–36 (Fall 2005).
WWW-ICT. 'Widening women's work in information and communications technology' from the European programme in IST (2002–4). [WWW document]. URL http://www.ftu-namur.org/www-ict/.
Yahomoto, M. and Lambert, D. R. (1994) 'The impact of product aesthetics on the evaluation of industrial products' *Journal of Product Innovation Management* 11, 309–24.
Zettl, H. (1999) *Sight, Sound, Motion: Applied Media Aesthetics* (USA: Wadsworth Publishing Company).

11
Tackling Ageism in Employment: Age the Final Frontier of Discrimination?

David Farnham

Introduction

Ageism is discrimination or prejudice against people on the grounds of their age and can affect the young, middle-aged or elderly. Ageism like all discrimination against individuals or groups stereotypes people, as having certain characteristics, or behaviours, based solely on their date of birth. Discrimination on the grounds of age can take place between individuals, within and between groups, in organisations, in communities, and in society-at-large. An elderly person, for example, may typically stereotype younger persons as being 'immature', 'irresponsible' or 'reckless.' Similarly, a young person may typically stereotype older persons as being 'inflexible', 'old fashioned' or 'forgetful.' Age discrimination takes place in different economic and social milieux. For example, it can occur in the provision and supply of goods and services, access to public services, and at work. Some providers of goods and services, for example, discriminate against their customers on the grounds of age, such as in motor car insurance premiums for the young or health care insurance premiums for the elderly. Public services may discriminate against individuals or groups on the grounds of age too, such as in access to certain types of medical care and treatment for health conditions. Also, when taking employment decisions, employers may discriminate against individuals or groups on the grounds of age in recruitment and selection, payment, promotion, the provision of training, selection for redundancy and so on.

This chapter focuses on age discrimination in employment and its relationship to the diversity agenda. The chapter has four aims. First, it outlines how the equal opportunities and diversity agenda have emerged in regulating employment and people management in the United Kingdom (UK). Second, it examines some of the issues reinforcing ageism in employment and the workplace. Third, it outlines the steps being taken in the UK, including legislation, to challenge ageism in the world of work. Fourth, it concludes by taking a wider perspective and provides a framework for combating ageism and developing age-related management strategies at work, based on the assumption that a multiplicity of parties has common interests in tackling age discrimination. The underpinning concern is that ageism in employment is not only socially unjust but also counterproductive economically. It is not beneficial to employers, employees or the wider community, where there are on the supply-side skills shortages and missing skills sets in the labour market and on the demand-side an ageing population in the UK and throughout the developed world.

Promoting equal opportunities and managing diversity

Challenging discrimination in employment on the grounds of age is only one element in promoting equality and diversity at work. This 'final frontier' of possible discrimination, 'ageism' and the promotion of equality of opportunity for individuals or groups and managing diversity through acknowledging the value of differences amongst individuals irrespective of their age, derives out of the wider societal movement that has aimed to eliminate social exclusion and advance human rights in the social and employment arenas since the 1970s. The original aim of this social movement was to further equal opportunities or equality of opportunity (equal 'rights' to disadvantaged groups) and remove discriminatory behaviours against individuals and groups within communities, organisations and government, where prejudice was shown towards them by others who were different from themselves. Governments have addressed the issue through legal, social and fiscal policies; organisations through the introduction of equality and diversity policies and practices; and individuals by asserting their legal rights to be treated equally and fairly in a changing society.

In organisations, the emphasis now is on managing diversity (or valuing differences amongst people) rather than on equal opportunities. In the area of employment, managerial focus is to harness the advantages to be gained from employing a diverse workforce through maximising the achievements of *all* employees, not just those covered by anti-discrimination legislation. The Chartered Institute of Personnel and Development (CIPD 2005a), the professional body for HR specialists, defines diversity as valuing everyone as individuals – whether as employees, customers or clients. In the world of work, managing diversity recognises the value of all employees in an organisation. The scope of diversity includes colour, ethnicity, disability, economic status, family/marital status, nationality, religious beliefs, sexual orientation, spent convictions, part-time working, political opinion/affiliation, gender re-assignment and age, which is the subject of this review.

In the field of work and employment, non-discriminatory employment practices against individuals or particular social groups are based on recognising the fact that certain people and groups experience disadvantage and inequality in the wider labour market and the workplace. Equality and diversity policies seek to eliminate these disadvantages by providing a level playing field for individuals. At organisational level, equality and diversity are about eliminating unlawful discrimination against people and introducing measures to remove the effects of any earlier disadvantages they might have had, drawing upon appropriate measures to do so. An employer's good practice model typically suggests that a systematic process of policy formulation, audit of existing provisions, action planning and implementation, and monitoring and policy review is the pathway to effective equal opportunity and diversity initiatives.

The primary vehicle at governmental level for promoting equality and diversity is anti-discrimination legislation, with age becoming what might be called, the 'final frontier' of anti-discriminatory law. This follows the Employment Equality (Age) Regulations (EEAR) 2006, which came into force on 1 October 2006. These are the final strand in the EU Framework Directive on Equal Treatment in Employment and Occupations being implemented in the UK. This Directive committed EU member states to legislate on disability, religion and belief, sexual orientation, and age.

The essential arguments for promoting equality and diversity in employment are social justice for individuals, penalty avoidance by employers and human capital optimisation for society. The general business case as promoted by the CIPD (2007), for example, is based on cost, where it has been estimated that age discrimination in the UK economy costs between £19 billion and £31 billion per year in lost output. The business case also argues that to be successful in an increasingly competitive market place, organisations need to attract and retain valuable employees and develop their talents. Another business argument stresses the value of employing people who mirror the needs and preferences of their customers, ranging from young to older people. Some key points against accepting ageist attitudes and age stereotyping in organisations, especially regarding older workers, are that more people are living longer active and healthier lives. Average life expectancy was 63 for men and 68 for women in 1945, rising to 77 for men and 81 for women in 2008. Between 1997 and 2021, it is estimated that the proportion of over-50s in the UK will have increased from a third to 40 per cent (Office for National Statistics 2008). Older people stay in their jobs longer than younger people, differences in absenteeism between age groups are slight, and many studies demonstrate that younger and older workers are, on average, equally effective in their work. Given the right training, older people are just as capable of learning new skills as younger ones. Another strong argument against age discrimination is that it leads to under-achievement, reduced self-confidence, poor motivation, lower self esteem, diminished personal income and loss of status for individuals subjected to it.

For businesses and public bodies, the business case for promoting equality and diversity is in terms of the benefits accruing to organisations as a whole, rather than how this might enhance the lives of workers. These benefits include improving customer satisfaction and facilitating deeper market penetration for organisations by employing diverse workforces. Another benefit is having a workforce whose composition is similar to that of the local population and being able to draw upon the skills of a diverse range of workers. This can improve the supply of labour to organisations, because organisations are seen as being 'good' employers, as well as enhancing worker motivation. Another benefit for organisations is avoiding costly discrimination cases, by adopting systematic and professional HR practices in selecting, reviewing performance and promoting staff. Promoting diversity as the main avenue for addressing equal opportunities issues at work, with the recognition that people from different backgrounds bring fresh ideas and perceptions to their work roles, not only makes the way work is done more efficient but also improves the products and services provided to customers and clients.

There are benefits to employees in promoting equality and diversity too. These include preventing ageism at work across all age groups and providing opportunities for flexible employment. Whilst people over 55 are twice as likely to suffer ageism as any other form of discrimination, younger workers are amongst the most vulnerable group at work. They often have less understanding of their basic employment rights and are less likely to recognise mistreatment than are older workers. Another is giving better information and guidance to people, so that they can re-skill and plan for their later careers and retirement. Providing learning opportunities for older people means that they can stay in work longer if they choose to. And linking with the 'age positive campaign' by government can help change employer attitudes to age and ageism at work.

The benefits for society of promoting equality and diversity at work, resulting in a more diverse workforce, include spreading the tax base, increasing employment opportunities, and increasing consumption choices. It also helps older people work longer, thus maintaining their standards of living.

Ageism at work

If the objective of the EEAR 2006 is to remove, or at least diminish, ageism at work, a fundamental obstacle working against this, as identified by the Employers' Forum on Age (EFA 2005), is the difficulty in defining precisely the nature of ageism. The EFA is an independent network of leading UK employers, who recognise the need to attract and retain valuable employees, whatever their age. Surprisingly, the main findings of a survey carried out by the EFA in 2005, and by other surveys, show that there is no consensus on what actually constitutes ageism. What was clear in this EFA survey and other surveys was that where individuals were at a disadvantage because of their age, they did not necessarily view certain practices or behaviours as discriminatory. This applied particularly to older respondents who had a sense of older people having earned advantages through time-serving in the workplace. This degree of self-interest makes it difficult for employers to keep everyone happy, as they implement changes to policies and behaviours to comply with age legislation. In general, the EFA found that people of different ages are affected by discrimination in differing ways, with younger people being particularly sensitive to different pay scales at different ages and older people being less likely to consider this discriminatory. Middle-aged people, in turn, had their own entrenched ideas about age and seniority.

To attempt to remove ageism in the workplace is to encounter a series of obstacles, some of which are outlined below. Re-writing all policies to remove age discrimination is necessary to comply with age legislation but this is not sufficient to safeguard employers from challenges of ageism. There needs to be a fundamental shift in everyone's perception of age and where the boundaries of acceptable behaviour are. Affecting culture change is possibly where the real challenge lies. This presents significant difficulties for employers charged with training employees and managers to avoid discriminatory behaviours. Two issues seem to be of particular importance to employers. First, employees do not really understand that the recent age law requires a complete rethink on attitudes towards age in employment. Second, most older people seem to be reasonably well informed about the age legislation rules, whereas younger people may well challenge policies, particularly on pay, that have traditionally favoured older people. Thus overcoming ageism may necessitate changes in attitude as well as conformity to the law. A key group in the workplace would appear to be middle-aged managers, since it is this group that recruits, manages, promotes and reviews employees and managers.

According to the EFA, age is a difficult strand in the equality agenda. In many cases, age is used as a measure of someone's experience but also to measure ability, maturity and potential. Unlike other strands of discrimination, there are sometimes good reasons for using age as a discriminator. But in reality it is rarely necessary to use age, and not other factors, such as competence or ability, to make employment decisions. The EFA gave respondents to one of its surveys a number of ageist scenarios. The figures shown in brackets below were the percentage of people who considered the notions described as ageist, representing between a third and two-fifths of all responses in each case:

- paying an older person more than a younger person irrespective of experience (33 per cent agreed)
- managing people differently depending on their age (targets enforced less or more aggressively) (36 per cent agreed)
- not employing or keeping someone on because their appearance doesn't match the firm's image (39 per cent agreed)
- employing someone of a similar age to one's colleagues to ensure a 'good' team fit (40 per cent agreed)
- assuming the oldest person in a meeting is the most 'senior' (39 per cent agreed).

The above examples of ageist attitudes could put employers at risk of tribunal claims. However, they are common behaviours which have been accepted practice in organisations for many years. For many people, ageist attitudes are in-built and age stereotyping and age discrimination are institutionalised. One of the biggest challenges for employers is that individuals cannot agree on what is or what is not age discrimination.

What is obvious discrimination to one person is fair and reasonable to another.

Further, the legal definition of age discrimination is very broad and anyone can be both a victim and a perpetrator of it. Ageism is a very personal thing, with people tolerating different levels of ageist banter, for example. This creates difficulties for employers to know where to draw the line. This raises fundamental questions, such as do all assumptions based on someone's age need to be re-evaluated? Are they fair and reasonable or simply ageist? In the above survey, of the 40 per cent of respondents who thought it was 'fair' to employ people of similar ages to ensure 'team fit', 60 per cent knew that this was unfair.

One of the most important findings of this EFA study and others was that age made a difference to the perception of age discrimination. Older respondents, for example, tended to have a greater awareness of age legislation. This probably reflects the media's focus on how legislation affects older people. Thus three-quarters of 55–64 year olds were aware of age discrimination legislation, compared with two-fifths of 16–24 year olds. However, whilst two-fifths of 55–64 year olds did not believe it to be discriminatory to pay an older person more because of their age, almost three-quarters of 16–24 year olds did. It would also appear that it is necessary to challenge the assumptions of middle-aged managers about age, since this is the group that recruits, manages, promotes and reviews employees.

A second factor giving rise to ageism at work is that there may be common perceptions regarding the relative speed, efficiency, reliability and flexibility of people of different ages. There may be a belief that these decline with the passing of time. In fact, these general perceptions need to take account of the facts, first, that people do not react in a homogeneous way to the biology of ageing. One has only to compare the performance of octogenarian musicians, such as Karajan and Rubinstein, for example, or artists such as Picasso, with people of the same age in a residential home for the elderly to see the truth of this. Second, social factors impact on the way people work. It has been found that the difficulties of employment sometimes experienced by older people can make them work harder than younger people. Lack of family commitments can also increase reliability of attendance at work amongst older workers.

Third, and related to the above, there is an individualistic culture in the UK that celebrates youth as against older age. It has been said that an individualistic culture, such as that of the UK or of the United States, is one that places a higher premium on youth than a collectivist culture does, such as in Japan – although under the pressures of westernising influences even Japan is changing. A collectivist culture is one that often includes older family members as an essential part of the collective group, with younger members of the group working actively to ensure the well-being and approval of these older members. This situation contrasts with that in many individualistic cultures where older family members are frequently disassociated from the family group by being removed to care homes in old age. The premium on youth brought about by an individualistic culture is likely to impact on attitudes both at work and in society as a whole.

Fourth, there are also economic incentives to employing younger people in some cases, because younger people, with less experience, can be recruited into lower points on a pay scale. In the public sector with a strong trade union presence, where criteria for appointment at different points of the pay scale are well-established, incentives to appoint younger people may be higher than in the private sector, where decisions on pay may be more fluid.

Fifth, there is the impact of what the EFA calls the 'servicescape' on employment decisions. This means that employees are frequently viewed as being an adjunct to the product or service being provided in the market place and that they need to blend in to the 'brand image' associated with what is being sold to customers. Many individual variables, such as gender, race, sexuality or age, or indeed a combination of these, are likely to be seen as 'in tune' or 'out of tune' with the brand image of the product. Thus fast food providers, for example, setting a premium on speed of delivery, seldom employ older workers. B & Q the do-it-yourself suppliers, on the other hand, although selling products to a young or middle-age market, have broken free from the imperatives of the servicescape by employing older people. There is also the perceived sexuality of women, which can be an additional factor in ageism. Are recruiters plainly oblivious to a woman's physical attractions? There are many anecdotes about women working in the media, public relations or fashion modelling, for example, who comment that when they reach middle age that their male managers or clients are no longer so keen to work with them or employ them. The same may be true of the employment of female airline stewards; but not of male airline pilots.

The legal framework

Since 1 October 2006, age discrimination in employment has been unlawful. In outline, under the EEAR employers must pay due regard to the law when people join them, when people are employed by them, and when people leave them (Employers Forum on Age 2006). Guidance from the Age Partnership Group (2005), funded and co-ordinated by the Department for Work and Pensions, shows that the new Regulations governing age discrimination are complicated. The Regulations cover people of all ages, both old and young, and relate to employment and providers of vocational training, including access to help and guidance, recruitment, development, termination, pay and perks. They also apply to trade unions, professional associations, employers' organisations and trustees, and managers of occupational pension schemes. Provision of goods, services and facilities, however, are *not* included in the Regulations. The main legal provisions of the Regulations are:

- the upper age limits for unfair dismissal and redundancy no longer apply
- a national default retirement age of 65 has been introduced, making compulsory retirement below 65 unlawful, unless objectively justified; this default retirement age is not due to be reviewed until 2011, to consider whether it is still necessary to maintain a retirement age or any at all
- all employees have the right to request to work beyond the retirement default age of 65 (or any other justified retirement age set by the organisation); employers must give advance notice of an approaching planned retirement date; and employers must follow the 'duty to consider' procedure to address these requests.

Heyday, the membership arm of Age Concern whose mission is to promote the well being of older people, challenged the compulsory default retirement age of 65 and the case went to the European Court of Justice (ECJ). In September 2008, the Advocate General of the ECJ found against the challenge. He ruled that the compulsory retirement age for employees aged 65 and over can in principle be justified in the context of national law. It was judged that a legitimate aim relating to employment policy and the labour market could be an objective and reasonable justification for the law. However, he also confirmed that the EU Directive requires the national default age to be justified by the British courts. An Advocate General's legal opinion is not legally binding but is taken into account by the ECJ in making its decisions. This decision was confirmed by the ECJ and the case returned to the High Court in September 2009, which upheld the law allowing UK employers to force employees retire at the age of 65.

Mr Justice Blake said that although he was ruling against the charities, the decision might have been different if the legislation had been introduced in 2009 rather than in 2006. The judge made it clear that forcing people to retire at 65 was unsustainable and needed reviewing. He added that if the government had not already ordered an examination and review of the issue, then he would have forced its hand. "I cannot presently see how 65 could remain as a DRA (Default Retirement Age) after the review" (http://news.bbc.co.uk, accessed 25 September 2009). Although Age Concern claimed the decision could leave some workers in financial difficulties, it decided not to appeal against the decision. It was heartened by the comments of the judge in the case and the fact that government had brought forward its review of the legislation to 2010.

Other provisions of the age Regulations include:

- occupational pensions are covered, as are employer contributions to personal pensions; but the Regulations allow pension schemes to work as they do now, and they do not affect state pensions
- both direct and indirect discrimination can be justified if the treatment or provision, criterion or practice in question is a proportionate means of achieving a legitimate aim
- length of service requirements for employment benefits practices of five years or less enjoy a special exemption and are deemed not to be unlawful age discrimination
- length of service requirements for employment benefits practices of longer than five years may also be justifiable, if the employer can show that they have awarded the benefit to reward loyalty, encourage motivation or recognise the experience of the worker.

When people join organisations, direct use of age limits is unlawful; indirect ageism, or where people of a particular age group are disadvantaged, is also unlawful. But the law allows employers to refuse to recruit people within six months of their retirement age or 65 if they do not have one.

For those employed in organisations, age harassment and victimisation are unlawful and are never justified. It is also unlawful to unjustifiably exclude a person from training on grounds of age. Similarly, pay and benefits based on age are unlawful, unless justified. Employers can pay as per national minimum wage bands and scales but no more, unless justified. Also, most but not all age related elements of occupational pensions are exempt.

When people leave organisations, as indicated earlier, the national default retirement age allows employers to compulsory retire people at 65 without justification, with employers having to objectively justify a retirement age below 65. Irrespective of whether employers set a retirement age below 65, at 65, or above 65, employers have to follow the retirement process. Individuals have a right to request to stay on beyond retirement age, and employers have a duty to consider that request. Selection for redundancy on the grounds of age or service is unlawful, unless objectively justified.

The statutory redundancy payment scheme remains in place. Only enhanced redundancy compensation schemes are automatically unlawful.

Combating ageism and developing age-related management strategies at work

It is now an oft-stated truism that over the next 50 years, as life expectancy increases and the birth rate remains low, the population over 60 will grow, both absolutely and relatively, in not only the UK but also throughout the developed world. With many people in this age group being healthier and wealthier than in the past, governments, employers (whether businesses or public organisations), trade unions and professional bodies, younger workers, the older individuals themselves, and society-at-large face challenges, arising out of these fundamental demographic and social changes. One challenge is for older people to continue to play active roles in their communities, including in employment and the world of work. The stark fact is that future age projections suggest that pensioners will outnumber children and, for most people, a third of their life will be lived post-50 years of age. Strategies for combating ageism affecting both the older population and younger adults are an immediate issue. These have the potential to be combined with the generation of positive age-related management strategies at work in the medium term. Values of active independence, quality of life and personal choice for working people, integrated with the search for efficient and humanised work organisations, can all be incorporated into these strategies, to the benefit of all age groups and the employers promoting them.

The challenges for employers, governments and workers

Most directly, the challenges and opportunities of an ageing population will affect all employers and organisations. They will have different customer bases and prospects for new markets but they will also have to accept that the workforce is changing and this must prompt new thinking about recruitment, job design, HR policies, employer responsibilities, working arrangements and managing retirement. Older people will be key players in their firms' successes. Employers have a key role to play in enabling society adjust to a new balance of life, where ageism will have to be discarded and the interests of the old and young integrated in workplaces. As the Vice-President for Rewards at Shell is reported as saying (CIPD 2008, p. 6):

> As a general rule, the company believes that having the right staff with the right skills at the right time is critical. The older worker phenomenon is of critical importance to Shell as the more experienced workers have a huge amount of expertise and many are reaching retirement age. Shell is a highly technical organisation. Many of the more experienced workers have a great deal of tacit knowledge that is very important to Shell. The company also realises that if we don't retain skilled individuals ourselves, they may end up working for a competitor.

Governments, in turn, will have to try and change attitudes and preconceptions about what an ageing society means. This will mean stimulating innovative ideas and technology to transform older people's lives. They will also have to rethink policies and approaches to public services, fostering independence and choice for older citizens and helping them improve their quality of lives. Governments will need to explode the myth that ageing is a barrier to positive contributions to the economy and society through work and active engagement in the community.

One of government's recent targets through its Age Positive campaign is to get a million older workers into work, over and above the million already working. This will enable the ratio of workers to non-workers in the economy to remain about the same in 2050, as it is now. People living longer, fitter lives means that government will have to make it easier for people to remain in employment and extend their working lives. Government aims to give workers new and attractive options to work longer when they want to such as part-time work, deferring the state pension, and re-skilling people. Government is also helping inactive and unemployed people over 50 into jobs and tackling the barriers the unemployed face getting back to work. Although critics would say that government is not doing enough, such as by having a default retirement age as outlined above, it is trying to tackle age discrimination in employment and vocational training. It has outlawed unjustified mandatory retirement ages below 65, employees have the right to request continuation of employment after 65, and it will review this in 2011, five years after implementation.

Everyone working or seeking employment will also have to shed outdated stereotypes and change mindsets about work, retirement and the process of getting older. Individuals themselves, all of whom will age, will need to take personal responsibility for planning and providing for a life course that is better than for previous generations. According to a former postal worker who had retired from the Post Office after 35 years of service, and who is now employed by Scotguide (Trades Union Congress TUC/CIPD 2007, p. 11):

> Employment isn't only about money. While the idea of retirement – no more work and time to pursue long-desired pastimes and hobbies – may seem wonderful, the reality for many turns out to be different... Changing social trends and economic realities mean that working can also be a necessity for many people if they are to avoid falling into poverty in later life. Remaining economically active should be seen as one way of maintaining a healthy and happy lifestyle.

What then do older workers want from their employers? From the case study material collected by the CIPD (2008, p. 9), the message to employers was 'that the needs of workers near to or beyond normal retirement may be different' from other workers. Pay and financial benefits may not be their only priority. In Molton Brown a London-based cosmetics company, opened in 1973, for example, it was reported that what older workers looked for included more flexible working arrangements, opportunity to use existing skills and experience, a worthwhile job, flexible leave arrangements, financial benefits they valued, and a participative, friendly culture. In the case study organisations examined, the CIPD concluded that there were 'very few organisations who have examined their current total rewards approach in the light of an ageing workforce. Most have simply taken a compliance approach with regard to the age legislation.'

A strategic response to combating ageism and attitudes towards ageing begins with employment, since it is with paid work that most people build the resources to lead a good life later on. Business productivity, and provision of public services, will increasingly depend on employers supporting the recruitment, retention and training of older workers, including offering more flexible opportunities for work and retirement. Although one-in-four people has experienced age discrimination when working or looking for work, there are proven benefits of an age-diverse workforce Businesses who are positive about age report: improved rates for keeping staff; higher staff morale; fewer short-term absences; higher productivity; better public image; wider range of skills and experience; and access to wider customer bases.

On the assumption that age discrimination is bad for business, is unfair, wastes talent, and is illegal, there are, in the short-term, some basic tasks for employers to respond to, if they are to combat ageism at work. For example, employers need to comply with the new legislation by checking that their employment policies and procedures are in line with the new requirements. Some larger employers such as ASDA, Barclays Bank, B&Q, GlaxoSmithKline, Nationwide and some public-sector employers are examples of promoting 'good practice' and they have adopted appropriate policies attracting older workers. Nationwide, for example, has a default retirement age of 75. Each stage in the employment cycle needs to be examined, since age discrimination can occur throughout any stage in an employee's working life. Everyone involved in employment decisions, managing people and learning and development need to understand the implications of age-stereotyping.

Developing proactive HR strategies

In recruitment and selection, for example, age, age-related criteria and age ranges should not be used in job advertisements, other than to encourage applications from age groups that do not normally apply for jobs. In advertising jobs, for example, employers need to remove all age limits, offer flexible working practices to attract older and younger workers, and create links with their communities to reach particular age groups. Employers also need to pay some attention to their brands, as employers, and promote their images as welcoming applications from all ages. ASDA, for example, has developed the brand of being a community business, so it is important for its employees to be representative of their communities (CIPD 2007). Other considerations to be taken into account are whether the date of birth and other indicators of age, such as the dates of qualifications and work experience are necessary on application forms. Alternatively, the dates can be removed from CVs before passing them on to the people doing the assessing. Similarly, asking for particular types of experience, rather than length of experience, in the person specification is good practice. It is also suggested that putting in place systems by which the performance of recruitment agencies on attracting age-diverse applicants can be monitored, by ensuring that the success of their contracts will be partly measured by this.

Nor should age criteria be taken into account in making employment decisions. Interviewers must not be subjective on the basis of physical characteristics and must ensure their decisions are based on objective criteria, relative to the job and merit. An individual's age should not be used to make judgements about people's abilities or fitness. Where a judgement is needed medical advice needs to be sought. To obviate age bias in making selection decisions, employers can use objective, criteria-based assessment and selection techniques. Those doing the initial screenings should not be given the applicants' ages, electronic screening can be used for first-stage screening, and telephone interviews may be used to remove age from the selection equation. In Marks and Spencer, for example, selection is based purely on talent screening; age is not a factor in this. Individuals apply on line, where age is not a factor at this stage. For those who are successful, they are then screened using on line talent screening. These tests assess the skills and experience against that required for the role being applied for.

Terms and conditions of employment, in turn, should not be based on age but reflect the value of the individual's contribution and standard of job performance. One research report recommends that employers examine the ways in which employers use their 'total rewards package' – or parts of it – to manage, reward and retain an ageing workforce (CIPD 2008). Experience suggests that they need to do this holistically to find out how their offerings meet the different needs of employees of all ages. This means understanding what these needs and preferences are, and aligning their total reward packages to them. Mercer Consulting categorises total reward as pay, benefits and careers. Pay includes base pay, short-term incentives, long-term incentives, and recognition. Benefits cover health and group benefits, work-life programmes, perquisites, and retirement. And careers incorporate learning and development, lateral career movement, 'stretch' assignments, and career incentives. The Hay Group model of total reward is more complex but is similar in content. Its six points of reference are inspirational values, quality of work, tangible rewards, work-life balance, an enabling environment, and future growth and opportunities. The principle of viewing a range of financial and non-financial factors as parts of the reward package appears to be the key issue.

A public sector case study organisation, Hertfordshire County Council, with about 30,000 employees, had taken a distinctive approach to managing an ageing workforce and was reported as employing a high proportion of older workers, which allowed the authority to address certain skills shortages, such as in social work and engineering, as well as reducing absenteeism. The Council's diversity strategy covered all aspects including age and consisted of a 'strong diversity brand' representing 'uniqueness' and 'individual contribution'. In October 2006, the Council removed its mandatory retirement age completely, so that employees can now choose to retire when they want to. Although older employees can continue paying into the Local Government pension scheme until they are 70, the scheme allows people to retire, draw their pension, and be re-employed on a part-time basis. Removal of a retirement age means that line managers have to use the Council's performance management system to address any performance issues relating to older workers. However, they are 'not to make assumptions based on age or about when the employee may wish to retire' (ibid., p10). Use of flexible retirement and flexible pension arrangements, in short, may prove effective ways of approaching the management of an ageing workforce.

Other benefits offered to staff by Hertfordshire Council include a number of health promotion schemes. These cover posture checks, blood pressure checks, stop smoking campaigns, and staff discounts on gym membership and health and dental insurance plans. It has an annual carers' conference and supports staff with caring responsibilities. The Council also runs support groups and an employee assistance programme. Use of flexible working arrangements helps the organisation meet service demands more effectively, as well as enabling employees balance work, home, and personal priorities. These include job sharing, term-time working, career breaks, compressed hours, annualised hours, and location flexibility such as home working. With its policy of wanting to retain and engage talent rather than lose it, the Council has found many workers want to move to part time hours when they decide to retire. One effect of all these schemes is reduced staff turnover and reductions in recruitment and training costs.

In terms of financial rewards, and given that these may be of less concern to older workers than are non-financial benefits, employers need to examine their pay structures, pay progression, pay levels and variable pay elements. This is to make sure that these help organisations attract, reward, motivate, and retain talent, irrespective of age, as well as sustaining high performance working and employee effort.

This requires examining the pay mix between fixed and variable pay, as well as between individual and collective rewards.

In terms of non-financial rewards, working patterns, work-life balance, and learning and development initiatives are key elements in total reward packages for ageing workforces. BT, for example, the telecommunications conglomerate, with over 100,000 employees and operating in 170 countries, has introduced a series of flexible working practices and has removed its retirement age completely. The firm's policies are designed to encourage older workers to stay with the business and ease the transition from employment to retirement (CIPD 2008, p. 16). To ensure older employees remain committed, engaged, and motivated, these arrangements include part-time working, reducing working time, being seconded to outside organisations, and planned demotion where senior staff take on less responsibility at work.

Creating an open workplace culture is regarded as another important factor in good practice diversity management. Social interaction also appears to be a key motivator in working after 65, whilst an ageing workforce requires a good physical working environment and good ergonomic design. Flexible working arrangements, a friendly working environment and appropriate job design are keys 'to engage and retain an ageing workforce' (CIPD 2008, p. 17).

All employees should be eligible for learning and development programmes, since there is potential to waste the talent of particular age groups. This applies especially to older members of the workforce, who may need to up-date their job skills, develop their knowledge about their organisation's changing customer and client bases, and understand and apply new technologies to their job roles. In practice, however, learning and development, career development and performance management have traditionally be neglected by employers in relation to older workers. The recent age Regulations, an ageing national workforce, and the potential removal of a mandatory retirement age, means that this neglect will have to stop. Historically, many employers have been reluctant to provide training to employees close to retirement, because of negative perceptions about the possible returns on investment in training. But from an economic standpoint, it is arguable that the learning and development of employees near or beyond retirement age will become an increasingly part of employer learning strategies and of the labour market.

Despite being at or near retirement, many older employees want to carry on making contributions at work, even if they are less interested in career development opportunities. As the size of the older workforce increases, it will be in the best interests of employers, especially in terms of knowledge management, to make sure that older employees are fully engaged in learning so that all an employer's talent is nurtured and not wasted. In this respect, it is interesting to observe that Sainsbury, a leading food retailer in the UK, has introduced apprenticeships across a range of craft-based careers. Originally limited to those aged 16–25 in 2006, there is now no age limit for entry to these apprenticeships. This is in line with the company's corporate social responsibility agenda and with the view that the benefits of removing the age limits outweighed its costs. Such initiatives provide clear advantages to both the company and its employees.

When releasing employees, organisations' future needs for knowledge, skills, and competencies need to be considered. Alternatives to redundancy should be considered such as shorter hours, part-time working, secondments, and employment breaks. Requests to work beyond retirement age need to be properly considered. As indicated above, there is substantial evidence that many older workers welcome opportunities for phased retirement, flexible working, working beyond normal retirement age, working on a self-employed basis, and working in the voluntary sector. However, it is the removal of mandatory retirement ages by organisations that lead to new, positive mindsets regarding age and retirement. As Gordon Mason, Senior Policy Advisor at the Department of Work and Pensions (DWP), has observed (TUC/CIPD 2007, p. 8):

> In 2006, the DWP decided to opt for having no mandatory retirement for all employees below Senior Civil Service (SCS)... Mandatory retirement is no longer an option for dealing with underperforming staff; management has to deal with the underlying issues to improve performance.

Discussion and review

Dealing with ageism and age discrimination in organisations is being driven, on the supply side, by rising numbers of workers who want to work beyond retirement age and, on the demand side, by the more progressive employers needing to retain their ageing workforces in the light of the changing structure of the labour force and labour market. The drive against ageism is also motivated by legislation aiming to remove age discrimination in organisations, in both the private and public sectors. Nevertheless, there are a number of obstacles to the eradication of ageism and age discrimination in employment. One set of obstacles turns on the economic incentives to employing people of certain ages, either because their pay can be lower than that of older/younger people, or because they fit into the 'servicescape' as outlined above. Another major set of obstacles turns on people's attitudes and perceptions about the abilities and attitudes associated with people at different points of the chronological spectrum. These attitudes may not be fixed but may, in turn, vary according to the age of the observer.

The introduction of the EEAR 2006 provides new opportunities for individuals claiming that they are being discriminated against in employment by employers. As a result, organisations are adapting their employment policies and practices to comply with the new legislation. These businesses have to scrutinise and revise all their HR policies, practices, and procedures, since age discrimination, both direct and indirect, can occur anywhere in the employment cycle from recruitment and selection, at one end of the employment spectrum, to redundancy and retirement, on the other. Employers taking these initiatives are implementing these policies as part of an approach to equality and diversity, using objective criteria for assessing employee performance and communicating these policies to all managers and employees. Learning and development programmes, in turn, are being designed to facilitate and embed these revised policies in organisations.

Effective age management strategies may start from a concern to protect older workers from discrimination, disadvantage, and redundancy. Alternatively, they may aim to strengthen the contributions that older workers can make to organisational performance, without undermining the interests of younger workers. Fundamentally, an effective age management strategy aims to produce a balanced approach to the treatment of different age groups in an organisation, rather than a balanced age structure. Case studies point to the importance of internal mobility to achieve this objective. This implies, amongst other things, generating more internal mobility in organisations than is strictly demanded by current business conditions. This accustoms workforces of all ages to changes in their work activities and job tasks. It means that this capacity can then be drawn upon when it is really needed, that is when older workers need to cope with mobility flexibility. Well developed internal mobility systems also benefit the operation of the external labour market, by making organisations consider a range of external recruits, including older workers, when they have labour shortages (Warwick 2006).

To be successful effective age management strategies also need support at institutional levels, beyond that of individual companies and employers. And these may not necessarily be compatible with one another at any single point in time. One of these is European Union (EU) and trans-national level. Here suitable frameworks and support measures promoting awareness of age management issues among member states can assist. The EU level can also encourage member states to develop national age management programmes. Another function is for EU institutions to engage in discussions with the social partners at European level to facilitate common interests between generations in the labour market.

The sorts of measures that can be facilitated at national level include aligning public-sector retirement practices with those being advocated for the private sector, promoting good age management practices generally, and seeking the co-operation of trade unions and citizens through relevant programmes, projects, and campaigns. There is also the need to promote balanced discussions and debates on possible intergenerational conflict about work and the labour market. At regional level, especially, there may be opportunities to provide specialist expertise to small and medium enterprises lacking practical knowledge of effective age management practices internally.

However, the key to developing effective age management strategies remains at company or employer level. These strategies need integrating at corporate level, including increasing the flexibility and internal mobility of all age groups and implementing career development for all age groups. Another is setting up of mixed age groups at work and organising knowledge transfers amongst them. It is also important to pay attention to the factors helping to make such internal strategies compatible. It is necessary too to examine the scope of adapting pay and pension schemes and working conditions to promote age management strategies. When dealing with trade unions, employers need to link age management and work ability perspectives to pay policies, working conditions, and access to learning and development for all age groups. Employers' associations and trade unions can play important roles in raising awareness of age management issues, as well as providing guidance on how to develop and respond to the implementation of age management approaches.

Trade unions are in a difficult position, because of their generally short term objectives. But they need to develop appropriate longer term strategies in response to demographic changes and communicate them to their members. Unions also need to develop a clearer position towards what is in the best long term interests of their members in relation to pay and pension schemes that inhibit job flexibility and mobility.

Lastly, if age is the final frontier of discrimination in employment, individuals themselves need to take responsibility for maintaining and enhancing their own job knowledge and work skills to sustain employability throughout their working lives. For this, they should expect to draw upon employer support for workplace learning, life long learning, and career development at critical stages in their cycles of employment.

References

Age Partnership Group (2005), *20 Key Facts Your Business Needs to Know*, London: Department for Work and Pensions.
CIPD (2005a), *Annual Survey Report for 2005*, London: CIPD.
CIPD (2005b), *Tackling Age Discrimination in the Workplace: Creating a New Age for All*, London: CIPD.
CIPD (2007), *Age and Employment*, London: CIPD.
CIPD (2008), *Managing an Ageing Workforce: The Role of Total Reward*, London: CIPD.
Employers Forum on Age (2005), *Defining Ageism*, London: EFA.
Employers Forum on Age (2006), *The Inside Guide to Age Laws*, London: EFA.
Office for National Statistics (2008), *Population Trends*, 133, Autumn, Basingstoke: Palgrave Macmillan.
Trades Union Congress/CIPD (2007), *Developing a New Mindset on Age and Employment: A Report on the CIPD/TUC Event on Managing Age and Retirement*, London: TUC/CIPD.
Warwick Institute of Employment Research/Economix Research and Consulting (2006), *Ageing and Employment: Identification of Good Practice to Increase Job Opportunities for Older Workers in Employment*, Brussels: Commission of European Communities.

12
Disabled People and Employment: Barriers to Potential Solutions

Marion Hersh

Introduction

Employment is very important for social integration and participation in society. In addition to providing an income and financial independence, employment provides a sense of identity and social status, an important source of (social) contacts and means of participating in society, as well as structuring the day, engaging in meaningful activity and having a purpose in life (Evans and Repper, 2000). Employment can also contribute to improving the quality of life and increasing self-esteem (Becker *et al.*, 1996), improving mental and physical health and making (disabled) people more optimistic about their future (Evans and Repper, 2000). Conversely, a lack of employment opportunities reduces the likelihood of social integration (Jongbloed and Crichton, 1990) and contributes to perpetuating negative stereotypes that, for instance, mental health impairments prevent people working.

Despite various schemes and policy measures to get disabled people into employment, they generally have much higher unemployment rates and are more likely to be underemployed or in low paid, low status jobs than non-disabled people (EBU, 2001; Roulstone and Warren, 2006). Since disabled people comprise an estimated approximate fifth of the population (EEOT, 2007; ONSLF, 2007), they are a significant potential source of talent, skills and expertise in the workforce and the lack of appropriate policies to support their employment could result in organisations not obtaining the best person for the job (EEOT, 2007). Since most disabled people become disabled during their working life, employers who do not take measures to retain employees who become disabled are likely to lose workers with valuable skills, experience and knowledge, as well as having to cover the costs of recruiting and training a new employee (DTS, 2005). Disabled workers have been found to have fewer absences and health and safety incidents than non-disabled workers (Graffan *et al.*, 2002; AEND, 2008) with associated reductions in costs. The costs of recruiting them are also significantly lower (AEND, 2008).

Although on average they earn less than non-disabled people, disabled people still have considerable spending power, for instance an estimated £80 billion per annum in the UK (DTS, 2005). Good practice in employing disabled people can be an important competitive advantage due to attracting the custom of disabled people, their families and friends and the fact that corporate reputation and ethical employment and environment policies are an important factor in the decisions on where to obtain goods and services of increasing numbers of consumers (DTS, 2005). Many countries have legislation against employment discrimination on the grounds of disability. Therefore, organisations which do not comply with this legislation are at risk of legal proceedings, which are time consuming and expensive and may lead to bad publicity.

However, despite the very clear benefits to organisations of employing disabled people, they still have high unemployment rates. This chapter will aim to provide an overview of some of the barriers to the employment, retention and promotion of disabled people in jobs with a career structure and that meet their needs and use their skills. In order to structure the discussion of these barriers, the Comprehensive Assistive Technology (CAT) model developed by Hersh and Johnson (2008a) will be used. The CAT model has a hierarchical tree structure model with the four main components of person, context, assistive technology and activity at the top level. A model which maps the interface between technology, contextual and other factors has been chosen due to the significant impacts of technology and, in particular, information and communications technologies (ICT) on the nature of employment, including the move from manufacturing to service industries. The availability of ICT and other new technologies presents both possibilities and threats for disabled people and their entry into the workplace. On the one hand technology is an enabler which can be used to overcome some of the barriers they might otherwise face. On the other hand, there are issues of whether or not technology is accessible and designed and implemented to promote inclusion, with the possibility of increasing disadvantage and exclusion, as well as the digital divide (Dobransky and Hargittai, 2006; RTC, 2006) if it is not.

The discussion will be from the perspective of the social (UPIAS, 1976; Barnes, 1994; Johnstone, 2001) rather than the medical model (WHO,

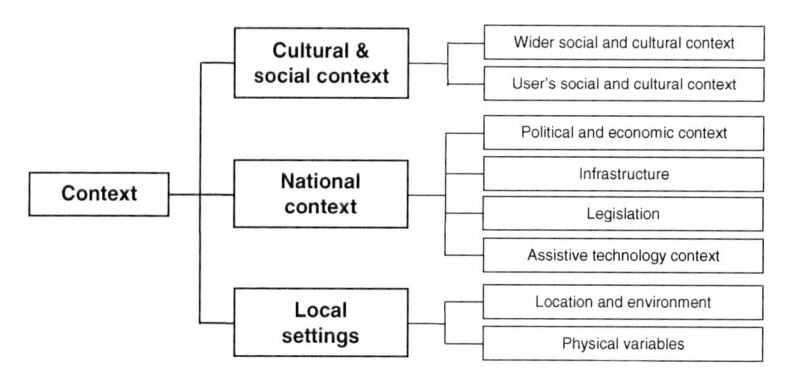

Figure 12.1 The context component of the comprehensive assistive technology model

1980, 2001) of disability. This represents a move away from a focus on individual impairments to the structural, environmental and attitudinal barriers to inclusion, leading to an examination of what types of change are required and where (Doughty and Allan, 2008) and leads to a focus on the context (Figure 12.1) rather than the person component of the CAT model.

The main barriers arising from the cultural and social; national and local contexts will be discussed in the second, third and fourth sections, with the third level components used to structure the discussion within each section. Conclusions, comprising a summary of the barriers to employment and suggested measures to overcome them are presented in the fifth section.

Due to space limitations, the national context will be restricted to the industrial countries and sections associated with some of the third level CAT model components have been omitted, though the barriers that would have been discussed in these sections are referred to in Figure 12.2 and discussed in the conclusions. The full version of the paper can be downloaded from http://www.gla.ac.uk/departments/assistivetechnology/.

Barriers arising from the cultural and social context

The user's social and cultural context

One of the determining features of the disabled person's context is the largely socially constructed negative identity of disability. This is in addition to other identities based on gender, race or ethnicity, age, interests,

218 Obstacles to Diversity Initiatives

```
                                    ┌─ Wider social and cultural context
                                    │  medical models & individual approaches
                  Cultural &    ────┤
                  Social context    │
                                    └─ User's social and cultural context
                                       negative constructed identities of disability

                                    ┌─ Political and economic context
                                    │  unhappy mix of market economics & welfare
                                    │  measures, low wages, inflexible benefits
                                    │
                                    ├─ Infrastructure
                                    │  educational and transport barriers
Context ──────── National        ───┤
                  context           ├─ Legislation
                                    │  omissions, insufficiency, lack of implementation
                                    │  and penalties
                                    │
                                    └─ Assistive technology context
                                       lack of information on availability, difficulties in
                                       obtaining it

                                    ┌─ Location and environment
                                    │  inaccessible buildings and facilities, uninformed
                  Local          ───┤  and sometimes prejudiced employers
                  settings          │
                                    └─ Physical variables
                                       noise, inappropriate lighting, heating and
                                       ventilation
```

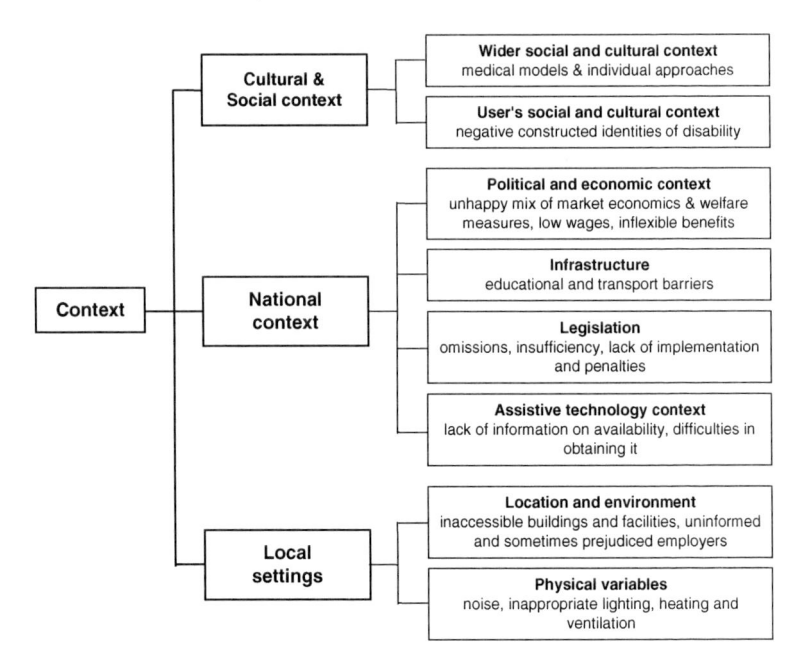

Figure 12.2 The main barriers to employment of disabled people related to the context component of the comprehensive assistive technology model

occupation or other factors. Many of these other identities will also be socially constructed to some extent, though the details are beyond the scope of this chapter. However, the existence of multiple discrimination should be noted. For instance, disabled women earn less than both disabled men and non-disabled women (Emmett and Alant, 2006).

Political, economic and other factors, as well as the market need or lack of it for disabled people in the workforce have contributed to shaping the details of this identity. Current constructions are largely an artefact of competitive market economies with their need for a flexible, relatively skilled workforce, which is available 24/7 and able to move to follow the availability of work. Perceptions of disabled people as unproductive and expensive workers (Kitchin et al., 1998) who have little role in meeting these needs and are therefore redundant have contributed to a constructed identity of disabled people as almost totally incapable, particularly of working. However, large numbers of disabled people are in employment, for instance nearly 3.5 million in the UK in spring 2002 (Stanley and Regan, 2003) compared to a total workforce of about 29 million (Stanley, 2008), assuming that the total workforce has not changed significantly between 2002 and 2008. The factors which convey and/or prevent challenges to this constructed image are negative images, fear, and the invisibility of disabled people, leading to a barrier to employment.

Disabled people generally have a low visibility in the media, advertisements, the arts and literature. Although campaigning organisations have recently started to use, for instance, people with Down's syndrome as models for their t-shirts, disabled people rarely appear in advertisements and they are still largely absent from literature, and soap operas and other popular television programmes, which have an important impact in developing people's perceptions of the world. Where disabled people have appeared in literature, the images used have generally been negative, either poor, pathetic victims, evil villains with their disability a symbol of this villainy, or heroically fighting against insuperable odds (Cameron, 2003). In particular, there is a lack of images of 'ordinary' disabled people doing ordinary things, but experiencing barriers and discrimination, rather than being 'evil' or 'heroic'. Although this has now changed, most of the major charities involved with disabled people have had a bad history of using negative images of disabled people to try and evoke pity and encourage donations, contributing to negative stereotypes of disabled people as being poor, pathetic and inadequate (Cameron, 2003), not the qualities most employers look for. In addition, the very association of disability with charity and the fact that many facilities for disabled people are provided by charities rather than as of right by the state (funded through taxation) contribute to perceptions of disabled people as dependent on the charity and pity of others rather than as competent workers in their own right.

Another factor is fear of becoming disabled. Since the incidence of impairment increases with age, people can become disabled at any point in their lives and many non-disabled people do make this transition, with less than 20 per cent of disabled people in the UK having been born disabled (Stanley and Regan, 2003). However, the very negative images many people, both disabled and non-disabled, have of disability (Ruiz and Moya, 2007) make this something to be feared and avoided at all costs, rather than something to be prepared for, including through combating discrimination.

While many countries now have a policy of mainstream education, historically many disabled people have been educated in segregated 'special' schools (Booth and Ainscow, 1998; Vislie, 2003; Avramidis and Kalyva, 2007). Consequently, most non-disabled people have had little experience of interacting with disabled people in the same way as they interact with non-disabled people. They also may not know whether there are disabled people amongst their friends, colleagues, acquaintances or even family members. Bad previous experiences and (often justified) fears of being mocked and treated differently or discriminated against, as well as the negative stereotypes of disabled people make it difficult for many disabled people to recognise or accept the fact they are disabled, never mind disclose it to other people. This apparent invisibility of disabled people is part of a cycle of lack of knowledge, misperceptions and fears leading to social exclusion. It both means that non-disabled people have little direct experience of disabled people to challenge stereotypes and lead to the 'normalisation' of disabled identities and contributes to an 'othering' process which views them as 'different' and 'defective'.

The wider social and cultural context

The cultural context in which disabled people are employed is dominated by medical models of disability, as well as a focus on individual rather than collective solutions. This has led to interventions to modify or rehabilitate disabled people to make them more employable and special schemes for their employment, rather than consideration of the wider socio-political context and the measures required to overcome attitudinal, infrastructural, societal and other barriers, including the lack of employment opportunities. Socio-political approaches based on the social model of disability recognise society as the source of the problems experienced by disabled people and the consequent need for external and structural changes (Lunt and Thornton, 1994). This does not exclude retraining or similar measures, particularly if organised in a proactive way to support a return to the (original) workplace after a person becomes disabled, but recognises that they will be insufficient on their own to open up interesting, well-paid employment with career prospects to disabled people.

However, in some countries there has also been a tendency to encourage some disabled people into a substitute career of training rather than employment in line with the still prevalent view that many if not most disabled people are unable to work. For instance, it has been suggested that services for people with mental health impairments are generally intended to support them '*out of work rather than in work*' (Grove, 1999) and the same could unfortunately be said for services for many other groups of disabled people. Particular groups of disabled people, such as those with mental health impairments may even be discouraged from working out of a genuine, but inappropriate desire to protect them (Evans and Repper, 2000). The training schemes provided for disabled people rarely lead to long term secure paid employment, often because they do not lead to recognised qualifications, and trainers may be patronising and assume they know best what disabled people require (Kitchin et al., 1998).

However, there is increasing recognition that improving the position of disabled people will require a focus on external barriers rather than individual skills, though this has not always led to policy changes (Jongbloed and Crichton, 1990) and programmes aimed at employment for disabled people have largely focused on increasing the employability of individuals rather than improving accessibility, working conditions and wages (Wilton and Schuer, 2006). In addition, some local government representatives and local projects on disability and employment have been found to have little experience or desire to engage with disabled people and to consider them 'other' (Piggott et al., 2005).

There seems to be a de facto assumption in a number of countries that people who become disabled or have long term sickness absence will not return to work. For instance, a 2002 survey by the Trades Union Congress in the UK found that just under a fifth of employers with union recognition agreements had five or more measures for reintegrating employees after a long period of sickness and only 8.6 per cent considered themselves to be successful at doing this (TUC, 2002). However, some countries do have (relatively) good practice. For instance, in Australia employers are required by law to establish a return-to work programme for injured workers, including vocational training if required, hold the injured worker's job open for six months, with some variations across the States, and provide suitable alternative employment if the worker is unable to return to the same job (Stanley and Regan, 2003). Another feature which is missing in many countries is 'disability leave' or a period of paid time off to adjust to the onset or increase in severity of an impairment (Stanley and Regan, 2003). This would, for instance, allow people who become blind as adults to both adjust psychologically and have training in orientation and mobility and basic living skills.

Support in obtaining work is likely to be useful to all workers, but disabled workers may require additional or different types of support to obtain and maintain work and may need this support to continue for an extended period. For instance, a study of visually impaired employees found that about half the respondents working in the legal profession and about a third of the respondents working in information technology had received assistance from one or more support organisations.

Other than one respondent, who was unable to obtain funding for workplace adjustments, all these respondents found the assistance useful. However, two respondents indicated that they preferred not to deal with organisations with bureaucratic procedures (Smith, 2002). Just as appropriate assistance, advice and support can be enabling factors, their absence or the need to navigate complex and bureaucratic procedures to access them can act as barriers to employment.

Due to the continuing prevalence of myths that disabled people are not able to work (Stanley and Regan, 2003) or are not highly competent and productive workers, very little consideration has been given to overcoming the barriers to promotion of disabled people or obtaining a career which is interesting and suited to the particular disabled person's interests and skills. This is clearly an area which needs to be addressed, or many disabled people will continue to be underemployed and society will not obtain the greatest possible potential benefits from their skills and talents. However, wider societal changes will probably be required before disabled people are employed in significant numbers in senior rather than entry level positions in most organisations.

Some disabled people require personal assistance with daily living activities in order to work. Therefore difficulties in accessing appropriate personal assistance can act as a barrier to employment. Unfortunately, the provision of personal assistance is still considered an individual or family rather than a social responsibility in many countries (Askheim, 2005). Where funding is available for employing personal assistants, the associated conditions vary greatly and may not make being a personal assistant to a disabled person an attractive career option. For instance, in the UK funding does not cover the costs of the employer's national insurance contribution or replacement staff to enable the assistant to take a paid holiday (Ungerson, 1997). In Sweden funding is provided, but only people requiring more than 20 hours of personal assistance are entitled to receive them. In some cases access to funding is limited by very stringent eligibility conditions and cumbersome and bureaucratic application procedures, thereby preventing a number of disabled people from engaging in employment and other activities (Barnes, 2000).

Barriers arising from the national context

The political and economic context

The current political and economic context is one of market economics, combined with some welfare measures, leading to the provision of benefits for those unable to compete in the market. It is also one of varying job availability, partly in response to external economic conditions. Disabled people are generally at the end of the queue into employment. They therefore may find it easier to obtain employment in conditions of high employment, when the shortage of labour forces employers to consider workers they might otherwise have turned away (Russell, 2002). They also experience greater problems than other workers in obtaining a job in conditions of high unemployment and are more likely to be dismissed in the event of redundancies in a worsening economic climate (Jongbloed and Crichton, 1990). It should also be noted, that unless jobs are available, removing the other barriers to the employment of disabled people will reduce their inequality in access to employment, but will do so by slightly reducing the employment rates of non-disabled people rather than improving employment prospects for everyone. The increase in the percentage of low paid unskilled jobs in the service sector (Dyck and Jongbloed, 2000; McDowell, 2004) also reduces the prospects of disabled workers obtaining high paid high status employment with a career structure.

The balance between the influence of market forces and concerns for welfare provision varies considerably between countries, leading to very different benefit systems. However, in many countries benefit levels are set at a relatively low level, often with additional or different benefits for disabled people. These benefits are often higher than those for non-disabled people, but frequently still at poverty levels. Thus the lower wages (despite anti-discrimination legislation) most disabled people can expect and higher benefits that many of them are entitled to, as well as the greater likelihood of working part time, force disabled people into a poverty and benefits trap which constitutes a structural barrier to their employment (Turton, 2001).

Thus, employment may lead to insignificant gains in income and sometimes even a reduction compared to benefits. Some disabled people need to be able to move in and out of employment in response to changes in their conditions, such as increasing fatigue, which affect their ability to work, and experience greater difficulties in finding a new job when existing employment comes to an end, since employment is rarely for life. Concerns about the potential drop in income if they have to move in and out of employment, as well as worries about having to yet again try to navigate the complex procedures for obtaining higher levels of benefit without certainty of success may act as disincentives to looking for employment. The fact that many disabled people lack accurate information about their entitlement to benefits and the security associated with a small, but known income from benefits, as opposed to the uncertainty of employment may also act as barriers.

However, it should be noted that the problem is the low wage rates which most disabled people can expect and the inflexibility of benefit systems which act as barriers to employment, rather than the higher rates of benefit of many (but not all) disabled people. These higher benefit rates are still generally far below the average wage, for instance only 56 per cent of national average earnings in April 1998 in the UK (Turton, 2001). Thus, the solution is not to reduce benefits for disabled people, but to take serious measures to counter discrimination and raise the income disabled people can expect in employment, as well as reform benefit systems to make it much easier for disabled people to move in and out of employment. This could include increasing the amount claimants can earn before their benefits are reduced and the rate at which benefits are reduced and tax paid with increasing income.

The availability of higher levels of benefit for disabled people and the assumptions behind these higher levels of benefit mean that disabled people who want to work are having to simultaneously present themselves as totally incapacitated and incapable of working to the benefit authorities and as highly motivated, skilled and capable employees to potential employers (Stanley and Regan, 2003). This inherent contradiction means that disabled people could experience difficulties in obtaining higher levels of benefit after a short period of employment, regardless of the existence of serious barriers to further employment, since they have obviously shown that they are not totally incapable of working.

The mixture of market and welfare approaches has led to sheltered employment programmes for many disabled people in many countries. The long standing sheltered workshop programme in the UK has been restructured, with stricter supervision and higher productivity targets being imposed on workers, leading to increased stress (Hyde, 1998). Sheltered workshops and transitional approaches are still being used, despite the fact that US research indicates that supported employment generally has greater benefits than sheltered or transitional approaches (Lehman, 1995) and that skilled support which is appropriate to the individual's changing requirements needs to be provided in real workplaces (Evans and Repper, 2000).

The assistive technology and support context

Assistive technology plays an important role in making workplaces accessible to many disabled people. For instance, a study of visually impaired people in the workplace found that 21 out of 26 respondents used assistive technology, including to access CD ROMs, computer databases and the internet (Smith, 2002) and a study of people with arthritis and other rheumatic conditions found that just over a third (38 per cent) of the 121 respondents had work adjustments, with one quarter using assistive technology, including special chairs and supports (Allaire *et al*., 2003). Therefore, concerns about the availability of assistive technology or other adjustments, as well as any delays or difficulties in obtaining them will act as a barrier to employment.

Many employers and workers have little knowledge of what assistive technology is available and do not know how to obtain this information (T-TAP, undated). This means that many workers will either not receive any adjustments or will not receive the adjustments best suited to their needs. This could lead to avoidable difficulties in carrying out work tasks. There is therefore a need for more widely available information in a variety of formats on assistive technology and workplace adjustments to overcome this barrier. Lack of information is not the only barrier to the implementation of workplace adjustments. An equally important factor is the attitude of employers.

Even in countries where there is a legal obligation to make workplace adjustments to support disabled workers, this legal obligation is often not translated into practical measures and, when it is, may require considerable effort on the part of the disabled worker. For instance, a recent study of the negotiation of adjustments in public sector workplaces (Foster, 2007) found that where successful adjustments had been made, a significant degree of responsibility had been devolved from management to the worker. Although the results of this study are not conclusive, there are indications that a significant degree of employee responsibility is required rather than management taking full responsibility for obtaining information about and implementing adjustments in consultation with the worker. This in itself is a barrier, since it requires employees to have sufficient knowledge, time, self-confidence and job security to take on the process of obtaining information about, negotiating and implementing adjustments. The individualistic and informal nature of the process also creates barriers by giving what should be a legal requirement an air of grace and favour, with success dependent on the relationship between the particular worker and manager, and making it difficult for the organisation to develop expertise and policy in providing adjustments for disabled workers (Foster, 2007). In addition, the individual nature of the process generally requires it to be initiated by the particular worker declaring themselves disabled and asking for adjustments.

This is problematic due to the reluctance of workers to disclose, which is discussed in the section 'The user's social and cultural context'. These barriers could be reduced by a proactive approach in line with the social model of disability of adjusting the working environment to remove barriers and improve working conditions for all workers, followed by asking workers whether they require any further adjustments.

Workers may experience particular difficulties in obtaining adjustments to hours of work or other aspects of the work itself, though flexible or non-standard working hours can be of great benefit to many disabled people. When such adjustments are made, they may be treated by the employer as a change in terms and conditions rather than a workplace adjustment (Foster, 2007). This disadvantages the disabled worker, particularly if associated with a reduction in the rate of pay or a reduced entitlement to workplace benefits.

Delays may also be experienced in accessing services which are required on a regular or occasional basis, such as sign language interpreters or lip speakers for deaf and hearing impaired people and large print or Braille materials for blind and visually impaired people, The UK Access to Work website suggests that it may be necessary to book communication support up to six weeks in advance (ATW, undated). While workers who regularly require interpreters in the workplace will probably have arrangements in place, problems may be experienced with meetings called at short notice.

Although employment for a number of disabled workers is dependent on access to assistive technology and other adjustments, expensive equipment is rarely required and the average costs of adjustments are quite low. For instance, figures provided by the Job Accommodation Network in the USA showed that 71 per cent of workplace adjustments cost no more than $500, with 20 per cent of these adjustments having no associated costs (Kittle, 1995). A study of organisations in one of the USA states found that the adjustments made for disabled employees by nearly half (46 per cent) the companies responding did not have any associated costs and that many adjustments, such as more flexible working hours and more frequent breaks, benefited all workers (Cleveland *et al.*, 1997). Estimates by the UK government of the costs of compliance with the Disability Discrimination Act 1995 have found that the average costs to employers of reasonable adjustments are £200 (Duckworth *et al.*, 1996). However, many employers have false perceptions that the employment of disabled people involves very high costs through the need for extensive adjustments to the workplace and/or expensive equipment (Kitchin *et al.*, 1998). It should be noted that some employers are very reluctant to make even minimal additional expenditure, so that even these low average costs can act as a barrier to the employment of disabled workers.

The relatively small number of disabled workers who require expensive equipment or other expensive adjustments will experience serious barriers to employment unless financial support for these adjustments is available, preferably from government and with a simple and speedy application procedure. This is available in many countries, but may be poorly publicised, leading to employers and workers with little knowledge of their entitlements to financial support, and/or require a financial contribution from the employer, which is often not easy to negotiate and can in itself act as a barrier. In addition, the procedures for obtaining this support are often bureaucratic and complex.

A case in point is the UK Access to Work Scheme. On the one hand it has enabled a large number of disabled workers to obtain assistive technology, interpreters and other workplace adjustments, 32,500 in 2000/01 (Stanley and Regan, 2003). On the other, it is badly publicised and has been described as a 'well kept secret' (ECU, 2008) and it is not unusual for the process of obtaining funding to take one to two years, which is not particularly useful to workers who require adjustments to be made speedily to enable them to start or continue working. There is also a threat of Access to Work funding being withdrawn from the public sector. Since it is unlikely that public sector employers would cover all the costs, this would leave some disabled workers trying to continue in employment with outdated equipment, while others would be forced out of their jobs with little likelihood of ever finding another one and disabled workers not yet in employment would have greatly reduced likelihoods of ever obtaining employment.

Barriers arising from the local setting

Location and environment

For most workers obtaining and maintaining employment is dependent on the ability to get to the place of employment, get into the building and use all relevant facilities, including toilets and washing facilities, and the equipment necessary to carry out required job tasks. The inability to access areas of the workplace, such as tea rooms and cafeterias, where workers spend their breaks and socialise can also act as a barrier and lead to social exclusion through lack of access to social networks and social contacts. In addition to leaving disabled workers socially isolated and without somewhere to spend their breaks, this can reduce their access to information about what is happening in the workplace, as well as opportunities to learn informally from other workers and share job-based knowledge.

Despite legislation in many countries, a number of workplaces or parts of them are still inaccessible, particularly to wheelchair users (Wilton and Schuer, 2006). Many (large) workplaces are also badly laid out, difficult to find one's way around and may require workers to walk long distances. All these factors create barriers for some groups of disabled people. Even where there is good (visual) signposting in large workplaces, little attention is given to the needs of blind and visually impaired people. Therefore, tactile signing is largely absent and visual signing is often inappropriately designed for visually impaired people with regards to location, colour contrast and size. The use of Braille or other tactile markings and audio announcements in lifts is still variable rather than universal. These issues are discussed in more detail in Hersh and Johnson (2008b). In addition, personal assistance in locating a particular room or department in a large workplace may not be available and there may not always even be someone in the reception area of large buildings to obtain directions from. It should be noted that barriers of this type are not absolute in that they do not totally exclude people from the workplace. Rather they add unnecessary difficulties and delays and increase the levels of avoidable stress.

Other frequently encountered features of the local context are increasing workloads and an expectation of increasing productivity and being available for work at any time and any place, partly in response to the use of information and communication technology. This has led to unreasonable pressures and unpleasant working conditions for all workers, and is likely to cause particular problems for many disabled workers. Expectations of high productivity and high speed in carrying out workplace tasks or always being available can act as barriers to disabled people (Garcia *et al.*, 2002). In some cases the only workplace 'adjustment' disabled workers require will be reasonable expectations of productivity, working hours and the pace of work. This will obviously have benefits for all workers and is a prerequisite for avoiding exploitation. Some disabled workers will additionally require a degree of flexibility in the scheduling of their hours, to be determined by the worker's needs rather than management. This type of flexibility can benefit many non-disabled workers, including those with small children.

Both actual and potential employers of disabled people may be influenced by the negative constructed identity of disabled people discussed in the section 'The political and economic context', and often exhibit ignorance and fear, resulting in discrimination and barriers to the employment of disabled people. However, supportive employers can facilitate the transition to work and maintaining employment. For instance a study of workers with epilepsy found that a supportive employer and co-workers who understood the condition were helpful in maintaining employment (Bishop, 2002).

Employers may also lack accurate information about how many disabled people they employ due the lack of monitoring of the workforce. For instance, a council involved in an action research project (Piggott *et al.*, 2005) had (mis)estimated the number of disabled people it employed by counting the number of cars parked in the spaces reserved for disabled people. Where monitoring is carried out, particularly if it is not anonymous, the data may be distorted due to underreporting as the result of often justified concerns about being stigmatised and discriminated against in decisions on employment, retention and promotion. For instance, participants in a focus group on barriers to the employment of people with epilepsy were very wary about disclosure, due to concerns that this would impact negatively on hiring decisions and that various pretexts were used to dismiss people with epilepsy when employers become aware of the condition even after several years of successful employment (Bishop, 2002).

While the right of disabled workers not to disclose should be respected, non-disclosure may have a number of negative consequences. Individual disabled workers will generally not be able to access appropriate support and adjustments (though it should not be assumed that they will be available if they do disclose), which may lead to difficulties in carrying out the job properly and expectations which the worker is not able to meet. In some cases, disabled workers may only disclose in order to seek adjustments when their working situation has become totally untenable. At this point, it may be more difficult to make adjustments and the time pressures for adjustments will be greater than if disclosure had occurred earlier. At the organisational level, non-disclosure will lead to totally inaccurate information about how many disabled workers are employed and reduce pressures to act proactively to make the workplace accessible and welcoming to them.

Many employers share the common misconception that the majority of disabled people are wheelchair users, though less than 5 per cent of disabled people are (Duckworth *et al.*, 1996). This results in a lack of awareness and knowledge of the adjustments that might be useful to other groups of disabled people, but unfortunately does not mean that employers are well prepared to make adjustments for wheelchair users.

Physical variables

A good working environment is important for all employees, but likely to have a particular impact on disabled employees, with problems leading to difficulties in carrying out work tasks, high levels of stress and associated absences and possibly even resignations if the problems are not resolved. While problems of this type are most likely to be experienced once employees are in place, concerns about, for instance, inappropriate lighting or high noise levels could act as barriers to seeking employment. Other physical variables which affect the working environment include temperature and ventilation.

Noise is likely to be problem for a number of disabled people, including those with hearing impairments, autistic spectrum conditions and tinnitus, and can itself cause hearing loss, with, for instance, an estimated more than one million workers in the UK exposed to noise levels which could damage their hearing (HSE, 2008). Proactive approaches to reducing noise levels will improve working conditions for all workers. They should start with an audit of noise in the work place and include a hierarchy of control measures based on elimination of noise sources, control of noise at source, control based on workplace organisation and layout, and the provision of protective equipment (OSHA, undated). Noise reduction can be achieved by a range of measures including regular preventative maintenance, the use of acoustically damping enclosures and barriers, and using quieter machinery and materials. Control measures include the appropriate installation and location of equipment, the use of sound absorbing materials and reducing the time people are exposed to noisy machinery (OSHA, undated). It is also important to recognise that some disabled people may be disturbed by levels of noise that other people do not even notice and may therefore require additional measures, such as a change of office or a change in some job requirements.

Changes in the nature of work with the increasing use of computer screens and other types of displays have increased the importance of appropriate levels of illumination to avoid stress, eye strain and eye damage for all workers. Many visually impaired people will be unable to do their jobs or move round the workplace if appropriate high quality lighting is not available. A more detailed discussion of illumination, with particular reference to visually impaired people is provided in Hersh and Johnson (2008b). However, it will be noted that both overhead lighting and desk lamps or other task lighting should be provided and overhead lighting is preferable to wall mounted lighting. A proactive approach should be taken to replacing existing fluorescent lighting by other types of lighting and providing sufficient shading, particularly underneath, for overhead lighting, without significantly reducing the illumination.

Disabled people are more likely to be sensitive to heat and cold or variations in temperature than non-disabled people and may have a greater need for ventilation. In general, heating and ventilation should be under the control of workers in a particular section of the workplace and, where possible, ventilation should be provided through windows rather than air conditioning, on the grounds of both energy saving and being less likely to cause irritation.

Discussion and conclusions: Barriers and solutions

This chapter has used the comprehensive assistive technology (CAT) model (Hersh and Johnson, 2008a) to structure the presentation of an overview of some of the barriers to employment experienced by disabled people. This overview has been presented from the perspective of the social model of disability, which considers the problems experienced by many disabled people to result from societal, attitudinal and infrastructural barriers and discrimination rather than their impairments. This has led to a focus on the context rather than the person component of the model. With the addition of a political and economic context component, the context component of the CAT model has been shown to provide a suitable framework for the discussion of these barriers. They are illustrated in Figure 12.2 and will be discussed in this section.

Barriers in the cultural and social context

The main barriers relating to the user's and the wider social and cultural context are negative constructed identities (of disability), and the domination of negative models of disability and the focus on individual rather than collective solutions respectively. The details of constructed disability identities are largely determined by the political and economic context and the need or lack of it for disabled people in the workforce. The factors which contribute to this construction are the fact that many non-disabled people do not (knowingly) have any contact with disabled people, due to separate education systems, though this is changing, the scarcity of 'ordinary' disabled people in the media, for instance in popular television programmes, and inaccessible facilities, buildings and public transport which prevent disabled people participating in many activities. This leads to an 'othering' of disabled people and the development of negative stereotypes and prejudices which, amongst other things, limit the range of job opportunities which are perceived to be suitable for disabled people or even the not uncommon belief that disabled people are incapable of working or will be unsatisfactory employees.

Potential solutions include setting measures in place to challenge this constructed identity, for instance by making disabled people more visible and less isolated. This could include continuing and speeding up moves to inclusive education, which should be adequately funded and resourced to ensure that disabled students have the full support they require, for example sign language teaching and facilities for learning Braille. Other measures involve improving the accessibility of facilities and the increasing visibility of 'ordinary' disabled people in the media, including in popular television series.

The wider social and cultural context is marked by a preference derived from medical models for individualistic approaches, such as training schemes to make disabled people more 'employable' and a devaluation of their experiences and lack of consultation by policy makers and project organisers, leading to often inappropriate policy measures. In addition, negative assumptions about the employability of disabled people have led to a lack of measures in many countries to support the return to work of people who are injured, have a long term illness or become disabled and an almost total neglect of measures to give disabled people access to career progression and promotion. Real change will require collective approaches to overcoming the societal, attitudinal, infrastructural and other barriers experienced by disabled people. Measures will be required at a number of different levels, to be decided on and implemented in consultation with and through the involvement of disabled people. They could include proactive approaches to make workplaces more accessible and welcoming to disabled workers, measures to support career progression and promotion and stronger legislation to support the rights of disabled people to work, with serious sanctions for non-compliance.

Barriers in the national context

The main barriers arising from the political and economic context are a consequence of the not always happy marriage of market economics and welfare measures. Disabled workers are particularly affected by the state of the economy and are generally at the end of the queue for obtaining employment in times of high unemployment. Inflexible benefits systems in combination with low wages create a benefits and poverty trap for many disabled people, which means that employment will not significantly improve their financial position compared to benefits and could even worsen it. It is also difficult for (disabled) people to move into and out of work in response to changes in their health conditions or other circumstances. Fears of losing higher rates of benefit if employment is not maintained may discourage them from looking for work.

Measures for removing this barrier should include a more flexible and much simpler benefits system, which makes it easy for people to return to benefits after short (or longer) periods of employment and significant increases in the amount people can earn before benefits are reduced, with a very gradual drop in benefit entitlements with increasing income. Equally important are widespread dissemination of information about benefit entitlements and significant increases in the real wages that disabled people can expect to earn. However, determining appropriate measures to improve the average wages of disabled people in employment is going to be considerably more difficult than changing the benefits system. It will probably also require changes in the barriers in the social and cultural context and, in particular, the negative constructed identity of disability.

The main infrastructural barriers considered relate to access to education and qualifications and transport. Many disabled people encounter barriers to accessing education on the same terms as non-disabled people, leading to a lack of qualifications. While this lack of qualifications acts as a real barrier to obtaining employment, obtaining qualifications unfortunately does not always translate into improved job opportunities for disabled people. Some improvements have been made in this area, though further measures will be required, for instance to ensure that the buildings and facilities of all educational institutions are fully accessible to all disabled people and that students who require materials in alternative formats can obtain them at the same time as other students. Additional resources will also be required to support disabled students, as well as to support teaching staff in making their courses fully accessible without loss of teaching content or interest.

Despite some improvements in many countries, public transport is still inaccessible or difficult to use for many groups of disabled people. This will prevent or make it difficult for them to travel to work unless they own and are able to drive a car or can obtain funding for taxis. Removing barriers for wheelchair users is a good starting point and an obvious first step, but barrier removal will need to have a much wider scope to cover the needs of all disabled people, as well as other minority groups. Where possible, design for all approaches, based on designing for as wide as possible a range of the population, regardless of factors such as size, age, gender, culture or disability, should be used.

Legislation has often acted as an enabler and aimed at removing barriers for disabled people in employment, education and leisure. Therefore the barriers are generally associated with inadequacies or omissions in the legislation or the lack of implementation, including the lack of serious punishments for non-implementation. There is also great variability in the legislation on disability in different countries. Therefore, there is a need for research to identify the (features of) legislation and measures for ensuring it is implemented across countries which have been most successful in eliminating discrimination and bringing about equality of outcomes in employment (and other aspects of life) for disabled people. Appropriate modifications to this best practice legislation to take account of national cultural and other factors will probably be required before it is implemented. Health and safety legislation has sometimes been used or served as a pretext to exclude some or all disabled people from particular types of employment. Information and education will be required to challenge the misconceptions which have led to this misunderstanding and the resulting misuse of the legislation.

The assistive technology and support context is marked by a lack of knowledge of what is available and difficulties in obtaining assistive technology and other workplace adjustments. Many employers have misconceptions about the high costs of employing disabled workers and/or try to displace responsibility for making workplace adjustments onto their disabled workers. Removing this barrier will require the introduction of improved schemes with simple procedures and fast response times for financing and otherwise supporting employers to introduce assistive technology and appropriate workplace adjustments, as well as strongly enforced legislation requiring them to do this. It will also require collective approaches by the trade unions, particularly in large workplaces, to negotiating proactive schemes for implementing assistive technology and other workplace adjustments.

Barriers in the local settings

Barriers in the location and environment include inaccessible workplaces and facilities, increasing workloads and a speeding up of the pace of work, as well as employers who lack information about how many disabled people they employ and a workplace climate which does not encourage disabled workers to disclose that they are disabled. In many cases funding will be required in order to make workplaces fully accessible. There is also a role for trade unions in taking a collective approach to negotiating confidential monitoring of disability (as well as other worker characteristics) and campaigning to change attitudes to and treatment of workers within their workplaces.

Physical variables that can give rise to barriers include noise and inappropriate lighting, heating and ventilation. While changes in this area will require some, though not high expenditure, they will generally be of benefit to all workers.

The relationships between the different barriers

Although the different barriers have been discussed separately and associated with different components of the comprehensive assistive technology model, there are connections between them, as illustrated in Figure 12.3 and will now be discussed briefly.

As shown in Figure 12.3, the unhappy marriage of market economics and welfare measures arising from the political and economic context either directly or indirectly affects all the other barriers. It has a direct impact on the development of medical models and individual

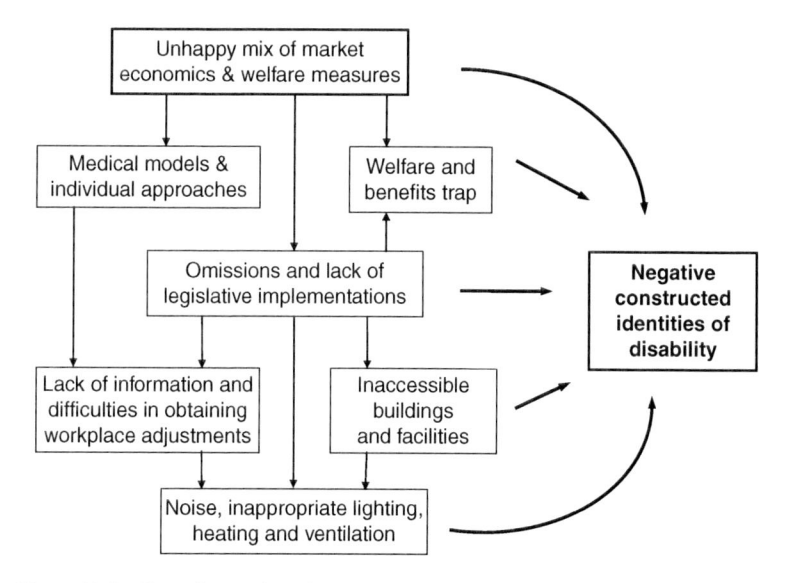

Figure 12.3 The relationships between the main barriers to the employment of disabled people

approaches, through the individualism associated with the market and contributes to the negative constructed identities of disability through the perceived redundancy of disabled workers. The focus on market approaches and limited impact of welfare measures leads to legislation which has important omissions and is not strongly implemented. Market economics and welfare measures are linked to the poverty and benefits trap, which is also affected by negative constructed identities of disability.

The limitations of legislation are one of the factors which lead to inaccessible buildings and facilities with excessive noise and inappropriate lighting, heating and ventilation and difficulties in obtaining workplace adjustments, since there are insufficient pressures on employers and other organisations to make changes to ensure accessibility and an appropriate environment. Inaccessible buildings also have what can be considered a feedback effect in perpetuating negative constructed identities of disability, since they contribute to the isolation of disabled people, and contact between disabled and non-disabled people is an important factor in challenging these negative identities. There is also interaction in both directions between medical models and individual approaches and negative constructed identities of disability, since medical model site the 'problem' in the disabled individual and negative constructed identities do nothing to challenge this.

Summing up

A number of different barriers have been discussed and shown to arise from the various contexts, local, social and cultural and national, in which employment takes place. Some solutions have been proposed and I would suggest that moves from individual to collective approaches and deconstructing the negative constructed identities of disability will be particularly important. While making changes will be to the benefit of employers and widen their pool of prospective employees, the wider changes will be difficult to implement under current political and economic systems.

Although solutions have been proposed, there has been less discussion of the actors who should be involved in their implementation. It should be noted that employers, government, campaigning organisations of disabled people and trade unions will all have important roles, but that their different interests may require trade unions and campaigning organisations of disabled people to put pressure on government and employers in order to achieve change.

Acknowledgements

I am very grateful to Dr Debbie Foster and Prof Mike Johnson for their very helpful comments and suggestions and to Prof Mike Johnson for drawing Figures 12.2 and 12.3.

References

AEND (2008). Fact sheet – business benefits of employing people with disability, The Australian Employers' Network on Disability, http://www.employersnetwork ondisability.com.au/images/Fact%20Sheets/Business%20 Benefits.pdf, accessed 4.1.09.

Allaire, S.H., W. Li and M.P. LaValley (2003). Work barriers experienced and job accommodations used by persons with arthritis and other rheumatic diseases, *RCB*, vol. 46(3), pp. 147–56.

Askheim, O.P. (2005). Personal assistance – direct payments or alternate public service. Does it matter for the promotion of user control? *Disability and Society*, vol. 20(3), pp. 247–60.

ATW (undated). Access to Work, http://www.direct.gov.uk/en/DisabledPeople/ Everydaylifeandaccess/Everydayaccess/DG_10037996, accessed 16.10.08.

Avramidis. E. and E. Kalyva (2007). The influence of teaching experience and professional development on Greek teachers' attitudes towards inclusion, *European Journal of Special Needs Education*, vol. 22(4), pp. 367–89.

Barnes, C. (1994). *Disabled People in Britain and Discrimination: A Case for Anti-Discrimination Legislation*, Hurst & Co., London.

Barnes, H. (2000). *Working for a Living? Employment, Benefits and the Living Standards of Disabled People*, The Policy Press, Bristol.

Becker, D.R., R.E. Drake, A. Farabaugh and G.R. Bond (1996). Job preferences of clients with severe psychiatric disorders participating in supported employment programs, *Psychiatric Services*, vol. 47, pp. 123–6.

Bishop, M. (2002). Barriers to employment among people with epilepsy: Report of a focus group, *Journal of Vocational Rehabilitation*, vol. 17, pp. 281–6.

Booth, T. and M. Ainscow (1998). *Creating an Inclusive School: The Influence of Teacher Attitudes*, Routledge, London.

Cameron, C. (ed.) (2003). *Getting a Job: Assertiveness Training and the Rights of Disabled People at Work for Young Disabled People*, Distance Learning Model, Dept. EEEng, University of Glasgow.

Cleveland, J., J. Barnes-Farrel and J. Ratz (1997). Accommodation in the workplace, *Human Resource Management Review*, vol. 7(1), pp. 77–102.

Dobransky, K. and E. Hargittai (2006). The disability divide in internet access and use, *Information, Communication and Society*, vol. 9(3), pp. 313–34.

Doughty, H. and J. Allan (2008). Social capital and the evaluation of inclusiveness in Scottish further education colleges, *Journal of Further and Higher Education*, vol. 32(3), pp. 275–84.

DTS (2005). The business case for employing disabled people, Disability Toolkit Sussex, http://www.disabilityequalsbusiness.org.uk/do/list.py/view?listid=23&listcatid=102&, accessed 4.1.09.

Duckworth, S.M. Freeney and M. Parkinson (1996). *Disability Matters, Managing Diversity at Work, A Good Practice Guide for Employers*, Lemos and Crane, London.

Dyck, I. and L. Jongbloed (2000). Women with multiple sclerosis and employment issues, *Canadian Journal of Occupational Therapy*, vol. 67, pp. 337–46.

EBU (2001). Survey on the employment of blind and partially sighted people in Europe (2001), European Blind Union, http://www.euroblind.org/fichiersGB/surveymb.htm, accessed 21.6.07.

ECU (2008). Response to Helping people achieve their full potential: Improving Specialist Disability Employment Services, Equality Challenge Unit Response to Department of Work and Pensions Consultation, www.ecu.ac.uk/news/2008/03/ecu/assets/ECU_response_to_DWP_March_2008.doc, accessed 16.10.08.

EEOT (2007). Why employ disabled people, Equal Employment Opportunities Trust, http://www.eeotrust.org.nz/toolkits/disability.cfm?section=whyemploy, accessed 4.1.09.

Emmett, T. and E. Alant (2006). Women and disability: exploring the interface of multiple disadvantage, *Development Southern Africa*, vol. 23(4), pp. 445–60.

Evans, J. and J. Repper (2000). Employment, social inclusion and mental health, *Journal of Psychiatric and Mental Health Nursing*, vol. 7, pp. 15–24.

Foster, D. (2007). Legal obligation or personal lottery? Employee experiences of disability and the negotiation of adjustments in the public sector workplace, *Work, Employment and Society*, vol. 21(1), pp. 67–84.

Garcia, L.J., C. Laroche and J. Barrette (2002). Work integration issues go beyond the nature of the communication disorder, *Journal of Communication Disorders*, vol. 35, pp. 187–211.

Graffan, J., K. Smith, A. Shinkfield and U. Polzin (2002). Employer benefits and costs of employing a person with a disability, *Journal of Vocational Rehabilitation*, vol. 17, pp. 251–63.

Grove, B. (1999). Mental health and employment: Shaping a new agenda, *Journal of Mental Health*, vol. 8, pp. 131–40.

Hersh, M.A. and M.A. Johnson (2008a). On modelling assistive technology systems part 1 modelling framework, *Technology and Disability*, vol. 20(3), pp. 193–215.

Hersh, M.A. and M.A. Johnson (2008b). *Assistive Technology for Visually Impaired and Blind People*, Springer Verlag, London, 978-1-84628-866-1.

HSE (2008). Noise at work, http://www.hse.gov.uk/noise/, accessed 31.12.08.

Hyde, H. (1998). Sheltered and supported employment in the 1990s: The experience of disabled workers in the UK, *Disability and Society*, vol. 13(2), pp. 199–215.

Johnstone, D. (2001). *An Introduction to Disability Studies 2nd Ed.*, David Fulton Publishers Ltd, London.

Jongbloed. L. and A. Crichton (1990). Difficulties in shifting from individualistic to socio-political policy regarding disability in Canada, *Disability, Handicap and Society*, vol. 5(1), pp. 25–36.

Kitchin, R., P. Whirlow and I. Shuttleworth (1998). On the margins: Disabled people's experience of employment in Donegal, West Ireland, *Disability and Society*, vol. 13(5), pp. 785–806. Published by Taylor & Francis.

Kittle, R. (1995). Job accommodation network – accommodating a person with a vision impairment, http://jan-web.icdi.wvu.edu/english/pubs/OtherPubs/VISION, accessed 31.12.08.

Lehman, A.F. (1995). Vocational rehabilitation in schizophrenia, *Schizophrenia Bulletin*, vol. 21, pp. 645–56.

Lunt, N. and P. Thornton (1994). Disability and employment: Towards an understanding of discourse and policy, *Disability and Society*, vol. 9(2), pp. 2223–37.

McDowell, L. (2004). Work, workfare, work/life balance and an ethic of care, *Progress in Human Geography*, vol. 28, pp. 145–63.

ONSLF (2007). Disability and employment statistics, Office for National Statistics Labour Force, http://www.shaw-trust.org.uk/disability_and_employment_statistics, accessed 4.1.12.

OSHA (undated). Noise reduction and control facts, European Agency for Safety & Health at Work, http://www.city.ac.uk/safety/dps/H%20&%20S%20Information/Noise%20reduction%20and%20control%20Fact58%20EN%5B1%5D.pdf, accessed 31.12.08.

Piggott, L., B. Sapey and F. Wilenius (2005). Out of touch: Local government and disabled people's employment needs, *Disability and Society*, vol. 20(6), pp. 599–611.

Roulstone, A. and J. Warren (2006). Applying a barriers approach to monitoring disabled people's employment implications for the Disability Discrimination Act 2005, *Disability and Society*, vol. 21(2), pp. 115–31.

RTC (2006). Disability and the digital divide: Comparing surveys with disability data, RTC Ruralfacts, http://rtc.ruralinstitute.unit.edu/TelCom/Divide.htm, accessed 17.12.08.

Ruiz, J. and M. Moya (2007). The social psychological study of physical disability, *Revista de Psicología Social*, vol. 22(2), pp. 177–98.

Russell, M. (2002). What disability civil rights cannot do: Employment and political economy, *Disability and Society*, vol. 17(2), pp. 117–35.

Smith, T. (2002). *Diversity and disability: Exploring the experiences of vision impaired people in the workplace*, *Equal Opportunities International*, vol. 21(8), pp. 59–72. Published by Emerald.

Stanley, K. and S. Regan (2003). *The Missing Million: Supporting Disabled People into Work*, IPPR, London.

Stanley, M. (2008). Civil service statistics, http://www.civilservant.org.uk/numbers.pdf, accessed 31.12.08.

T-TAP (undated). Assistive technology as a workplace support fact sheet, http://www.worksupport.com/research/viewContent.cfm/504, accessed 18.12.08.

TUC (2002). *Rehabilitation and Retention: The Workplace View*, Trades Union Congress, London.

Turton, N. (2001). Welfare benefits and work disincentives, *Journal of Mental Health*, vol. 10(3), pp. 285–300.

Ungerson, C. (1997). Give them the money: Is cash a route to empowerment? *Social Policy and Administration*, vol. 31(1), pp. 45–53.

UPIAS (1976). *Fundamental Principles of Disability*, London, UPIAS (Union of the Physically Impaired Against Segregation).

Vislie, L. (2003). From integration to inclusion: Focusing global trends and change in the western European societies, *European Journal of Special Needs Education*, vol. 18(1), pp. 17–35.

WHO (1980). *International Classification of Impairments, Disabilities and Handicaps*, World Health Organisation, Geneva, Switzerland.

WHO (2001). *International Classification of Functioning, Disability and Health (ICF)*, World Health Organisation Publication, ISBN-13 9789241545426, ISBN-10 924 154 5429, Geneva, Switzerland.

Wilton, R. and S. Schuer (2006). Towards socio-spatial inclusion? Disabled people, neoliberalism and the contemporary labour market, *Area*, vol. 38(2), pp. 186–95.

13
Barriers to Diversity: The Case of Advertising Creatives

Jim Blythe

Advertising creatives are at the sharp end of creativity. The people who design and develop new advertising (the so-called creatives) are usually talented artists, musicians or wordsmiths who have found a commercial outlet for their talents – it has been said that advertising copywriters would sell their souls for a potted message: the ability to convey a message in a few words, or a single image, or a few bars of music is at the root of all advertising success.

Of course, the artistry is constrained by the client. Advertising creatives are given a brief, from which they need to develop a rough outline of what they intend to do: the client then approves the rough (or not) and the work either goes ahead to a full treatment, or is adapted to suit the client's needs. This is the area in which the creatives sometimes become bogged down, because they then find that their creative urges are curbed by the client's wish to do something incremental, that is something which follows on from previous advertising and which is therefore not seen as being as original as the creatives might have liked it to be. The need to present solutions that the client will like therefore presents a potential obstacle to the achievement of diverse, creative solutions.

This chapter builds on research carried out with advertising creatives in London. The research was carried out using a grounded-theory approach involving an in-depth analysis of qualitative data: because this approach is perhaps less well-known to many readers, some explanation of the methodology is probably in order.

Methodology

The grounded theory approach to research operates under an interpretivist paradigm. The intention is to generate theory rather than arrive at an objective truth. In the words of Corbin and Strauss (1990):

> Grounded theorists share a conviction with many other qualitative researchers that the usual canons of 'good science' should be retained, but require redefinition in order to fit in the realities of qualitative research and the complexities of social phenomena...significance, theory-observation compatibility, generalisability, consistency, reproducibility, precision and verification.

Grounded theory follows a set of ten procedures, but (by its nature) the procedures are not necessarily followed in strict order, and several iterations of a given procedure might be needed before the researcher moves on to the next phase of the research. The activities involved are summarised in Table 13.1.

Part of the problem with using a grounded-theory approach is that it relies on the establishment on the part of the researcher of a long-term relationship with the data. Final results may easily take a long period to analyse; the research itself can never be considered to be 'finished'; and the interpretation of the data is necessarily subjective and requires considerable navel-gazing on the part of the researcher.

In common with other interpretivist methodologies, grounded theory does not pretend to arrive at an objective, generalisable truth: what it is intended to achieve is a development of theory, some of which is explained by a return to the literature.

Method

The research was conducted with eight advertising creatives and one branding consultant, all based in the London area. A breakfast meeting was convened, and the group were encouraged to talk about their experiences in creating and interpreting brand personalities. The discussion was initiated by asking each member of the group to say what kind of animal they most resembled personally, and how this had affected their approach to their creative work. As an approach, this started the conversation going, but was only partially successful in eliciting a direct response: interestingly, the five animals mentioned were the fox

Table 13.1 The processes of a grounded theory study

Activity	Description
Collect data	Semi-structured interviews and observation are most commonly used, but any textual data may be used.
Transcribe data	A full transcript of the interview or other data is made.
Develop categories	Open coding of the transcripts is used to categorise comments.
Saturate categories	The data is analysed according to the categories developed, the researcher proceeding through the transcripts as often as is necessary until all the examples of comments in each category have been gathered.
Abstract definitions	Formal definitions of the categories are developed by reference to the data gathered.
Theoretical sampling	Relevant samples of comments are abstracted with the aim of testing and developing the categories further.
Axial coding	The development of relationships between the categories.
Theoretical integration	A core category is identified around which the other categories are linked to existing theory.
Grounding the theory	The emergent theory is grounded by returning to the data and validating it against actual segments of text.
Filling in gaps	Further collection of data to fill in any missing detail.

Source: Adapted from Bartlett and Payne (1997).

(because it is sly and is able to get its own way without giving anything away), the hyena (for similar reasons to the fox), the unicorn (because it is magical, colourful and mythical), the chameleon (because it is adaptable), and the bear (because it can appear large and friendly, but can also be aggressive).

The creatives were also asked to bring samples of their best work, a task which they interpreted as meaning samples of their favourite work. The intention in doing this was to encourage discussion about the relationship between the individual and the communications they had produced.

Collecting and transcribing the data in a grounded-theory study is a somewhat time-consuming task: fortunately, once the interview data has been transcribed, much of the remaining analysis can be assisted by the use of computers. Open coding of the transcripts led to the development of data categories: the initial reading of the transcript generated

Table 13.2 Categories of data

Category	Description
Conflict vs. co-operation	This category is concerned with conflict between work colleagues (the other half of the team) much of which was regarded as positive. The conflicts largely arise as a result of personality differences, leading to creative solutions.
Sensitive vs. insensitive	At times creatives need to be sensitive in order to empathise with the target audience and with the marketers from the firm, but also need to be insensitive when their work is criticised.
Career vs. creation	Some creatives are career-orientated, others are more motivated by the impulse to create.
Passion vs. discipline	Becoming emotionally involved in the creative process is necessary, but also creatives need to be disciplined in order to produce finished work which meets the brief.
Creatives vs. agency	Some creatives are able to be 'company men' while others see themselves as 'free spirits'.

almost 30 possible categories, but these were amalgamated into a final five categories of data, which were defined as shown in Table 13.2.

The transcript was then re-examined, and the data divided up between these categories; several iterations of the process were needed in order to ensure that data was correctly attributed to the appropriate category. In some cases, respondents' statements could be considered under more than one category, but these cases were surprisingly few.

Given the way creatives work, there is a natural bias in favour of diversity: this naturally led to dichotomies and even to conflicts in the reported data. In the next section, we will see that conflict is not necessarily a bad thing as we expand on the elements in Table 13.2.

Conflict vs. co-operation

Broadly speaking, conflict is a psycho-social outcome of interaction (Ruekert and Walker 1987) and can be described as a breakdown or disruption in normal activities in such a way that the individuals or groups concerned experience difficulty working together (Reitz 1977; Hellreigel and Slocum 1988; Hodge and Anthony 1991; Daft 1998; Hatch 1997). Traditionally, conflict is viewed as being dysfunctional, in other words we tend to see conflict as a bad thing, as something that gets in the way of getting the job done. Conflict is often seen as impacting negatively on the organisation, reducing productivity, and decreasing morale, because attention focuses on the conflict rather than on organisational aims.

However, conflict is inevitable where people have a diversity of background, interests and talents. In the case of advertising creatives, conflict is the sand in the oyster shell, creating an irritation that leads to original ideas. This is known as the interactions or functional view of conflict, and implies that conflict can be a positive force which helps effective performance and encourages creativity. Far from diverting attention away from the aims of the organisation, conflict ultimately generates more effective ways of achieving those aims.

Creatives usually work as part of a two-person team. This is a time-honoured system in advertising agencies, producing conflicts which lead to creative solutions. The creatives were clear about the importance of this type of relationship, as these quotes show:

> I think personalities get quite interesting as well when they're full of contradictions. You know, I think I know what he's going to say next and then he'll throw something in and it'll contradict...

> Keith did a lot of the work in terms of the concept, and the stuff that went out actually ended up being critical with them going through them but without Keith it wouldn't have worked. He would definitely call himself a bowler, and he needed a batsman. It's quite interesting, an interesting scenario.

The concept of the batsman and the bowler, on opposite sides but playing the same game, was mentioned on other occasions.

> I think that teams are brought together through experience, and what you've got to do out of that and sometimes that could be XXX who was a production person, a producer, a project manager, but those kind of definitions and those boundaries don't matter, I think personality depends on how you work together, as a group, that dynamic group.

> I think my best work has been done with other people. It may be possible to be an artist, to be an absolute artist, to have complete control of your work but even that's a bit unnatural...and you do want to do it all yourself, but you reach a point where you can't release it, you react with other people, otherwise you can't achieve it within the time-frame.

You also think that you're going to try to find either one, whatever you get, so if there isn't a conflict with you, in the brief they've given you, you need a partner who'll create that in order to get the best out of you.

There was no evidence in this category that the personalities of the team members were expected to have an effect on the outcome of cracking the brief, in other words there was no expectation that the creatives would try to impose their collective personality on the finished brand identity to any extent. This may be because of a feeling that the aim of the exercise is to crack the brief rather than be independently creative.

> The brief is not necessarily what gets you, it's the idea you come up with to crack the brief that gets you.

Sensitive vs. insensitive

The mental anguish of being a creative came through strongly, especially in terms of having to put one's work up for criticism by outsiders. This is an area in which being different can be painful – the creatives had often felt that their natural propensity to be original and different had been met with some hostility, and they therefore found themselves creating defensive barriers against this kind of response.

> In advertising you have to be sensitive and insensitive at the same time. Eh???

> I think you're asked to wear your heart on your sleeve.

> You have to be very tenacious to make it happen. I had a friend who was a junior at XXXXX and they taught their marketing people not to respond, at all, in meetings. So you'd go, you'd turn into an animal, swoosh around, turn into a shell, hard work explodes, and there's.... (PUTS ON A BLANK EXPRESSION) (LAUGHTER) It's the kind of behaviour you hate.

> People like to show their work, and you come up with the most original funny TV ad and you have to show it to the most cynical people in the world and you're expecting, you know, a barrel full of laughs and get half a titter, yeah, that's horrible.

> I think what else is interesting is that adverts will try and use every personality in the creative process. We are actually creating you know

> sometimes a piece of work we can be quite precious about it saying, it's my baby, and we are creating something and I think in terms of what we just said is that we give something hopefully arms and legs and something that can go and live and breathe and whether it's gone through an agency or whatever hopefully there's enough kind of tools and bits to that thing that it can go off and continue to live.
>
> Producing new raw material.... There's this huge melting pot of creative people, much bigger than the whole advertising industry, much hungrier than the advertising industry, earning less money, and there's this huge cultural creative beast that, has the stage and TV and drama where the opportunities are for celebrity and all those things, a whole world which is kind of.... glossier than advertising.

This was an area in which the creatives felt that the individual's personality was likely to have an effect on the brand personality. Partly this was due to the ability of a professional, sensitive creative to understand and add to the brand identity proposed by the client, and partly it was due to the affinity the creative's personality might have for the brand personality.

> I brought in a programme which was designed as a passport. Basically it took you into the London Eye and put on an arts festival, for G8, a celebration of Africa, but I thought why it's my favourite, I think probably it's not even the biggest or the best but I really I had such passion for the fact that I really think we could make a difference to people's lives on it, and so we brought over African growers, and we thought that it was really important that they bought into it and that they, in there own way got what we were trying to do and you could see the difference it made to them, and in the context of the G8, and then each show has got basically a different passport.

There is clearly an issue here involving emotional labour, which is defined as 'the management of feeling to create a publicly observable facial and bodily display [which] is sold for a wage and therefore has exchange value' (Hochschild 2003). In the original work on emotional labour, the emphasis was on low-paid service sector jobs where staff were compelled to smile and say 'Have a nice day' to each customer. In the business-to-business context, emotional labour is no less important, but it operates in a somewhat different way: the creatives were expected to display enthusiasm, competence, and passion when showing the client their work. This took a certain toll on their sensitive, artistic natures, and in the long run could have an effect on the degree to which they are prepared to be diverse in their work.

Career vs. creation

The relationship between career aspirations and diversity is not unique to advertising industry creatives, but it is certainly an area in which the creative's personality is likely to play a role in developing the brand personality. Career and creativity are not always in conflict: in some cases, a particularly creative piece of work is rewarded by the industry, and this can lead in turn to lucrative contracts and job offers.

> But for me, when I was young and creative, I was working to win an award a lot of the time... It was probably, I went too far that way, I wanted the glory, I wanted to be on the podium, and that's the basis...

> I've changed a bit in the interim, I don't think awards add much, they're still great I don't think you can base a career on going out for awards, these days it's not as true that I feel like that. Probably because I haven't got any!

> In big agencies, the highest accolade you can win in advertising is the D&AD Black Pencil, and it actually guarantees you a job for the next ten years.

> You know if it's somewhere like (well known agency) which has got a bit of name as, like, the song and dance agency, very successful in what they do, with the Halifax, with Johnny Ball, with whatever his name is, you would think of that as a great place to work, it's very very successful mainstream advertising, I can't do that sort of stuff. You could put me in there and pay me £150,000, £450,000 a year and I couldn't do it.

> That mainstream stuff is not going to win awards. You stay outside of that, on the margins, doing something different that hasn't been done before, they know that stuff like that, there isn't, at the end of it, ...

The issue coming out here is that the creative is likely to choose to work in an area that suits his or her personality – either in an environment where career is important, or in one in which creativity is important.

The view was expressed that producing a creative, original piece of work was not necessarily the way to please the client: clients and agencies almost seem to operate a bias against diversity.

> If you genuinely want to produce bags of work you have to be pretty sly about it. I don't think most people want genuine creative work I think most people want progress from the thing they had before... So I would say, having said that, having said that I would say I'm a fox.

This respondent admits to being like a fox in personality, but the next respondent talked about being more like a chameleon. The reference to paedophiles comes from an example provided by the interviewer, suggesting that creating a campaign for greater understanding of paedophiles would be a real challenge to the creatives.

> I think that's the best thing about this business, it's like a chameleon, you try and fit in somebody else's shoes and you can be the other guy, and you can probably get to Paedophile, the intellectual one, what it would be like, so being aware that it wouldn't stick, that would be terrible but you could probably get to close enough, and go to the uncomfort zone, get to the discomfort zone, where you start thinking about it from that point of view, and so you do a job that other people couldn't possibly do...

For this respondent, the key to creativity was the challenge: trying to understand paedophiles without actually becoming one. (The interviewer offered an alternative scenario, that of being asked to develop a campaign for golfing equipment if one were a keen golfer. This was generally regarded as being much less interesting.) The overall implication of this part of the research was that creatives enjoy and embrace diversity, whereas clients and agencies tend to shy away from it.

Passion vs. discipline

Becoming passionate about cracking the brief while at the same time retaining the necessary professional detachment to carry out the task was another area the creatives regarded as a personality issue.

> Passion's useless if you can't focus, if you can't discipline yourself. Unless you can focus that, that thing you've got, that spark,...

> Of course you use that inspirational force, to get a lot of other people going.
>
> The most important is you should get the passion to support the work.

Part of the passion is the challenging brief: challenges are often about avoiding the obvious.

> It goes back to when I was working in an agency, they'd say 'Oh, it's a tampon brief, let's get the girls in on that' and we'd go like No, a lot of great ads are in those sort of ways buzzing.
>
> In reality it's all about challenge, you don't have like months off to celebrate you're into the other job that's fallen by the wayside or picking up the next thing.
>
> What you mean by that, going back to your example of the golf balls or the paedophile, to be honest you'd probably want the paedophile brief because you'd know that would be...

In other words, passion is necessary but not sufficient – creatives also need to stay focused and remember that, as soon as one job finishes, another one will follow on.

Creatives vs. agency

It is in the area of relationships between the creatives and the agency (and hence the client) that one would expect the greatest impact on the brand personality. Creatives tend to have an uneasy relationship with those who set the brief, whether this is done by the client, by a branding agency or in-house. This often results in attempts to circumvent the agency in some way, or outwit them.

> When you go in as a creative and try to do something more from the thing you're doing that's the thing... I don't think the money would be there, you want the reward of the commission, seeing something made, and feeling that, that you know your heart's in it and all of that which is the kind of thing you need, has been you need an opportunity to nail the job to the ground you know the commercial reality here is I don't think there are really that many opportunities to be creative unless you really want to smash something. Not an appealing prospect for most people who have to work with you or work

within the confines of.... So there's always the challenge. So I would say, having said that, having said that I would say I'm a fox.

It's funny, something we've been going through for the past few weeks, I had a brief I had no idea what the branding was I had a blank piece of paper and a completely incomprehensible brief, and so you get work, you get a phone conversation and, you know, you get, a rubber stamp, all you need to do is what's expected of you.

You rewrite the brief in your own language

We worked, in this kind of work, we can't look into the corporate side of things the classic corporate communications type of thing...whereas in an agency it's like being a piece of meat chucked to the dogs sometimes and they're hungry dogs.

There's a sort of them and us, corporate agencies and innovation agencies...And that's partly because venture capital got in the way and tried to move everybody who's got a salary upstairs, so there's loads of energy, lots of good stuff coming out, but there's no continuity, there's no kind of thrust in new ideas and you know radical new ideas, and the whole industry was driven by that.

When the client wields so much power that you can't turn around and go No, this is really good, it's going to work for you, and they go and the whole agency goes...you can't, you, know, the industry's f***ed.

Quite interesting from a client's side as well, what you said earlier about being paid for thinking, for ideas, I think that what clients pick by instinct are personalities, and a lot of the time clients are buying a relationship, you'll have a pitch to sell on personality.

I agree with that, the relationship has always been there. Obviously you do get major personalities, with major causes, for major relationships. It's always been there, but we're only starting to think about it.

It's interesting to have this conversation because I think in branding it's a tad different in that usually in terms of a piece of work you work on the brand and then maybe that brand will then go to a marketing, advertising agency so I think that when you're developing or creating a brand there's more of an input for putting your personality or personality shape in there.

252 Obstacles to Diversity Initiatives

The group (not surprisingly) became very animated when asked to show their best pieces of work. The first pieces of work (three pieces in all) were from a creative in his late 30s, an experienced and confident man with a calm, laid-back personality.

> The other thing I want to show you is we did a campaign for the National Railway Museum. I had to go up there and have a look round before we planned the campaign, and railway museum is something I wouldn't normally go, but I was really kind of knocked over by the trains and all the stuff there, and I wanted to kind of convey some of that to people and so we did a whole campaign, and I actually got the signwriter who did the lettering on some of those carriages, and it actually did increase the number of people going to the museum. And the last piece is for an opera, I think this is good because it sort of sums up part of the beauty and a kind of ragged... I created it as a poster, and then had it printed as a poster, and stuck it up on concrete and then distressed it.

For this creative, the satisfaction in the pieces of work came from learning something new about the brand, and (in the second instance) from producing something which was in itself creative and evocative. Note the almost surprised tone in the statement that the advertising 'actually did increase the number of people going to the museum.'

The next piece of work was from a young team of creatives (in their early 20s) who had produced an on-line game to promote a sporting event. In the manner typical of a creative team, they told the story together, alternating the sentences.

> (Creative 1) We sort of pushed the boundaries slightly on the brief we'd been given, which was to find an on-line way to selling the Guardian Life Cup, we incorporated a drop-down banner all the scores were updated on all the drop-down banners anywhere on the Web so you either went on the Team America or Team Europe, and so the scores which country or which sub-continent won, and... (Creative 2) I don't say it's our best piece of work but I say it's like, one that's quite personal, and also it's an idea that like, we got challenged by the client to do it, and they said, (Creative 1) Yeah, cool, do it. (Creative 2) It was good fun too because again it's not linear it's not a piece of paper it's not something.... It's something you look at, and ten thousand people went there and played with it and

interacted with it, (Creative 1) I mean that's brilliant, and you can see something....

In their case, the promotional material reflected their relative youth and their connection with other young people who would use the website. It is unlikely that anyone else in the room would have created anything like this (and it is entirely possible that most of them would not have known where to begin).

The next piece of work has become iconic for advertising creatives. The various campaigns for telecoms provider Orange have been widely-acclaimed throughout the industry.

> The piece of work that I brought, the reason that it connects with me on a personal level, is Orange. It was a defining moment for what subsequently developed, and I really liked this idea that the whole essence of Orange at the time was about a brand, or a product, it was a personality, it was a child moving into the future, and that's what connects for me.

The next piece of work was developed by a young woman creative: she had a strongly idealistic personality, and clearly related strongly to the aims of the campaign.

> I brought in a programme which was designed as a passport. Basically it took you into the London Eye and put on an arts festival for G8, a celebration of Africa, but I thought why it's my favourite, I think probably it's not even the biggest or the best but I really I had such passion for the fact that I really think we could make a difference to people's lives on it, and so we brought over African growers, and we thought that it was really important that they bought into it and that they, in their own way got what we were trying to do and you could see the difference it made to them, and in the context of the G8 and then each show has got basically a different passport.

The personalities of the creatives had a very clear influence on the work they produced (as might be expected). As creative people, they have a direct connection to the concept of diversity – they earn their living from being different, from thinking differently, and from developing new ways of looking at things. The problem for advertising creatives is that they often want to be a great deal more diverse than their clients will allow them to be.

Conclusion

Diversity is obviously both a positive and a negative factor in organisations. Diversity can create conflicts, and in fact frequently does, which in many cases leads managers to resist allowing diversity. In fact, what this short-sighted approach fails to take account of is that conflict is not necessarily a bad thing since conflict can lead to creative solutions.

Advertising creatives provide us with an extreme example. Creativity is what they are about: it is the lifeblood of their work as well as their individual personalities, so their systems of working are designed to exploit diversity (and hence conflict) in order to generate a dynamic, creative atmosphere. Creatives typically work in teams of two, and say openly that their best work comes about when they are teamed with someone who has a different approach to work and life. This illustrates the positive aspects of diversity, in which it becomes something which leads to growth, creative solutions, and progress for the organisation.

The other area in which advertising creatives provide an example is in their relationships with advertising agencies and clients. Here diversity is often regarded as a problem: creatives who are too far out of step with the agency or the client simply find that their work is rejected, and they are forced off the job. This is the downside of diversity – the area where being overtly different from the others will lead to a definite disadvantage. The natural upshot of this is, of course, that clients will tend to pick teams or agencies that fit in with their own views rather than seek out diversity. In turn, this encourages agencies (and creatives) to become foxes (or chameleons) and fit in with what is expected rather than actually do something truly creative. For the creatives working on the account, this often means looking for ways to rewrite the brief in order to maintain their professional and personal integrity.

References

Bartlett, D. and Payne, S. (1997). 'Grounded Theory – Its Basis, Rationale and Procedures'. In *Understanding Social Research; Perspectives on Methodology and Practice*. Eds. McKenzie, G., Powell, J., and Usher, R. (London: Falmer Press).

Corbin, J. and Strauss, A. (1990). 'Grounded Theory Research: Procedures, Canons and Evaluative Criteria', *Qualitative Sociology*, 13, 1, 3–21.

Daft, R.L. (1998). *Organisation Theory and Design*, Sixth Edition (Ohio: South Western College Publishing).

Hatch, M.J. (1997). *Organisation Theory – Modern Symbolic and Postmodern Perspectives*. (Oxford: University Press).

Hellreigel, D. and Slocum, J.W. Jr. (1988). *Management*, Fifth Edition (London: Addison-Wesley).

Hochschild, A.R. (2003). *The Managed Heart: Commercialisation of Human Feeling* (Berkeley: University of California Press).
Hodge, B.J. and Anthony, W.P. (1991). *Organisation Theory – A Strategic Approach*, Fourth Edition (London: Allyn and Bacon).
Reitz, H.J. (1977). *Behavior in Organisations* (Homewood, IL: Richard D. Irwin Inc.).
Ruekert, Robert W. and Walker, Orville C. Jr. (1987). 'Marketing's Interaction with Other Functional Units: A Conceptual Framework and Empirical Evidence', *Journal of Marketing*, 51, January, 1–19.

Name Index

Abrams, L.C., 62
Acker, 142
AEND, 216
Agars, M., 165
Age Partnership Group, 202
Ainscow, M., 219
Alant, E., 218
Alas, R., 93
Alban-Metcalfe, J., 9, 112
Alimo-Metcalfe, B., 9, 112
Allaire, S.H., 225
Allan, J., 217
Allen, R., 12–13, 161
Allen, R.S., 143
Allen, T., 61
Allport, G.W., 124, 126
Alps, T., 164
Alschuler, R.H., 126–8
Altervia Consulting, 76
Alvarez, E.B., 3, 12
Alvesson, M., 4
Amit, R.P., 37
Anderson, B., 46, 54–5
Anderson, P.M., 171
Andriopoulos, C., 156
Anthony, W.P., 244
Argyris, C., 24
Arnold, J., 173
Aronson, E., 126
Askheim, O.P., 222
Attfield, J., 163
ATW, 226
Avolio, B., 112
Avramidis, E., 219

Baden-Fuller, C., 150
Bajaria, H.J., 60
Bakan, D., 79, 86
Bales, R.F., 79
Balogan, J., 162
Banks, 30
Barbosa, I., 137, 139–40

Barletta, M., 151, 153, 157
Barnes, C., 216
Barnes, H., 222
Barney, J.B., 20, 26
Baroudi, J.J., 156, 179
Bartel, K., 173
Bartlett, C.A., 61
Bartlett, D., 243
Bass, B.M., 112, 114
Batstone, M., 153
Becker, B.E., 26–7
Becker, D.R., 215
Beer, 147
Berning, C., 174
Berscied, E., 121
Billing, Y., 4
Bilsky, W., 85
Bird, K., 77
Bishop, M., 229
Blake, S., 11, 33
Bloch, P.H., 119, 132, 149, 172
Blythe, J., 7, 171, 179
Bonfour, A., 66
Bontis, N., 66
Booth, T., 219
Boxall, P., 159–60, 162
Braun, W., 51, 62
Bremner, C., 5
Brennan, L., 64
Brizendine, L., 121
Brock, T.C., 121, 158
Brooke, S., 157
Buchanan, R., 123
Buckley, C., 163
Buck, N., 152
Burgoyne, C.B., 47–8
Burke, R., 159
Burke, R.J., 94, 112, 144
Burnes, B., 147
Burt, R.B., 129
Byrne, D., 121, 161

Name Index

Cabral-Cardosa, C., 137, 139–40
Cadwalladr, C., 157–8, 164, 166
Caldwell, B.S., 65
Cameron, C., 219
Cameron, K., 46
Campbell, A., 21, 31
Carlozzi, C., 12
Castellanos, A.R., 66
Caterall, M., 127
Cellar, D., 165
Chiang, K.-H., 65
Cianni, M., 4
CIPD, 195–6, 205–8, 210–11
Clark, T.A.R., 62
Cleveland, J., 226
Clifton, R., 158, 164, 166
Cobban, A., 46–7, 54
Cohen, W.M., 19, 22–3, 29–30
Collins, J.C., 61, 66
Colman, A., 129, 149
Commission for Racial Equality or (Kochan, T.), 143
Cook, C., 7, 9
Coolican, H., 96
Corbin, J., 242
Cornelius, N., 4, 140
Cox, T., 11–12, 161
Cox, T.H., 33
Cox, T.Jr., (93, 01), 19, 26
Crichton, A., 215, 221, 223
Crimp, M., 95
Crosby, F., 161, 164–5
Crosby, F.J., 3, 6
Cross, B., 61, 71
Crozier, W., 121, 158
Currie, E., 6

Daft, R.L., 244
Damasio, A., 140–1
Daunton, L., 145–6
David, A., 7, 24, 34
Davidson, M., 94, 112
Davies, J.K., 63
Davis, A., 6
Davis, H.L., 152
Dawson, P., 156
Day, G.S., 22–3, 32, 37
Dechant, K., 12
De Chernatoney, L., 121, 159

DeEtta, J., 20
de Ferran, F., 7, 76–7, 79, 82
De Long, D., 63
De Pelsmacker, P., 77–8
The Design Council, 153, 155
Dhanaraj, C., 61
Dickson, R., 5
Di Dio, L., 80
Diekema, D.A., 65
Diploye, R., 121
Dix, A., 172
Dobransky, K., 216
Donovan, R.J., 121, 158, 172
Doughty, H., 217
Doward, J., 157–8, 163
Drake, L., 5
Driscoll, D.M., 160
DTS, 216
Duckworth, S.M., 226, 229
Durisin, B., 34
Dussault, C., 64
Dyck, I., 223

Eagly, A., 94, 112
EBU, 215
E-Consultancy, 155
ECU, 227
Eden, C., 8, 34
EEOT, 215
EFA, 198–201
Emmett, T., 218
Equalities and Human Right Commission or (Ryan, M.), 145
Erikson, E.H., 126
Eurostat, 91
Evans, J., 215, 221, 224

Fahey, L., 63
Fancher, R.E., 124
Farnham, D., 7, 9–10
Feather, N.T., 80
Ferrario, M., 94, 112
Firat, F.A., 127
Fiske, N., 153
Flanagin, A., 173
Fleishman, E.A., 25
Fliaster, A., 37
FLO International, 75
Flood, P., 61

Foster, D., 225–6, 237
Franck, K., 128
François-Lecompte, A., 77
Fuchs, D., 47
Fullerton, J., 3, 5, 12, 23, 26, 28

Gagnon, S., 4
Garcia, L.J., 228
Gardiner, M., 94, 112, 165
Garvin, D.A., 28, 38
Geary, D.C., 79
George, G., 22–3, 29
Ghoshal, S., 61
Glaser, B., 95
Globokar, T., 66
Golembiewski, R.T., 19, 24–5
Goold, M., 21, 31
Gornik, K., 165
Govindarajan, V., 31
Graffan, J., 216
Graham, J., 144
Granrose, 140
Greene, A., 3–4, 9
Greenhalgh, P., 121, 158
Griscombe, K., 12
Gropius, W., 123
Groppel, A., 121, 158, 172
Grove, B., 220
Grunert, K.G., 76–7, 81
Grunert, S.C., 81
Guba, E., 95
Gummerson, E., 95
Gunn, R., 6, 129–31, 149, 171–3, 178–81, 190
Gupta, A.K., 31
Gutman, J., 81–2

Haberberg, A., 20, 26
Haig, A., 173
Hall, D.T., 28–9
Hammer, E.F., 125–8
Hammer, M., 9, 119, 121, 131, 149, 158, 174
Hanover, J., 165
Hargittai, E., 216
Harris, A., 126
Harris, L., 63
Hassenzahl, M., 119–20, 132, 149, 172–3

Hatch, M.J., 244
Hattwick, W., 126–8
Havelaar, M., 76
Heide, 127
Heilman, M., 5
Heimlich, J.E., 172–3
Hellreigel, D., 244
Hellstrom, T., 60
Hersh, M.A., 216, 228, 230–1
Hersh, M., 6, 11, 63, 66
Hewett, T.T., 172
Hickson, D.J., 47
Hillman, A., 12
Hilton, T., 42
Hochschild, A.R., 247
Hodge, B.J., 244
Hoffmann, R., 171–3
Hoffman, W.M., 160
Hofstede, G., 51, 66–7
Holden, N., 51
Hollingsworth, J., 63
Holst, E., 94
Hope-Hailey, V., 162
Hopkins, W.E., 20, 22, 23, 30–1, 33
Horsman, M., 163
Horvath, G., 6, 9, 173, 180
HSE, 230
Hubbard, E., 20, 23–4, 27, 38–40
Hughes, D.R., 77
Husted, K., 60
Hyde, H., 224

Igbaria, M., 156, 179
Ipsos, 75–6
Ipsos Marketing (08), 76

Jackson, S., 127
Jackson, S.E., 3, 12, 61–2, 66
Janz, B.D., 61–2, 66
Jasuna, B., 116
Jehn, K., 12
Jennex M., 60
Joergensen, J., 171, 179
Johnson, L., 151
Johnson, M.., 94, 112
Johnson, M.A., 216, 228, 230–1, 237
Johnstone, D., 216
Jongbloed, N., 215, 221, 223

Jonsson, F., 171–2
Jordan, P.W., 172
Judge, T., 114

Kahle, L.R., 79
Kale, S.H., 45
Kalyva, E., 219
Kandola, R., 3, 5, 12, 23, 26, 28
Kanter, R., 94, 112
Kaplan, R.S., 23, 27, 39
Karande, K., 119, 121, 149, 152, 158, 174
Karnite, R., 93–4
Kelly, G.A., 81
Kiepper, A., 25
Kim, W., 61
Kirkham, P., 163
Kirton, G., 3–4
Kirton, M.J., 8–9
Kitchin, R., 218, 221, 226
Kittle, R., 226
Klein, D., 157–8, 163
Klingemann, H.-D., 47
Knapp, R.H., 129
Kolman, L., 52, 57
Konno, N., 61, 66, 68
Korgaonkar, P., 173
Kossak, E.E., 24
Kotler, P., 172
Kottke, J., 155, 165
Krauss, K., 171–3
Kréziak, D., 79
Kroeck, K., 112
Kubacki, K., 6–7, 65
Kupshik, G.A., 65
Kurdek, L.A., 80

Laczniak, G.R., 31
Laitin, D., 46, 48, 53
Lai, A.W., 79
Lambert, D.R., 121, 158, 172
Lavie, T., 179
Lawler, E.E.III, 25
Lawrence, E., 138, 144
Learned, A., 151
Lehman, A.F., 224
Leonard, D., 61
Leonard, J., 12
Lepak, 159, 162

Levinthal, D.A., 19, 22–3, 29–30
Levitt, T., 49–50
Levy, 128
Lewis, D., 63
L'Huillier, M.A., 52
LIAA, 93
Liff, S., 8, 139
Lincoln, Y., 95
Lindgaard, G., 119
Lipovetsky, G., 76
Lobel, S.A., 24
Lockwood, N.R., 23–4
Lorenz, T., 121
Lowe, K., 112
Lowell, B., 24
Luce, J.A., 63
Lunt, N., 220
Lupotow, L., 127, 130
Lusch, R.F., 31

Macan, T., 121, 161
Maclaran, P., 127
Maignan, I., 53
Mair, P., 46, 48
Majewski, M., 128
Margolin, V., 123
Mariampolski, H., 96
Marion, G., 76
Marr, R., 37
Martins, L., 12
Mason, G., 211
Mathiyalakan, S., 19, 23–4, 37
Mattis, M., 12
Mauborgne, R., 61
Maughan, L., 120
Mayer, F.C., 48
McAlister, D.T., 53
McAllister, M., 12
McClean, 79
McDowell, L., 223
McEachern, 79
McEnrue, M.P., 23–4
McNiff, K., 126–8
McSweeney, B., 62–3
Mediaweek, 174
Meek, V., 59
Mercado, S., 52
Michnik, A., 55
Microsoft Windows Mobile, 146

Miller, D., 4
Miller, H., 173
Miller, J., 64–5
Milliken, F., 12
Mirzoeff, N., 123
Mohan, M., 153
Mohrman, A., 25
Mohrman, S., 25, 41
Montgomery, K., 161
Mooradian, N., 60
Moore, J., 61, 66
Moss, G., 3–13, 20, 26, 42, 59–71, 91–115, 127–31, 145–6, 149, 151–5, 157, 159, 164, 171–90
Moya, M., 219
Murphy, P.M., 65
Murray, J.P., 63

Nelson, D., 121, 159
Nelson, G., 123
NetRatings, 173
Neuman, J., 161
Ng, E.S.W., 12
Nieto, M., 24, 30
Nill, A., 53
Nkomo, S., 4, 9
Nochlin, L., 126
Nohria, 147
Nonaka, I., 60–1, 66, 68
Norton, D.P., 23, 27, 39

Oakeshott, I., 6
OECD, 66
Office for National Statistics, 197
Ogbonna, E., 63
Olson, J.C., 82
ONSLF, 215
OSHA, 230
Oshagbemi, T., 66
Ozcaglar, N., 77–8

Pedersen, D.M., 65
Pahl, J., 152
Palmer, 165
Palmowski, J., 48
Parasuraman, 156
Parasuraman, S., 179
Parker, V.A., 28–9

Parsons, T., 79
Paul, H., 31
Payne, S., 243
Peppas, S., 155
Piccolo, R., 114
Pieters, R., 84
Piggott, L., 221, 229
Pitts, R.E., 78
Polyani, M., 60
Pophal, R., 124
Porras, J.I., 61, 66
Porteous, J.D., 121
Powell, 161
Prasarnphanich, P., 61–2, 66
Preece, A., 8
Preyer, W., 124, 126
Pugh, D.S., 47
Purcell, J., 159–60, 162
Putrevu, S., 80

Quevedo, P., 24, 30

Ramina, B., 93
Read, H., 122–3, 129
Rees, C.J., 93
Regan, S., 11, 218–19, 222–2, 224, 227
Reitz, H.J., 244
Repper, J., 215, 221, 224
Reynolds, T.J., 81–2
Rieple, A., 20, 26
Rigaux, B.P., 152
Rigby, D.K., 24
Rivza, B., 94
Roberts, J.A., 78
Robertson, M., 156, 179–80
Robinson, G., 12
Rogoff, 123
Rokeach, M., 79–80, 82
Romberger, B., 4
Rosen, E., 128
Rosener, J., 9
Roulstone, A., 215
Rousseau, D., 65
Routh, D.A., 47, 48
Rowley, C., 62
RTC, 216
Rubin, L.G., 171
Ruekert, R.W., 244

Name Index

Ruiz, J., 219
Russell, M., 223

Sambamurthy, V., 19, 23–4, 37
Sarros, J., 112
Schenkman, N., 171–2
Schlosser, A.E., 173
Schneider, B.(87), 161
Schneider, R., 4, 161
Schoemaker, J.H., 37
Schon, D., 25
Schuer, S., 221, 228
Schwartz, S.H., 79, 85
Seeman, M., 65
Selwyn, T., 60, 65
Senge, P., 61, 66
Senge, P.M., 19
Sensiper, S., 61
Shaw, D., 77–8
Shaw, S., 142–3
Sheehan, M., 173
Shneiderman, B., 172
Shore, C., 50, 65
Shui, E., 77–8
Silverstein, M., 153
Simon, J., 155
Singh, V., 159
Sirieix, L., 77–8
Skinner, H., 7, 53
Slack, N., 66
Slocum, J.W.Jr, 244
Smith, T., 222, 225
Snell, 159, 162
Souter, P., 159–60
Sparke, P., 163
Spittal, 142
Sriskandarajah, D., 48
Stanley, K., 11, 218–19, 221–2, 224, 227
Stanley, M.(08), 218
Steger, U., 47
Sterman, J.D., 19
Sterns, P.A., 75
Stilma, M., 128
Stockdale, M., 161, 164–5
Stockdale, M.S., 3, 6
Stores, 174
Storey, J., 62
Strauss, A., 95, 242

Strong, C., 86
The Sunday Times, or (Toomey, C.), 145
Sveiby, K., 61

Tagbata, D., 77
Taha, L.H., 65
Takeuchi, H., 60
Thelwall, M., 155, 179
Thomas, H., 60
Thomas, R., 4, 25–6, 161
Thornton, P., 220
Tiggerman, M., 94, 112, 165
Todorova, G., 34
Tractinsky, N., 173, 179
Trompenaars, F., 51, 66
T-TAP, 225
TUC, 206, 221
Tung, R.L., 12
Tunnelle, A., 125
Turton, N., 223–4

UNESCO, 63
Ungerson, C., 222
UPIAS, 216

Vanags, A., 93
Van den Bosh, 150
Van den Bulte, C., 22–3, 32, 37
Van der Heijden, H., 171, 173
Van de Ven, A.H., 150
Van Iwaarden, J., 172, 179
Vantomme, D., 77
Vass, E., 6
Vega, G., 64
Vernon, P.E., 124, 126
Villinger, R., 52
Vinnicombe, S., 159
Vinten, G., 62
Vislie, L., 219
Vogler, C., 152
Von Krogh, G., 61
Vos, O., 128

Waehner, T.S., 126, 128
Wajcman, J., 139, 159
Walker, B.A., 82
Walker, C., 164
Walker, O.C.Jr, 244

Walsh, A., 164
Walster, E., 121
Wang, K., 172–3
Warner, F., 153
Warner, M., 48, 51, 62
Warren, J., 215
Watson, W., 11
Webb, J., 8
Wedande, G., 171
Weigand, R., 12
Wheeler, M.L., 23, 35, 38–9
White, J., 127
Whitfield, T.W.A., 173
WHO, 216
Wildman, S., 6
Williams, L., 46–7, 54

Willmott, H., 60
Wilton, R., 221, 228
Windolf, P., 162
Wolff, A., 129
Wolin, L., 173
Wright, L., 95
WWW-ICT, 180

Yahomoto, M., 121, 158, 172
Yalom, I.D., 71

Zahra, S.A., 22–3, 29
Zanini, M., 24
Zettl, H., 172
Zielonka, J., 46, 48

Subject Index

Absorptive capacity, 29–30, 33
   diversity knowledge, 30, 33
Access to Work Scheme, 227
advertising, 156–7, 162, 163–4
   advertising creatives, 241–2
Age Concern, 202
ageism, 10–11, 194–214
   Chartered Institute of Personnel and Development (CIPD), 195–6, 205
   combating ageism, 204
   discrimination, 194–214
   Employers' Forum on Age (EFA), 198–9
     servicescape, 201
   Employment Equality Age Regulations (EEAR), 196, 198, 201, 212
agentic orientation, 79
Age Positive Campaign, 205
agility, 19, 27, 30, 35
   customer and partnering agility, 35
   operational agility, 35–6
artistic expression, 123
art therapy, 126
ASDA, 207
assistive technology, 224–5
augmentation hypothesis, 114
Australia, 6, 62, 66–8

Belgium, 52
birth, 53
Brainwriting, 124, 126
Brown, Molton, 206
BT, 210
Bunnyfoot, 120
Burnett, Leo, 162
business benefits, 11–13
B&Q, 207

California State University Sacramento, 121
Carrefour, 50
Centrality of Visual Product Aesthetics (CVPA), 120
Chartered Society of Designers (CSD), 153–4
China, 4
colours, 175–6, 184–5
communal orientation, 79
complementary approach, 28
Comprehensive Assistive Technology (CAT) model, 216–17
conflict, 244–5
congruity principle, 119, 131, 149, 164
   design diversity, 149–51, 159
   inside-out & outside-in perspective, 150, 152
   similarity-attraction paradigm,
     see also matching hypothesis
   strategy innovation approach, 150
   see also mirroring principle
convergence approach, 48
   see also etic approach
creative capacity, 29
creatives, 241–54
creativity, 248
Currie, Edwina, 6
Czech Republic, 53–5

Demographics design profession, 154
dialogic idealism, 53
divergence approach, 49
   see also emic approach
Diversity, 3, 5–8, 10–15, 19–37
   behavioural diversity and cognitive diversity, 22, 32
   benefits, 11–12, 22, 24

Subject Index

Diversity – *continued*
  business diversity and global diversity, 22–3
  diversity density, 23, 31, 33
  diversity mindset, 23, 31–3
  measuring, 27, 34–5
  structural diversity, 22
  workforce diversity, 21–2
Diversity approach, 127
diversity management, 26
diversity orientation, 23, 31, 33
  see also diversity density
diversity scorecard, 20, 23–4, 36–7, 41
  see also scorecard
domicile, 54

E-consultancy, 155
emic approach, 49
  see also divergence approach
emotional labour, 247
emotional management, 97
empathy principle, 121
Employment, 214
Equality Act, 142
Equality specialist, 137–9, 143
Equal Opportunities (EO) approach, 3–4, 8
  ontological equality, 4
ethical issues, 53
etic approach, 48
  see also convergence approach
European Court of Justice (EJC), 202–3
European Economic Community (EEC), 45
European identity, 47
  cultural convergence, 47
  cultural divergence, 47–8
European Union (EU), 45–8, 57–8, 91, 213
  cultural heterogeneity, 52
  economy, 50
  history, 45
  labour market, 92
  members, 46
  segmentation, 50–1
    cross-border clusters, 52
  trade, 75
executive mindset, 31
  see also global mindset

explicit knowledge, 60, 61
  see also Knowledge Management (KM)

Faico Information Solutions, 182
Fair trade, 75
  Artisans du Monde and Oxfam, 76
  consumers, 77
  eco-design approach, 87
  European and French market, 75
  labour market, 93, 105–6
  north/south imbalances, 78
  produits portage, 77
  purchasers' motives, 84–8
Female managers in Latvia, 91–2, 94–5, 103, 112, 115
  employment barriers, 108–12
  promoting factors, 103–8
Female style of management, 96–103, 112
  attitude to risk, 103
  consensual approach, 100–1
  decision-making, 99–9
  emotionality, 97–8
  focus on results, 99
  long- & short-term focus, 100
  teamwork, 101–2
France, 53–5, 75
  France's President, *see also* Sarkozy, Nikolas

gender marketing, 75, 77
  primary and secondary communication axes, 87
gender stereotypes, 86
Globalization, 49
  adaptation and evidence, 49
  multinational enterprises (MNE), 50
  standardization, 49
  see also global market
global market, 19, 34, 49, 58, 75
  see also globalization
global mindset, 31
  see also executive mindset
Grounded theory approach, 241–2
  conflict, 244–5

Harman, Harriet, 5–6
Hay Group model, 208

Herder, Johann Gottfried, 46
Hertfordshire County Council, 209
Higher education, 60
Hofstede's framework, 51
Hofstede's dimension, 66
Homogeneity principle, 161–2
Human Computer Interaction (HCI), 172–3
  aesthetic design continuum, 180–81
  visual aesthetics, 172–3
  gender index, 176–8
  masculine aesthetics and feminine aesthetics, 174
Hungary, 53–5

Image-Line Software, 182
Institute of Practitioners in Advertising, 156–7, 158
Intellectual Capital Management (ICM), 60–1, 67
  transformation process, 66
interactionist perspective, 122
Internal labour market, 159–60
Intro wizard flash website builder 1.0, 182
isolation, 9, 63–6, 68
  see also social isolation
IT gender distribution, 156

Japan, 50

Kirton's Adaptor/Innovator, 8–9
Knowledge Creation (KC), 60–2
  see also tacit knowledge
Knowledge Management (KM), 60–2, 66
  organizational culture, 63
  see also explicit knowledge

laddering technique, 81
  hard-laddering & soft-laddering, 82
language, 54–5
Latvia, 7–8
  education, 91, 94
  history, 92
  Latvia's President, see also Vaira Vike-Freiberga
  society, 94, 107

learning organisation, 26, 28–9
  complementary approach, 28–9
Legislation, 141, 195
level-playing field theory, 144
live expectancy, 197

Marks&Spencer, 208
matching hypothesis, 121
MBTI psychometric test, 8–9
means-end chain, 81–2
  coefficients of centrality and prestige, 84–5
  hierarchical value map, 82–4
  motivation dimensions; hedonistic; universalistic & transcendental, 85–6
Men's leadership style, 113–14
Mercer Consulting, 208
merit, 4–6
Michael Hammer, 119
Microsoft frontpage 2002, 183
mirroring principle, 120–21, 131, 158, 174, 190

Namu 6-website editor, 2, 183
National culture, 66
  collectivism, 66, 200
  individualism, 66–7, 200
National identity, 46, 53
  domicile and language, 54
  Eurobarometer, 46, 47
  parentage, 53–4
  place of birth, 53
  traditions, 55
Nationwide, 207
Nestle, 50

Old-boy network, 110

Pablo Software Solutions, 181
Photonfx, 182
Poland, 53–5
  Polish consumer preferences, 56
  preference aesthetics, 130, 151, 178
  production aesthetics, 151
psychology of personal constructs, 81
purchasing patterns, 152

266 Subject Index

Race Relations Amendment Act, 142
recruitment, 162, 165
Research Assessment Exercise (RAE), 62
Research Quantum (RQ), 60
Rokeach typology, 80

Sainsbury, 211
Sarkozy, Nicolas, 5
scorecard, 24, 36–40
  community perspective, 40
  diversity leadership commitment and learning and growth, 40
  workforce profile and workforce climate, 40
  see also diversity scorecard
Shell, 205
sheltered workshop programme, 224
Slovenia, 6, 66–8
social isolation, 63, 67
  causes, 63; structural and psychological, 65
  effects, 64
  experience, 63
Somerfield, 177
Soviet Union, 92, 104
stakeholder approach, 52–3
stereotyping and age, 199
Switzerland, 75

tacit knowledge, 26, 60–1
  see also Knowledge Creation (KC)
Talentor, 95
Tesco, 177
total rewards package, 208
transactional leadership, 112, 114–15
transformational leadership, 112, 114–15
Trendyflash website builder 1.0, 182
Trompenaar's framework, 51
typography, 177, 186

UNESCO, 63
United Kingdom, 53–5, 195
United States of America, 50

Value chain, 21, 26
Vike-Freiberga, Vaira, 92
visual culture, 123
Volkswagen, 50

Wal-Mart, 50
web design, 155–6, 171
web design software, 181–4, 190
  see also individual software names
web usage, 173–4
white male norm, 3
Women's leadership style, 113–14
Workforce diversity, 21–2
Wraptech Limited, 181

Race Relations Amendment Act, 142
recruitment, 162, 165
Research Assessment Exercise (RAE), 62
Research Quantum (RQ), 60
Rokeach typology, 80

Sainsbury, 211
Sarkozy, Nicolas, 5
scorecard, 24, 36–40
  community perspective, 40
  diversity leadership commitment and learning and growth, 40
  workforce profile and workforce climate, 40
  see also diversity scorecard
Shell, 205
sheltered workshop programme, 224
Slovenia, 6, 66–8
social isolation, 63, 67
  causes, 63; structural and psychological, 65
  effects, 64
  experience, 63
Somerfield, 177
Soviet Union, 92, 104
stakeholder approach, 52–3
stereotyping and age, 199
Switzerland, 75

tacit knowledge, 26, 60–1
  see also Knowledge Creation (KC)
Talentor, 95
Tesco, 177
total rewards package, 208
transactional leadership, 112, 114–15
transformational leadership, 112, 114–15
Trendyflash website builder 1.0, 182
Trompenaar's framework, 51
typography, 177, 186

UNESCO, 63
United Kingdom, 53–5, 195
United States of America, 50

Value chain, 21, 26
Vike-Freiberga, Vaira, 92
visual culture, 123
Volkswagen, 50

Wal-Mart, 50
web design, 155–6, 171
web design software, 181–4, 190
  see also individual software names
web usage, 173–4
white male norm, 3
Women's leadership style, 113–14
Workforce diversity, 21–2
Wraptech Limited, 181

Herder, Johann Gottfried, 46
Hertfordshire County Council, 209
Higher education, 60
Hofstede's framework, 51
Hofstede's dimension, 66
Homogeneity principle, 161–2
Human Computer Interaction (HCI), 172–3
  aesthetic design continuum, 180–81
  visual aesthetics, 172–3
  gender index, 176–8
  masculine aesthetics and feminine aesthetics, 174
Hungary, 53–5

Image-Line Software, 182
Institute of Practitioners in Advertising, 156–7, 158
Intellectual Capital Management (ICM), 60–1, 67
  transformation process, 66
interactionist perspective, 122
Internal labour market, 159–60
Intro wizard flash website builder 1.0, 182
isolation, 9, 63–6, 68
  see also social isolation
IT gender distribution, 156

Japan, 50

Kirton's Adaptor/Innovator, 8–9
Knowledge Creation (KC), 60–2
  see also tacit knowledge
Knowledge Management (KM), 60–2, 66
  organizational culture, 63
  see also explicit knowledge

laddering technique, 81
  hard-laddering & soft-laddering, 82
language, 54–5
Latvia, 7–8
  education, 91, 94
  history, 92
  Latvia's President, see also Vaira Vike-Freiberga
  society, 94, 107

learning organisation, 26, 28–9
  complementary approach, 28–9
Legislation, 141, 195
level-playing field theory, 144
live expectancy, 197

Marks&Spencer, 208
matching hypothesis, 121
MBTI psychometric test, 8–9
means-end chain, 81–2
  coefficients of centrality and prestige, 84–5
  hierarchical value map, 82–4
  motivation dimensions; hedonistic; universalistic & transcendental, 85–6
Men's leadership style, 113–14
Mercer Consulting, 208
merit, 4–6
Michael Hammer, 119
Microsoft frontpage 2002, 183
mirroring principle, 120–21, 131, 158, 174, 190

Namu 6-website editor, 2, 183
National culture, 66
  collectivism, 66, 200
  individualism, 66–7, 200
National identity, 46, 53
  domicile and language, 54
  Eurobarometer, 46, 47
  parentage, 53–4
  place of birth, 53
  traditions, 55
Nationwide, 207
Nestle, 50

Old-boy network, 110

Pablo Software Solutions, 181
Photonfx, 182
Poland, 53–5
  Polish consumer preferences, 56
  preference aesthetics, 130, 151, 178
  production aesthetics, 151
psychology of personal constructs, 81
purchasing patterns, 152